THE REPUBLICAN EVOLUTION

THE REPUBLICAN EVOLUTION

From GOVERNING PARTY
to ANTIGOVERNMENT PARTY,
1860–2020

KENNETH JANDA

Columbia University Press
New York

Columbia University Press
Publishers Since 1893
New York   Chichester, West Sussex
cup.columbia.edu

Library of Congress Cataloging-in-Publication Data
Names: Janda, Kenneth, author.
Title: The Republican evolution : from governing party to
antigovernment party, 1860–2020 / Kenneth Janda.
Description: New York : Columbia University Press, [2022] |
Includes bibliographical references and index.
Identifiers: LCCN 2022009147 (print) | LCCN 2022009148 (ebook) |
ISBN 9780231207881 (Hardback : acid-free paper) | ISBN 9780231207898
(Trade Paperback : acid-free paper) | ISBN 9780231557160 (eBook)
Subjects: LCSH: Republican Party (U.S.)—History. | Conservatism—
United States—History. | United States—Politics and government.
Classification: LCC JK2356 .J36 2022 (print) | LCC JK2356 (ebook) |
DDC 324.273409—dc23/eng/20220518
LC record available at https://lccn.loc.gov/2022009147
LC ebook record available at https://lccn.loc.gov/2022009148

Columbia University Press books are printed on permanent
and durable acid-free paper.
Printed in the United States of America

Cover design: Elliott S. Cairns
Cover images: Valya Trait/Shutterstock.com

My wife, Ann Janda, who helped with early chapters,
joins me in dedicating this book
to our teenage grandsons,

Leo Alexander Janda Milne

and

Benjamin Ryder Janda Milne.

We hope that they will live as adults under
a democratic two-party system.

Evolution may be defined as any net directional change or any cumulative change in the characteristics of organisms or populations over many generations—in other words, descent with modification.

—J. A. ENDLER, *NATURAL SELECTION IN THE WILD*

A NOTE ON THE COVER

Both colors on the book's cover relate to Republican history. Originally, blue was the Republican color. The Union Army fought in blue uniforms against Confederate forces in gray. After the war, government soldiers enforcing Reconstruction were called "the blues." The speaker at a Republican rally in Chicago in 1888 praised the weather "as clear as the record of the Republican party" and the glorious blue sky, which was "True Republican blue at that."

In contrast, red symbolized the 1917 Russian Revolution. So it became associated with communism, socialism, and leftism. Into the 1920s, a "Red scare" of communism filled American media. After World War II, the Republican senator Joe McCarthy led a second "Red scare." In 1953, the Cincinnati Reds baseball team's owner officially changed its name to Redlegs. Founded in 1881, the team dared not reclaim its original name until 1961.

That history of hues led many political scientists to color Republican and Democratic victories blue and red respectively on election maps. The *Atlas of U.S. Presidential Elections* website still plots all election results since 1789 in blue for Republicans and in red for Democrats.

Television reversed the historic colors for the two parties in reporting results for the historic 2000 election. The November 7 election was not decided until December 12. Jodi Enda in the *Smithsonian Magazine* wrote: "The 2000 election dragged on until mid-December, until the Supreme Court declared Bush the victor. For weeks, the maps were ubiquitous. Perhaps that's why the 2000 colors stuck."

Today's Republican Party celebrates a traditionally communist color. The cover captures the irony, *Republican* in blue and *Evolution* in red. Momus, the Greek god of mockery, must be smiling at the new "red scare" for Democrats.

CONTENTS

PART IV. REPUBLICANS AS TEAM, TRIBE, AND CULT

PART V. REPUBLICAN RESTORATION

PREFACE

We all have biases in what we see, like, and think. Readers deserve to know some of mine. I admit to Democratic inclinations. I have usually—but not always—voted for Democratic candidates. I also am biased toward legislatures as instruments of democratic government and as objects of study. My doctoral dissertation dealt with the Indiana General Assembly. I felt then and now that legislatures have closer links to citizens than elected executives—for example, governors or presidents. Legislatures are physical and visible. One can visit their chambers and talk to the legislators. In contrast, political parties (which I study now) are intangible and invisible. They are leprechauns in a political forest.

In the spring of 1965, my bias toward legislatures made me receptive to a phone call from the American Enterprise Institute, a conservative Washington think tank. AEI invited me to contribute to its planned book on the U.S. Congress, to meet in Washington on the project in the summer, and to submit my work by early fall for publication in 1966. Involved at the time in other work, I initially declined but promptly accepted after learning that AEI would pay me $2,000, about one-quarter of my assistant professor salary then at Northwestern University.

AEI undertook its book project in reaction to the results of the 1964 presidential election. Democratic president Lyndon Johnson had won

61 percent of the popular vote and 90 percent of the electoral vote over Republican Barry Goldwater. Becoming president after John F. Kennedy's assassination in 1963, Johnson was elected president in 1964 and was expected to run again in 1968. Anticipating rule by a liberal Democratic administration for two more presidential terms, AEI foresaw an onslaught of undesirable policies and looked to Congress as a shield. Adopting a defensive posture, the conservative think tank assembled an ideologically diverse group of scholars to write about the virtues of a strong Congress.

The ten other scholars who accepted AEI's generous invitation and gathered in Washington that summer of 1965 were established authors in American politics.[1] I had not written anything noteworthy in that field, but earlier that year I had published the first book on computer applications in political research.[2] Accordingly, AEI asked me to write on improving Congress through computer use. My piece appeared in AEI's book *Congress: The First Branch of Government*, published in 1966.[3] The Washington think tank quickly flooded the nation's newspapers with press releases about Congress as the people's bulwark against executive rule. Each contributor received sixteen-by-twenty-inch montages made from scores of newspaper clippings from Maine to California.

Numerous clippings featured my contribution, "Information Systems for Congress." In the fall of 1967, the Association for Computing Machinery invited me to give a plenary address at its semiannual conference in Anaheim, California.[4] Soon afterward, AEI asked me to coauthor a book on Congress's use of program budgeting, a method for tracking project revenues and expenses that was well suited to computers.[5] AEI even contributed modestly to my new NSF-funded cross-national study of political parties.

In November 1968, Republican Richard Nixon defeated Democrat Hubert Humphrey by 0.7 percent of the popular vote in the presidential election. Suddenly the American Enterprise Institute lost interest in Congress and in me. With Republicans now in charge of the presidency, AEI no longer viewed Congress as a bulwark against undesirable governmental policies. And so I learned, in a personal way, how party politics trumps political philosophy. I had naively thought that AEI wanted to empower Congress—"the First Branch of Government"—as a matter of principle. However important that was to the conservative think tank, it was less important than regaining control of "the Second Branch"— the presidency.

I wrote this book believing that both of our major parties should value maintaining the democratic foundation of our two-party system above winning any election. Unlike my other academic studies of cross-national political parties and comparative party politics, *The Republican Evolution: From Governing Party to Antigovernment Party, 1860–2020*, has a political purpose. It aims not to trash the party but to help restore the GOP to its former grandeur. By documenting the party's original principles and how they have changed over time, I hope to remind Republicans of their party's history of promoting national unity while governing for the public good. Today, the party operates in reverse, opposing national government while sowing sectionalism by pursuing the Democrats' old "states' rights" philosophy.

Codifying Republican principles in 2,722 planks identified in all forty-one party platforms since 1856, I describe the Republican Party's experience over three different historical eras. The party's illustrious nationalism era lasted from 1860 to 1924, during which Republicans emphasized order over anarchy. In their neoliberalism era, from 1928 to 1960, Republicans downplayed government, favoring the individual over the state. In 1964, the party entered an era of ethnocentrism, demeaning national government and favoring white Christians over others. During this era, Republicans have acted increasingly as a political tribe catering to their dwindling tribal base.

The Grand Old Party once governed the nation effectively and compassionately under presidents Abraham Lincoln, Theodore Roosevelt, and Dwight Eisenhower. The party today moves in a different direction, sparked by presidential nominee Barry Goldwater and led by presidents Ronald Reagan and Donald Trump. It opposes government policies that would reduce income inequalities, lessen social inequalities, advance health care, improve the environment, and combat climate change, ostensibly because such policies might infringe on personal freedom. Whereas in 1953, Eisenhower told Congress that Social Security was "an essential part of our economic and social life," Goldwater in 1960 wrote that its 6 percent tax "compels millions of individuals to postpone until later years the enjoyment of wealth they might otherwise enjoy today."

As a citizen, I admit a bias to Democratic policies. As a political scientist, I care more about maintaining the vigorous two-party system that has sustained our American version of democracy for over two hundred years. Current Republican leaders are quick to abandon responsible party politics for short-term electoral gains. My book analyzes Republicans acting as a political party, an electoral team, a political tribe, and a personality cult. Republicans today behave less like a principled political party whose electoral team accepts the outcome of democratic voting than like a political tribe or personality cult claiming transcendent superiority to rule.

Parties can change. For a century after the Civil War, the Democratic Party's southern wing stained their national party with racism. Then in 1948, Democrats had a political epiphany; they awakened to their sordid silence on civil rights. The 1948 Democratic National Convention adopted the party's first civil rights plank, causing southern delegations to walk out of the convention. The Democrats gained far more in stature than they temporarily lost in electoral support. Perhaps my historical account of how their party reversed its principles will encourage some Republican activists to engineer a comparable Republican epiphany, become the party's new heroes, and make the Grand Old Party grand again.

THE REPUBLICAN EVOLUTION

INTRODUCTION

I admit to Democratic partisanship, but I am more loyal to democratic government. More than fifty years of research and writing on democracy and party politics have convinced me that no nation can practice democratic government in the absence of a responsible, competitive party system.[1] Given its constitutional structure, the United States cannot endure as a democracy without two major parties—two that compete for popular votes, accept election outcomes, and govern responsibly.[2] Until 2020, both major parties, at different times to varying degrees, admirably fulfilled those requirements. Now one doubts whether the Republican Party—the Grand Old Party of the republic—will continue to behave like a democratic party.

I wrote this book for contemporary Republican activists who are uneasy with the trajectory of their party, hoping some among them will act to restore the GOP's old grandeur. Of course my assessment reflects my personal views, but those views are informed by extensive research into the party's own principles, as reflected in 2,722 planks culled from all Republican Party platforms since 1856. Reviewing the planks from their party's past for themselves, Republican activists can discover how far the GOP has strayed from its proud history. I show when and why their party scrapped key principles. In some cases, the party changed course because the principles became historically and socially outdated.

Other times, it temporarily slighted its principles to win votes. In 1964, however, Republicans deliberately deserted their honorable party's heritage and began catering to racial prejudices.

Before abandoning the party's founding principles in 1964, Republicans, unlike Democrats, could be justifiably proud of their party's past. Historically, the Democratic Party was saddled with a southern wing stained with racism since the Civil War. Nevertheless, the 1948 Democratic National Convention squarely faced its dark past and adopted its first platform plank calling for civil rights, causing some southern delegations to walk out of the hall. By endorsing civil rights for minorities in 1948, Democrats began dismantling their sordid racial legacy. Perhaps knowing what Democrats did nearly seventy-five years ago will encourage Republican activists today to act to restore their party, to make it responsibly competitive.

My reading and assessment of the Republican Party is not new. Other political analysts have shared their concerns about changes in the Republican Party since the Eisenhower era. Thomas Mann and Norman Ornstein at the conservative American Enterprise Institute published several books about the party's dysfunctional role in government. *The Broken Branch* (2006) criticized both parties for failing to cooperate in Congress but came down harder on Republicans.[3] Mann and Ornstein in *It's Even Worse Than It Looks* (2012) described the Republican Party as an "insurgent outlier," and they (along with E. J. Dionne) showed in *One Nation After Trump* (2017) that the party's radicalization had been going on for decades before Trump.[4] According to Geoffrey Kabaservice's book *Rule and Ruin* (2012), the Republican Party underwent its fundamental change in the 1960s.[5] Recently, in *At War with Government* (2021), Amy Fried and Douglas Harris claim that Trump was continuing a war with government that began with Barry Goldwater in 1960.[6] My complementary study of the party's change is based on different information and new data. It also takes note of Donald Trump's cultlike effect on the Republican Party.

The party's politics crystallized at the 1960 GOP convention that nominated Richard Nixon over Barry Goldwater. Facing Nixon's inevitable win, Goldwater supported Nixon's nomination but also challenged conservatives to "grow up" and "take back" the party. After Nixon's 1960 loss to John F. Kennedy, frustrated Republicans nominated Goldwater in 1964. Today, conservatives need to "own up" to what happened to their party in 1964 and has happened since. They should "take it back," not with the hollow MAGA boast, making their party "great again," but with a vision of reclaiming its former morality—of restoring grandeur to the GOP.

When a major political party changes its political philosophy, it affects the public. Founded in 1854 to prevent the expansion of slavery outside southern states, the Republican Party won the 1860 elections for president and won both houses of Congress. In complete control of the national government, the Republican president fought the South's attempt to secede from the Union. The Republican Party later guaranteed political equality to newly freed slaves. The Republican Party began as a governing party, one willing to use its power to shape the nation.

Today, the GOP has evolved into an antigovernment party. In his book *The Conscience of a Conservative*, Barry Goldwater, the 1964 Republican presidential nominee, laid out his libertarian views for limited government: "I have little interest in streamlining government or in making it more efficient, for I mean to reduce its size. I do not undertake to promote welfare, for I propose to extend freedom. My aim is not to pass laws, but to repeal them." He continued: "The government must begin to withdraw from a whole series of programs that are outside its constitutional mandate, from social welfare programs, education, public power, agriculture, public housing, urban renewal and all the other activities that can be better performed by lower levels of government or by private foundations or by individuals."[7]

In his inaugural address on January 20, 1981, Republican president Ronald Reagan voiced his party's understanding of the nation's economic condition: "Government is not the solution to our problem; government is the problem." The party that had fought a Civil War against states' rights on slavery and battled against states' rights arguments in enacting civil rights had become an advocate of states' rights and an opponent of government programs that serve the public and promote social equality.

The party did not change to its present state abruptly; it evolved over time. This book documents how the party's principles evolved in nearly three thousand planks that I identified in all forty-one Republican Party platforms since 1856. Other researchers may have come up with more or fewer planks, but they will not be very different from mine. I analyzed those planks for underlying principles in terms of four organizational forms—*party*, *team*, *tribe*, and *cult*—that Republicanism has exhibited since 1856. The story divides this book into five parts.

PART I: POLITICAL PARTIES AND PRINCIPLES

Part 1 consists of three short chapters. Chapter 1 describes Republicans' four organizational forms. At core is the *party*—the organization that attracts activists to its political principles. A related entity but sometimes a conflicting one is the *team*, which aims at winning votes in elections. The *tribe* comprises the hardcore party identifiers who often align more closely with team than party. Very recently, a fourth form, *cult*, formed around the person of President Donald Trump. After President Trump's loss in the 2020 election, the party entered an uneasy relationship with his cult.

Chapter 2 identifies four principal benefits of government: *Social order*, the maintenance of which is government's original and fundamental benefit. Providing adequate *freedom* to citizens while maintaining order is not per se a benefit of government but a happy outcome of successful government. Using government to promote *equality* among citizens is a controversial benefit that did not emerge until the nineteenth century. (In the 1780s, our Founding Fathers balked at ending the slave trade and so even failed to recognize equality among human beings. After assuming control of government in 1860, however, the Republican Party promoted political equality among U.S. citizens.) The fourth and final benefit of government is providing *public goods* (for example, building roads and operating schools).

Chapter 3 inquires into how American political parties formulate their principles and announce them in party platforms—called "election manifestos" in foreign lands. Because American party platforms originate in a highly decentralized process involving party activists across the country, they provide the most authoritative statement of party principles and can be considered as more legitimate than speeches by presidential nominees.

PART II: REPUBLICAN PARTY PLANKS

Part 2 has two short chapters. Chapter 4 considers and rejects a historical analysis of party platforms on a liberal-conservative continuum. It examines at length John Gerring's alternative classification of ideological epochs in the Democratic and Whig/Republican parties from 1828 to 1998.

Chapter 5 reports on cataloging 2,722 planks in forty-one Republican platforms from 1856 to 2016. The planks were coded into 114 categories under four primary headings—Order, Freedom, Equality, and Public Goods. It also classified them under four secondary headings— Government, Military, Foreign Policy, and Symbolic.

PART III: PRINCIPLES OF REPUBLICANISM

Part 3 has eight chapters. Chapter 6, "Original Principles," traces how the Republican Party, founded to prevent slavery's spread outside the South, used national authority to establish political equality within the United States before becoming a states' rights party opposed to enforcing social equality.

Chapter 7, "Financing Government," details two switches in party principles: first, from embracing the protective tariff as its signature policy to becoming a free-trade party and, second, from proposing an income tax to provide additional revenue to opposing tax increases for erasing budget deficits.

Chapter 8, "Economic Affairs," discloses that Republicans, backed by manufacturing industries, once closely regulated those industries before their party, as a defender of free enterprise, switched to opposing government regulations.

Chapter 9, "Law and Order," examines the party's complicated positions on death and life. On the surface, Republicans seem to favor using government power both to kill (favoring the death penalty) and to prevent killing (opposing abortion of a fetus). Incongruously, the party still opposes government action against buying firearms while having favored government action against same-sex marriage.

Chapter 10, "Culture and Order," considers shifts in Republican immigration policy. In the nineteenth century, the party welcomed immigrants, despite worries about admitting more Catholics. In the twenty-first century, the party shied from admitting nonwhites and non-Christians. Except for its successful opposition to polygamy, the party generally lost its battles against the practice of alternative lifestyles in marriage and gender.

Chapter 11, "Conservation and Conservatives," recounts the party's retreat from championing conservation of the natural environment to advocating its development for economic gain.

Chapter 12, "Elections," reviews the party's changing positions on government's responsibility to ensure voting rights and the role of the Electoral College in choosing the president.

Chapter 13, "Evolving to Ethnocentrism," reviews the findings of the six previous chapters and charts the Republican Party's evolution from Gerring's nationalism epoch to its neoliberalism epoch. I contend that in 1964 the Republican Party left neoliberalism and entered an era of ethnocentrism.

PART IV: REPUBLICANS AS TEAM, TRIBE, AND CULT

Part 4 has chapters on each of three organizational alternatives to the formal party organization. Chapter 14, the longest, analyzes the Republican Party as an electoral team. It identifies major occasions when the

Republican Party chose between holding true to its principles and departing from them to win votes in presidential elections.

Chapter 15 relies on survey data to argue that many Republicans, originally attracted as fans to the Republican team, began to act as if belonging to a tribe. As tribal members, they intensified the difference between "we Republicans" and "those Democrats" in lifestyle as well as politics.

Chapter 16 sees some of the Republican tribe transforming into a cult around the person of Donald Trump. Party principles became less important than personal pronouncements. Evidence took a backseat to assertions. Democracy lost.

PART V: REPUBLICAN RESTORATION

Part 5 ends the book with two chapters and an epilogue. Chapter 17, "A Party in Peril," assesses the state of the Republican Party in 2022, torn between fealty to former president Donald Trump and to others seeking to reestablish the party as guided by principles, not by personality.

Chapter 18, "A Republican Epiphany," urges Republicans to acknowledge where their party stands morally and electorally. It contends that the GOP could improve its moral and electoral standings by abandoning its ethnocentric politics—if anyone could appear to lead the epiphany.

"Epilogue: The New Era" offers suggestions for remaking the Republican Party.

I

POLITICAL PARTIES
AND PRINCIPLES

1

POLITICAL PARTIES

The term "political party" warrants examination. It implies an organization, a group of individuals who interact with one another to pursue a common goal with some division of labor and role differentiation, but that's true of all organizations. Parties differ from other organizations by their goal: *to place their avowed representatives in government positions.*[1] The term "avowed representatives" is important. It means that they must be openly identified with the party name or label. That excludes such organizations as the National Association of Manufacturers and the AFL-CIO, a federation of labor unions. Both endorse candidates in elections but do not nominate them to run as their avowed representatives. If they did, they would qualify as political parties.

Also, the term "placing" in government positions should be interpreted broadly to mean through the electoral process (when a party competes with one or more others in pursuing its goal), *or* by a direct administrative action (when a ruling party allows no electoral competition), *or* by forceful imposition (when a party subverts the system and captures the governmental offices).

Applying this definition and its interpretations allows for ruling out and ruling in various organizations calling themselves parties. For example, the Black Panther Party, active in the 1960s to the 1980s, did not seek to place its members in government positions and so does not fit the definition. A decade ago, some elected Republican members of Congress professed belonging to the Tea Party, which also did not nominate and run its own candidates.[2] As a distinguished parties scholar wrote, "The recognizable label (which may or may not be on the ballot) is the crucial defining element."[3]

What about political organizations that do not compete with others in elections, such as former communist parties in Russia and Eastern Europe? In his 1956 book *Modern Political Parties*, Sigmund Neumann wrote, "Only the coexistence of at least one other competitive group makes a political party real," and continued: "A one-party system is a contradiction in terms."[4] Nevertheless, Neumann's book included an article on the Communist Party of the Soviet Union. Despite the way he defined a party, even Neumann found it awkward not to regard communist parties as political parties.[5] If organizations seek to place their avowed representatives in government positions, they are political parties.

This thumbnail cross-national and cross-time review of political parties has relevance for studying party politics today. First, it establishes that not all organizations that call themselves parties qualify for the label; second, that parties differ in the extent they compete in elections and how well they perform; and third—and most important—that political parties exist in governments across the world. That leads one to ask: Why do they? Authoritarian regimes may create parties for the illusion of linking with citizens, but why do parties always arise in democratic governments?[6]

John Aldrich addressed this question in his classic book *Why Parties?*:

> Election requires persuading members of the public to support that candidacy and mobilizing as many of those supporters as possible. This is a problem of collective action. How do candidates get supporters to vote for them—at least in greater numbers than vote for the opposition—as well as get them to provide the cadre of workers and contribute the

resources needed to win election? The political party has long been the solution.[7]

Winning a majority of votes from a large number of voters requires organized collective action from a set of individuals, hence the need for a political party. In democratic governments, contests for political office typically engender multiple parties, hence the creation of a party system. Every nation classified as a democracy has a system of at least two parties that seek to place its members in government by competing in elections. Since 1856, American politics has been structured by the same two competing parties: Republican and Democratic.

PARTIES, TEAMS, TRIBES, AND CULTS

Granting that both parties want to elect their candidates to government positions, what binds Republicans and Democrats together in opposing parties? What motivates partisans to work collectively? Writers propose at least four different sources of motivation: *principle, winning, identity,* and *authority.* Each source underlies one of four organizational manifestations: *parties, teams, tribes,* and *cults.*

PARTIES

The most familiar term, "political party," fits the popular view of politicians organized around common interests. Commenting on British politics in 1790, Edmund Burke held that parties joined politicians "united for promoting by their joint endeavours the national interest upon some particular principles in which they are all agreed."[8] I reserve the term "political parties" for such organizations, ones pursuing political principles. In truth, Burke wrote when parties were only factions within Parliament. British political parties did not compete for votes in popular elections until the 1830s.[9] Nevertheless, Burke's definition stands as the oldest, most accepted, and most noble rationale for their existence. This book inquires at length into the principles underlying the Republican Party.

TEAMS

Writing in the mid-1950s, Anthony Downs described parties as teams "seeking to control the governing apparatus by gaining office in a duly constituted election."[10] Although Downs believed that parties proposed policies based on political principles, he argued that they mainly adopted policies and principles to win elections. Senator Mitch McConnell of Kentucky, the long-time Republican leader in the U.S. Senate, endorsed that pragmatic view. Speaking about candidates running in the 2020 elections (over a month after Donald Trump's supporters stormed the U.S. Capitol and McConnell denounced President Trump's role in the insurrection), McConnell said, "I personally don't care what kind of Republicans they are, what lane they consider themselves in. What I care about is electability."[11] For Downs, and presumably for McConnell, winning elections is key to implementing policies. This book documents times when the Republican Party sacrificed its principles in order to win elections.

TRIBES

In two prominent 2018 publications, Lilliana Mason held that partisan behavior could be driven by another motivation: identifying with a social group linked to a party.[12] When social identity merges with party identity, party losses and wins become not just significant politically but also internalized personally. The party becomes a political tribe. Instead of contests between teams, elections become conflicts between tribes. Political symbolism acquires new meaning to members of warring tribes. During the COVID-19 pandemic, for example, wearing or not wearing a mask became a social and political statement.[13] A national survey in mid-June 2020 found Republicans "much more likely than Democrats to say that masks should rarely or never be worn (23 percent vs. 4 percent)."[14] On the last day of the Minnesota state legislature's special session in June, a reporter wrote: "Every Democrat entered the room with a face covering, but not one Republican wore a mask."[15] A national survey a year later found 86 percent of Democrats were vaccinated against COVID-19 versus 60 percent of Republicans.[16] Today, neither of our two national parties is actually a tribe, but scholars have observed increases in tribal behavior among individual partisans, especially among Republicans.

CULTS

In 1922, the German sociologist Max Weber wrote on the concept of charisma, used to describe leaders with "expansive personalities who establish ascendancy over other human beings by their commanding forcefulness."[17] Their followers grant them wholesale authority to act for them on political matters. Adolf Hitler's hold over the Nazi Party exemplified charismatic leadership, and scholars have referred to the "Cult of the Führer."[18] The term "personalist" refers to cultlike charismatic leadership in Latin America, where parties are sometimes named after their leaders—for example, Juan Perón, whose followers were called Perónistas. These terms, "charisma," "cult," and "personalism," have not figured prominently in the history of American party politics. Certainly, Teddy Roosevelt attracted followers and even led them in a fruitless split from the Republican Party in 1912. His distant cousin, Franklin Delano Roosevelt, also had devotees, as did Ronald Reagan and Barry Goldwater. The independent presidential candidate Ross Perot also won 19 percent of the vote in the 1992 presidential election. Yet the comprehensive review and analysis of personalist parties by Kostadinova and Levitt in 2014 mentions none of these names and no American parties.[19]

Before Donald Trump was elected president, American parties were not marred by personalist rule. Since then, waves of Republican partisans have succumbed to Trump's authority, acknowledging that the

Republican Party was "his" party and giving him the right to rule it. Observers soon began writing that the party had become a cult.[20] Cults may not have scruples, but do they have principles?

Most definitions of "principle" refer to "a basic truth, law, or assumption" used as a foundation for a system of belief or behavior.[21] The "basic truth" need not be demonstrably "true" but only assumed to be true. Consider slavery. Slave owners in colonial times and into the nineteenth century regarded slaves as fundamentally inferior beings. In southern states, slavery was a principle of the Democratic Party. Meanwhile, abolitionists in northern states believed that Negroes were fully human. On that principle, they formed the Republican Party in 1856 to prevent slavery's expansion outside the South. In that sense, both parties were "principled," but their principles were contradictory. A "principled" party may or may not be universally admired. For the purposes of discussion, let me stipulate that all four of the political groupings described earlier have principles, but they vary:

Parties offer *philosophical* principles with social, economic, and military significance: Consider the parties' positions on slavery in the nineteenth century.

Teams create *instrumental* principles with electoral significance: Think of the Republican Party's opposition to statehood for Washington, DC.

Tribes acquire *symbolic* principles to differentiate themselves from other tribes: Reflect on Republicans' refusal to wear masks.

Cults rely on *messianic* principles based on leaders' pronouncements: When accepting the Republican presidential nomination in 2016, Donald Trump proclaimed a crisis in America and said, "Only I can fix it."

Throughout American history, Democrats and Republicans have acted mostly as political parties and as teams. Each group of partisans coalesced around political principles they widely shared, and both typically campaigned on those principles to win elections. The Democratic and Republican parties were founded at different times, but both were founded on philosophical principles that were very different from their principles today.

FOUNDING PRINCIPLES OF AMERICA'S TWO MAJOR PARTIES

If political parties have principles, they most likely appear in their party platforms.[22] Throughout most of its history, two major political parties have governed the United States, sporadically alternating in power. The Democratic Party was formed in 1828, a quarter-century before the Republican Party in 1854. Historians say that the Democrats adopted the world's first national party platform at their 1840 nominating convention.[23] That brief early platform consisted of nine resolutions, the first one stating: "That the federal government is one of limited powers, derived solely from the constitution, and the grants of power shown therein, ought to be strictly construed by all the departments and agents of the government, and that it is inexpedient and dangerous to exercise doubtful constitutional powers."

You read that correctly; the Democratic Party platform once advocated restricting federal power to those specifically granted in the U.S. Constitution. Its position, 180 years ago, was similar to what the Republicans believe in today—"limited government, separation of powers, federalism, and the rights of the people"—as stated in the 2016 Republican platform and readopted in 2020.[24]

This is not the only example of a crossover by the parties on a key principle. The Republican Party was formed to oppose slavery and its spread to new territories and states. Running on that platform in 1860, the Republican candidate, Abraham Lincoln, won election, became president, fought a war against southern states defending slavery, freed the slaves, and became a hero to Black citizens at the time and over the next century. But today, Black Americans no longer identify with "the Party of Lincoln." Instead, they vote overwhelmingly for candidates of the once racist Democratic Party that had suppressed Blacks for over a hundred years.

There is no simple explanation for why—over time—the two major American parties crossed over in their positions on such core political principles as the role of government and support for ethnic groups. Did party leaders truly change their political philosophies, or did they compromise on their principles in order to win elections? Did they behave more like a team than a party? Most of this book will deal with Republicans considered as a political party versus an electoral team. Later sections will identify when Republicans began to exhibit tribal behavior and cult traits.

2

GOVERNMENT BENEFITS

The Republican Party styles itself as a conservative party. Conservative thought has a long history. Since time immemorial, rulers have lived better than their subjects. Having much to conserve, monarchs were politically "conservative" in the sense of opposing change—one meaning of that multifaceted term.[1] They sought to monopolize force to retain the status quo—the existing state of affairs. Over time in the Western world, autocratic rule evolved into oligarchical governments and eventually into representative governments chosen by restricted electorates. After being elected, leaders still lived better than their citizens and remained politically conservative. Like hereditary monarchs, they maintained order by monopolizing force within government; governments maintained order to support rulers and leaders. Whereas to conservatives today government is bad, to conservatives then government was good.

Inevitably, ambitious citizens banded together in political parties hoping to win elections, gain office, and personally share in the various benefits of government. Seeking to win votes, enterprising politicians promised more government outlays to an expanding electorate. After the Civil War, rational politicians seeking office in the United States aligned with either the Republican or Democratic parties. Ironically in today's politics, the Republican Party is regarded as a conservative party *because* of its opposition to government—especially the government in Washington. Mirroring the irony, the Democratic Party is regarded as liberal because it favors national government. Historically, that assessment went the other way.

Slavery had long been established in the South when the Democratic Party was founded to elect Andrew Jackson president in 1828. Jackson was a southerner, owned slaves, and wanted to conserve his property. Almost three decades later in 1854, northerners founded the Republican Party to oppose what was called the South's "peculiar institution." Seeking to maintain the status quo in the South, Democrats were the conservative party. They were opposed by Republicans, who pledged to confine slavery to southern states and to prevent slavery in new states, while retaining the Union in the process. Witness the 1856 Republican platform, which resolved against "establishing Slavery in the Territories of the United States by positive legislation, prohibiting its existence or extension therein." The Republican Party did not begin as a conservative party. In today's terms, it would be a liberal party.

From this point, the labels "liberal" and "conservative" will seldom reappear. Chapter 4 argues that they do not apply very well to politics across history. Instead, we analyze party politics using the core values that manifest in governmental principles. The original principle of government was to maintain order—which matched the desires of monarchical rulers. While imposing order, rulers were forced to grant citizens some degree of freedom, which became a second principle of acceptable government. A third principle was to provide public goods and services to citizens. Eventually, a fourth principle arose: to promote equality among citizens—a principle that became controversial. I incorporate these four core values into a framework for tracing and evaluating the trajectory of Republicanism over time.

ORDER AS A GOVERNMENT BENEFIT

Government's oldest and chief benefit has been *maintaining order,* a phrase rich with meaning. Let's start with "law and order." Maintaining order in this sense means establishing the rule of law to preserve life and protect property. To the seventeenth-century English philosopher Thomas Hobbes, preserving life was government's most important function. In his 1651 philosophical treatise *Leviathan*, Hobbes described life without government as life in a dangerous "state of nature."

A state of nature lacked behavioral rules, without which, Hobbes held, people would live as predators, stealing and killing for their personal benefit. In his classic phrase, such a life "under danger of violent death" would be "solitary, poor, nasty, brutish, and short." He believed that a single ruler, a sovereign, must possess unquestioned authority to guarantee the safety of the weak and protect them from the attacks of the strong. He believed that complete obedience to the sovereign's strict laws was a small price to pay for the security of living in a civil society. Hobbes named his all-powerful government "Leviathan," after a biblical sea monster.

Not everyone agrees that government is necessary for people to live in harmony. According to anthropologists, egalitarian stateless societies without rulers are "anarchist," after the Greek term *anarchos* ("having no ruler").[2] Hence, anarchism is defined as the absence of government. Anarchy typically results in lawlessness. Hobbes lived in a time perilously close to anarchy. The complicated English Civil Wars (1642–1651) occurred between Royalists and Parliamentarians. Hobbes argued that a strong, absolute ruler could prevent civil war. Unfortunately for King Charles I, he was not Leviathan-like and was beheaded in 1649. Eventually, a victorious Parliament consented to restore the monarchy as a constitutional monarchy. Anarchism still has its fanatics who violently protest against authority, but most people prefer a substantial degree of order from their governments.

RELEVANCE TODAY

Relatively few politicians would say they were attracted to the Republican Party out of a desire to promote order, a vague philosophical value. However, that value defines one of the four overarching political principles that encompass other specific principles embedded in practical politics that do motivate party partisans. Consider these examples of Republican platform policies embraced within the concept of order:

- Stopping crime and punishing criminals
- Controlling national borders
- Banning same-sex marriages
- Imposing tariffs on imported goods
- Mandating English as the national language

Such policies have, within recent times, been endorsed in Republican Party platforms. They all reflect the party's concern with maintaining social and economic order in American society. I capitalize "Order" in subsequent discussion when it stands for an abstract value.

FREEDOM AS A CHECK ON GOVERNMENT

Governments at any level require citizens to surrender some freedom. Although some governments minimize infringing on personal freedom, no government seeks to maximize personal freedom. Governments exist to control; "to govern" means "to control." Why do people surrender their freedom to this control? They do so to live in safety. Nevertheless, citizens do not surrender their freedoms willingly or completely.

Hobbes's conception of life in the cruel state of nature led him to view government primarily as a means of guaranteeing people's survival. Other theorists, taking survival for granted, believed that government should also preserve private property (goods and land owned by individuals) while allowing certain freedoms in economic and social life. Foremost among them was the English philosopher John Locke. In *Two Treatises on Government* (1690), he wrote that the protection of life, liberty, and property was the basic objective of government. Indeed, the state's role in religious freedom was central to the English Civil Wars. Locke's thinking strongly influenced the Declaration of Independence. It is reflected in the Declaration's famous phrase identifying "Life, Liberty, and the Pursuit of Happiness" as "unalienable Rights" of citizens under government. Locke's defense of property rights became linked with safeguards for individual liberties in the doctrine of *liberalism*, which holds that the state should leave citizens free to further their individual pursuits.[3]

To John Locke, liberalism referred to limits on government. That was liberalism's meaning then, and it is still understood that way in other countries. British colonists in American knew about Locke's ideas and wrote state constitutions "guarding against the apprehended mischief of the government" long before the Bill of Rights was appended to the U.S. Constitution.[4] Technically, rights—like dining in a public restaurant—require government action to secure. Freedoms—like freedom of religion—are guarantees against government interference. So the Bill of Rights is more properly a Bill of Freedoms. Especially in recent years, Republicans have rallied around "freedom" as an abstract value—as witnessed in many Republicans' refusal to wear protective face masks to prevent the spread of the COVID-19 virus. Consider these other examples of contemporary policies embraced under the concept of freedom:

- Oppose restrictions on the purchase of firearms
- Allow businesses to deny service to those who violate their religious beliefs
- Protect private property against seizure for public purposes
- Reduce income tax rates
- Support family choice of private over public schools

Such policies have become increasingly popular in Republican Party platforms. They all reflect the party's enhanced concern for personal Freedom, hereafter capitalized to stand for the value.

BENEFITS OF PUBLIC GOODS

After governments have established basic order and guarantee certain freedoms, they can pursue other ends. Using their coercive powers, governments can tax citizens to raise money to spend on *public goods*—benefits and services theoretically available to everyone, such as education, the postal service, sanitation, and parks.[5] Public goods benefit all citizens but are unlikely to be produced by the voluntary acts of individuals. The government of ancient Rome, for example, built aqueducts to carry fresh water from the mountains to the city. Road building was another public good provided by the Roman government, which also used the roads to move its legions and maintain order.

Government action to provide public goods can be controversial. During President James Monroe's administration in the first quarter of the nineteenth century, many people thought that building the Cumberland Road (between Cumberland, Maryland, and Wheeling, West Virginia) was not a proper function of the national government, the Romans notwithstanding. Over time, the scope of government functions in the United States has expanded. Although Republican president Dwight Eisenhower was opposed to big government, he launched the construction of the massive interstate highway system, at a cost of $275 billion (in 2020 dollars). Yet some government enterprises that have been common in other countries—running railroads, operating coal mines, and generating electric power—are politically controversial or even unacceptable in the United States.

Studies show that governments in European countries generally spend a far larger share of their Gross Domestic Product (GDP) than does the United States.[6] Most of the difference occurs in fund transfers to lessen household income inequality, but Europeans spend more for public goods, too. Americans disagree about how far the government ought to go in using its taxing power to provide public goods and services. Parents with school-age children may favor increased taxes for education more than adults without such children, and wealthier people may prefer to spend their money on private consumption rather than public goods. Studies also show that ethnic majorities are less supportive of public spending that benefits ethnic minorities.[7] Democrats and Republicans also differ in spending for public goods, and both parties devote much of their platforms to such issues. Recent Republican platforms have disagreed over:

- Extending broadband capabilities across the nation
- Maintaining highways and bridges

- Conserving and developing natural resources
- Supporting Medicare for the elderly
- Funding free community college education

RELEVANCE TODAY

In truth, Republicans today do not seem as motivated to provide public goods as they have in the past. The very first Republican Party platform in 1856 proposed building a railroad to the Pacific Ocean and using government funds to improve rivers and harbors. During President Grant's administration in 1872, Republicans created the national park system. The party's 1888 platform criticized the Democratic administration for refusing to start work on a canal to link the Atlantic and Pacific oceans. Assuming power in 1892, the party supported the canal's construction as "of the highest importance to the American people." In 1906, under Teddy Roosevelt, Republicans created new national parks and designated national landmarks and national monuments. Since World War II, only Dwight Eisenhower's Interstate Highway initiative in 1952 compares with those Republican expenditures for Public Goods, hereafter capitalized when indicating the value.

EQUALITY: A DISPUTED BENEFIT

Private charity (voluntarily aiding the poor) has a strong basis in Western religious traditions; public welfare does not. Charles Dickens's 1838 novel *Oliver Twist* dramatized how England imprisoned poor people. Only in the twentieth century, in the aftermath of industrialization and urbanization, did the United States begin taking steps to promote equality—to improve life for the poor—and such actions proved controversial. Under the emerging concept of the welfare state, government's role expanded to provide individuals with medical care, education, and a guaranteed income "from cradle to grave." Sweden, Britain, and other nations adopted welfare programs aimed at reducing social inequalities.[8]

Using government to enforce equality was a radical idea, set forth by Karl Marx as the ultimate principle of developed communism: "from each according to his ability, to each according to his needs."[9] This extreme has never been realized in any government, not even in communist states. But over time, taking from the rich to help the needy has become a legitimate function of most governments but a very controversial one to some citizens.

People often oppose taxation for public goods (building roads and schools, for example) because of cost alone. Government spending for highways, schools, and parks benefits nearly every citizen, and such services merely cost money. People are more likely, and more strongly, to deny on *principle* funding government programs to promote economic and social equality. Using government to promote social equality—busing school children to integrate schools, granting women equal rights, recognizing same-sex marriages—has proved to be politically disruptive. The cost is greater than money; funding for social equality usually means a tradeoff in basic values: such spending conflicts with Order and Freedom. These contemporary planks in Republican Party platforms exemplify Republican opposition to social equality:

- Opposed to raising the minimum wage
- Opposed to the Equal Rights Amendment to the Constitution
- Against using ethnicity as a factor in college admissions
- Against funding American and Alaska Native tribal governments
- Preventing same-sex couples from adopting children

RELEVANCE TODAY

Especially since the Great Depression of the 1930s, the government's role in redistributing income to promote economic and social equality has been a major source of policy debate in the United States. Whereas the Republican Party was founded in 1856 to end slavery and had a platform plank promising "liberty of conscience and equality of rights among citizens," equality as a principle occupies a lesser status in the party's values today. Equality too will be capitalized in what follows.

BENEFITS TO PARTISANS

How heavily do government benefits weigh in the attention that the electorate pays to the offerings of political parties? Research on the electorate's voting behavior suggests that relatively few voters know very much about the specific policy proposals of the candidates for whom they vote or know anything specific about the platforms of the Democratic or Republican parties. Instead, most variation in voting behavior can be explained by the citizens' party identifications. With which of the parties does the voter identify? Typically, over 75 percent of the American electorate votes for the party with which they identify.

What causes people to identify with political parties? Whatever the factors, they have less influence today than in the early 1950s. In 1952, almost 75 percent of the electorate called themselves Democrats or Republicans. Almost 50 percent identified with Democrats and almost 30 percent with Republicans then. In 2021, less than 60 percent identified with either party. Only about 33 percent remained Democrats, but about 25 percent were still Republicans. Did Republicans keep a better hold on their partisans because of their superior principles?

Research shows that about half of the electorate simply adopts their parents' party preference—much as they adopt their parents' religious affiliation. As a result, state counties with little population change over time tend to back the same parties over decades. When young people move away from parents, become educated, and have different life experiences, they often depart from their parents' partisanship. Also, the electorate's social composition changes over time from immigration and differential birth rates. These factors produce partisan change along with changes in party principles.

In the 1950s, people in small towns and rural areas, women, college-educated voters, and Blacks living in the South were more likely to identify as Republican than Democrat. Today those relationships are reversed. Then the South was solidly Democratic; today it is strongly Republican. The Republican Party—once closely identified with Wall Street—now considers its base to be blue-collar wage earners and white Christians outside New York. In an earlier book, I analyzed the changing social bases of the Democratic and Republican parties since 1952.[10] In this book, I look for an explanation for changes in Republican Party principles, but not just since the 1950s. I study 2,722 planks included in all forty-one Republican Party platforms since 1856.

3

PARTY PLATFORMS AND PRINCIPLES

A physical platform is an elevated place to stand. In early England, a written plan was also called a platform.[1] *Safire's Political Dictionary* indicates that as early as 1803 in the United States the term described a set of political principles.[2] The U.S. Democratic Party was founded to back Andrew Jackson's election in 1828, and it formally adopted the world's first party platform at its 1840 national convention. Since then, scores of different political parties in the United States have formally adopted platforms announcing their political values and policies. Most minor party platforms have been printed in books.[3] Today, all Democratic and Republican platforms, as well as those of the more important other parties, are available on the internet, courtesy of the American Presidency Project.[4]

Party platforms are supposed to declare "the principles, objectives, and promises of the national party as proclaimed by the national convention";[5] provide "the single avenue by which parties can make their comprehensive policy positions known to voters";[6] "articulate party policy commitments";[7] and—simply—tell "what the party stands for."[8] Writing in 1967, Gerald Pomper, a major student of the subject, said that the platform adopted at a national party convention "most fully represents the party's intentions." Nevertheless, he continued, platforms "have received more scorn than attention."[9]

Observers' scorn for party platforms goes far back in American history. In 1888, James Bryce (later Britain's ambassador to the United States) wrote, "Neither platforms nor the process that produces them have a powerful influence on the maturing and clarification of public opinion."[10] In 1902, Moisei Ostrogorski, another foreign observer of American politics, said, "The platform, which is supposed to be the party's profession of faith and its programme of action is only a farce."[11] In 1936, the American Richard Browne's doctoral thesis found that nearly everyone who wrote before 1912 substantially agreed "that the national party platform has had little or no significance."[12]

Writing thirty years after Browne, Pomper still found writers who dismissed a platform as "meaningless,"[13] frequently quoting the popular saying "A platform is something to run on, not stand on." Pomper was one of the first researchers to demonstrate that political parties actually deliver on most of their platform pledges. Since Pomper's early work, a great deal of research has established that party platforms are reasonably good predictors of party behavior. While this book reviews some of that research, it does not rate Republicans' fidelity to their party platforms. It focuses instead on how party principles, especially in the Republican Party, have changed over time.

PLATFORM CONTENTS

Describing the contents of a party platform in the simplest terms, Browne said,

> It consists of three general parts:
> 1. An elaboration of the record and achievements of the party [pointing with pride].
> 2. A denunciation of the opposing party, its record, or its proposals [viewing with alarm].[14]
> 3. Various statements on the issues of the day, "as to what the party believes in, approves, favors, advocates, stands for, demands, or pledges itself to do."[15]

Browne held that the platform's heart lies in point 3, typically its longest part, which includes:

a. Statements of general principles.
b. Expressions of sympathy [e.g., for Armenians in 1920].
c. Actual statements of policy to be pursued, sometimes clearly stated, sometimes vague.[16]

Later scholars expanded on classifying platform contents. Most have been based on Gerald Pomper's 1967 breakdown, given here (omitting Pomper's illustrative examples):

1. Rhetoric and Fact
2. Evaluations of the Parties' Records and Past Performances
    (a) General Approval
    (b) General Criticism
    (c) Policy Approval
    (d) Policy Criticism
3. Statements of Future Policies
    (a) Rhetorical Pledges
    (b) General Pledges
    (c) Pledges of Continuity
    (d) Expressions of Goals and Concerns
    (e) Pledges of Action
    (f) Detailed Pledges[17]

Pomper updated his research in 1980 to include the 1976 platforms,[18] and Lee Payne extended Pomper's analysis of party platforms through 2008.[19] Subsequent researchers have adopted or expanded on Pomper's classification, with special attention to how specific were the party's "pledges."[20] Others have modified how pledges were interpreted. For example, Royed and Borelli scored economic pledges for proposing a policy change, adhering to the status quo, expanding, cutting, or reviewing.[21]

Curiously, while virtually all American parties formulate platforms, parties in other countries do not write platforms; they issue "manifestos." The *Oxford Universal English Dictionary* says that "manifesto"—a public declaration of intentions—appeared in seventeenth-century English. In 1848, the term famously appeared in German—*Manifest der Kommunistischen Partei*. Perhaps the "Communist Manifesto" heritage led parties abroad to favor using that term. Regardless, "manifesto" is not mentioned in the eight-hundred-plus-page *Safire's Political Dictionary*. This minor difference in terminology (platform versus manifesto) accompanies a major difference in how party principles are studied by academics and employed in politics.

Empirical research on the content of party platforms and party manifestos exploded following the publication of Pomper's 1967 article and 1968 book. Many studies, if not most, focused on how well governmental parties fulfilled their platform or manifesto pledges. Research of this type proved to be especially popular in countries with competitive parties and parliamentary systems, which often have coalition governments. Party scholars eventually banded together to create a "Party Manifesto Database" of over four thousand manifestos drawn from about fifty countries—including the United States—to support cross-national research.[22]

Studies soon focused on how well political parties kept pledges they made in party platforms and party manifestos. Petry and Collette identified and reviewed many such studies, asking whether "political parties keep their campaign promises once elected" and finding: "[Our] review of 21 cases in 18 separate published studies reveals that parties fulfill 67 percent of their promises on average. Contrary to popular belief, political parties are reliable promise keepers. Why people underestimate the capacity of political parties to keep their election promises remains an open research question."[23]

One team of eleven scholars from multiple countries studied "fulfillment of over 20,000 pledges made in 57 election campaigns in 12 countries" and concluded: "Parties that hold executive office after elections generally fulfill substantial percentages, sometimes very high percentages, of their election pledges, whereas parties that do not hold executive office generally find that lower percentages of their pledges are fulfilled."[24] While research has established that most parties everywhere tend to fulfill their election pledges, scholars studying European manifestos place more importance on fulfilling pledges than those studying party platforms in America.

PARTY PLATFORMS VERSUS PARTY MANIFESTOS

American parties adopted platforms before European parties issued manifestos. The British Conservative Party was founded in 1832, only four years after the U.S. Democratic Party. However, the researchers Thackeray and Toye found that British parties did not publish manifestos until 1900. They noted that the new prime minister, Sir Robert Peel, wrote and distributed an election manifesto in 1834, but that was a personal statement and not a true party document.[25] By the end of the century, the practice of party leaders issuing election addresses became established in Britain. Nevertheless, Thackeray and Toye said, "Manifestos became mere 'shopping lists' made without reference to general principles" until 1900.[26]

British party manifestos also tend to be shorter than American party platforms. Thackeray and Toye counted words for twenty-seven British manifestos from 1900 to 1997 for both the Conservative and Labour parties. Their counts can be compared with counts for twenty-six Democratic and Republican platforms from 1900 to 1996.[27] British manifestoes are much shorter. The average Conservative manifesto was 7,611 words to 12,014 for the average Republican platform. British Labour manifestos averaged 5,482 words to 11,222 for Democratic platforms. Over time, both British manifestos and American platforms increased in length, which narrowed the differences between the two party systems. However, the 2015 Conservative and Labour manifestos of 30,146 and 18,178 words respectively were still shorter than the 35,467 and 26,058 words in the 2016 Republican and Democratic platforms.[28]

Are American party platforms longer than party manifestos in other countries because the United States is larger in size and population? While that factor may apply, the difference may be attributable more to the unique nature of American political parties. Both American political parties operate in a highly decentralized political system.[29] The United States has a federal form of government with fifty state governments, three coequal branches of national government, and a national legislature with two coequal branches. These factors, and the larger size of the United States, disperse political power across the country.

Unlike most other parties across the world, both American parties publicly nominate their candidates for congressional offices and publicly elect delegates to party conventions that nominate presidential candidates. This combination of governmental and party structure results in highly decentralized national political parties. Different people and groups can influence the policies of their preferred party at various points while building the platform for adoption at the party's national convention.

BUILDING PARTY PLATFORMS

In comparing the processes of producing American party platforms and writing British party manifestos, two British scholars pointed to "the structural difference between the federal and unitary system," citing many of the points made here about the decentralization of power in the United States, and they noted "the importance of state representation in the making of national party policy."[30] In sum, American party platforms differ from British party manifestos—and manifestos in other countries—mainly because the American governmental structure is decentralized, the party organization is decentralized, and the process of drafting the party document is itself decentralized.

In the United Kingdom and especially in its Conservative Party, national party leaders figure prominently in starting and then influencing the drafting of the manifestos, and leaders are often pictured in the glossy print versions.[31] In the United States, presidents and presidential candidates have often steered the content of their party's platform, but they tend to exercise their influence at the end of the process rather than the beginning. The drafting process typically begins by involving state and local activists and leaders.

Historically, partisans at the state and local levels were always involved in drafting party platforms. Richard Browne's 1936 dissertation devoted a forty-page chapter to the process as practiced a century ago. Even then, it was too simple to say they "are adopted by the national party conventions after having been drafted by the Resolutions Committees of the conventions." Instead, Browne said, "The actual drafting takes place only after weeks and months of preliminary work, dating back several months before the convention meets."[32] He then outlined the work of various organizations, groups, and individuals who aided the drafting, devoting short sections to each of these participants: "The National Committee . . . Advisory Committees . . . Dominant Candidates . . . Party leaders . . . State and Party Conventions . . . Non-party Organisations . . . Non-party Individuals . . . Public Hearings . . . Subcommittee on Drafting . . . The Resolutions Committee."

Since Browne's detailed 1936 study, later accounts have confirmed the decentralized nature of the complex drafting process. Cooke's account of drafting the 1952 platforms stated: "With hundreds of persons officially involved, and scores of others working behind the scenes, we may at best ascribe certain areas to the craftsmanship of one or more of the main agencies involved in the platform-making process. The genesis of the Republican platform may be traced to the subcommittees, the drafting committee, the special advisers, the full committee, and the party legacy." The genesis of the Democratic platform goes back to the White House draft and the McCormack revision, the drafting committee, the special advisers, the full committee, and the legacy of past platforms.[33]

In 1968, Paul David studied how both parties created their platforms. Because "the platform has to be voted by the platform committee of the convention before it can reach the floor," David explained, "every platform committee in recent decades has involved a heterogeneous membership of more than 100, with two from every state delegation." Moreover, "Since 1960, it has been customary for the platform committees of both parties to come into session at the beginning of the preconvention week, first to hold public hearings and then to complete committee work on the final text of the platform."[34]

Concerning the 1976 Democratic platform, Jeff Fishel wrote that its construction began four years earlier, in 1972:

> When reform, anti-war, McGovern Democrats were bitterly opposed by major figures in the AFL-CIO and by many party regulars like the Daley organization from Chicago . . .
>
> Representatives of the Carter campaign came into the first national platform hearings, held in Washington, May 17–20, 1976 . . .
>
> The actual hearing produced the typically large (more than 140) parade of witnesses, from Michael Harrington speaking for "Democracy '76" . . . to Hubert Humphrey.[35]

Susan Fine's study of 1988 party platforms focused on the role that nonparty actors played. She stated: "The wheels of the platform writing process begin turning during the primary/caucus season. Each party holds regional hearings so that interested groups and individuals may express their views to the party executive committees which in turn draft the document. No restrictions are placed on who can testify."[36]

A large portion of those outsiders testifying before the platform writing committees represent interest groups. An interest group whose perspective is reflected in a platform benefits in several ways because its view is endorsed by party leaders and delegates representing the party faithful.[37]

Sandy Maisel, however, found that the parties produced more "presidential-centered platforms" in 1992:

> Each party's platform went through three public drafts. Staff produced one draft; that draft went respectively to the subcommittees of the Republican Committee on Resolutions and to the Drafting Committee of the Democratic Platform Committee. The second draft emerged from the Republican subcommittees and the Democratic Drafting Committee. The third draft emerged from the two full committees

and in each case was adopted by the national convention without amendment.[38]

In truth, American party platforms have always been subject to presidential adjustment. As early as 1936, Browne wrote, "After the platform is adopted, it may be interpreted, perhaps altered, by the nominee himself."[39] Part 4 discusses important impacts of presidential nominees on their election platforms.

Finally, we should note that nonparty groups also influence the content of party platforms. A comparative study of organized groups' testimony before platform committees found both parties' platforms in 1996, 2000, and 2004 "responsive to organized interests that are ideologically similar to the party status quo and to those who have demonstrated loyalty to the party."[40]

THE 2020 PARTY PLATFORMS

Evidence of party leaders' control, not just influence, emerged at both parties' conventions in 2020. Because of the COVID-19 pandemic, the Democratic and Republican parties did not gather thousands of delegates at national conventions to nominate their presidential candidates and adopt party platforms. By April 2020, Senator Bernie Sanders had withdrawn as a presidential candidate in the Democratic Party, conceding the nomination to former vice president Joe Biden. While the Democrats' nominee was no longer in question, the party platform had not been drafted. Knowing that the Democrats would not hold their customary convention, the party's centrist candidate and presumptive nominee, Joe Biden, met with his left-of-center challenger, Bernie Sanders, to discuss the platform. They agreed to submit to the Platform Committee a 110-page document of policy recommendations from a "joint task force."[41] After some confusion about procedures, the Democratic Party managed to endorse an unusually long platform made outside the usual drafting procedures. One cannot know what to make of the 2020 Democratic platform, which at 42,092 words was by far the longest in its history.

The Republican Party followed a comparably strange route. For the first time in their history, Republicans adopted no platform in 2020. Directed by President Donald Trump, the National Committee simply published resolutions about the missing platform prefaced by these remarks:

> WHEREAS, All platforms are snapshots of the historical contexts in which they are born, and parties abide by their policy priorities, rather than their political rhetoric;
>
> WHEREAS, The RNC, had the Platform Committee been able to convene in 2020, would have undoubtedly unanimously agreed to reassert the Party's strong support for President Donald Trump and his Administration . . .

The RNC then resolved to continue "to enthusiastically support the President's America-first agenda" and to adjourn the 2020 convention "without adopting a new platform until the 2024 Republican National Convention." This was its concluding resolution: "*RESOLVED*, That any motion to amend the 2016 Platform or to adopt a new platform, including any motion to suspend the procedures that will allow doing so, will be ruled out of order." In effect, the 2020 Republican Party decided to readopt its 2016 platform. Only the 2016 platforms of the Democratic and Republican parties will be considered in this book.

The pandemic year 2020 broke almost two hundred years of tradition in drafting party platforms. True, Maisel found party platforms more "president-centered" in 1992, but drafting party platforms still originated in a highly decentralized process. That is clearly illustrated by considering who participated in drafting the 2016 platform of the Republican Party, its most recent platform. Over several pages at the end of the document, the party named all the individuals who helped draft the document:

- The Republican Platform Committee, headed by RNC Chair Reince Priebus, consisting of nineteen members.
- Two RNC members from each of the fifty states and two RNC members from six territories and the District of Columbia, for a total of 110 members.
- The Platform Staff of thirty-six named employees.
- Others mentioned for "special thanks," numbering eighty-four.

A total of 249 people were identified by name as helping draft the 2016 Republican platform, which was later presented for adoption to 2,472 Republican delegates at the nominating convention. In 2020, however, neither party followed standard practices in drafting their platforms.

II

REPUBLICAN PARTY PLANKS

4

BEYOND LIBERAL
AND CONSERVATIVE

P olitical observers across the world describe parties as being liberal or conservative, as being on the left or right of a political continuum. The Manifesto Database, discussed in chapter 3, contains about twenty variables that indicate parties' left-right (L-R) ideological positioning. In his thoughtful appraisal of that project, Gemenis Kostas noted that manifesto data "have been used in hundreds of PhD theses, monographs and journal articles," adding, "Undoubtedly, its popularity lies in the rich time-series data which run for more than two dozen countries since 1945 and include parties' positions on the L-R scale." Nevertheless, he continued, "the most criticised aspect of the project is its 'standard' scale measuring parties' and governments' L-R positions."[1] He cited studies finding "that some scale items do not 'fit' in the underlying 'left' and 'right' dimensions" and "a lot of published evidence" that the L-R scores in the data sets "do not provide valid and reliable estimates regarding parties' L-R positions."[2]

The extensive Manifesto Database is more suitable for studies across space (different nations) than across time within the same nation. Although the data consist of thousands of manifestos for scores of countries, less than 5 percent date before 1950. This book does not use those data. It analyzes data specifically collected on forty-one American party platforms since 1856 and avoids using the L-R continuum, despite its common use by political observers.

Many analysts view the Democratic and Republican parties on a left-right continuum or scale, in which the left-hand side represents the "liberal" position favoring more government and the right-hand side stands for the "conservative" position of less government. Placed on the left, the Democratic Party is called a liberal party, and the Republican Party, on the right, a conservative party. Mass media typically use these terms, as frequently do political scientists and historians. While the terminology has validity and utility for political analysis at given points in time, it fails miserably in trying to track the parties' ideology over long stretches of history. Verlan Lewis indicts such research as succumbing to the "Static Spectrum Fallacy."[3] In reality, the meanings of party policies change over time.

We begin by examining the concept of party ideology.[4] A political ideology can be defined as a coherent and consistent set of values and beliefs about the proper purpose and scope of government.[5] "Coherent" means that the values and beliefs are organized and logically constrain one another. "Consistent" means a person's opinion of the proper role of government on one issue matches the person's opinion on a different but similar issue. Although the term "ideology" has been used historically in other ways,[6] Frances Lee's research finds that in contemporary political science research it "denotes interrelated political beliefs, values, and policy positions."[7] Studying congressional politics, Lee counted references to ideology and to closely related terms—liberal and conservative—in professional journals and in the *New York Times* from 1900 to 2003. "Prior to the 1950s," she wrote, "scholars generally spoke only of particular liberal or conservative coalitions or legislators"; not until the 1960s were the terms commonly applied to "individual legislators' policy orientations."[8]

Steeped in contemporary politics of ideological polarization, today's readers may be surprised—even astounded—by Lee's finding that legislators were not commonly described as liberal or conservative until the 1960s. Today, politicians are routinely painted as spendthrift liberals or backward conservatives. In the past, the words "liberal" and "conservative" were not so negatively colored.

Moreover, the further one goes back in history, the less the terms correspond to what we today would recognize as either liberal or conservative. Verlan Lewis's comprehensive analysis of party positions since the republic's founding convincingly demonstrates the changing meaning of the terms and the parties' switches in positions "on virtually every enduring public policy issue in American history."[9] Lewis wrote: "For the past eight decades or so, virtually whatever the Democratic Party does is termed 'liberal' and whatever the Republican Party does is termed 'conservative.'"[10] Although these terms differentiate the parties for their followers, their meanings have changed notably over history.

IDEOLOGICAL TERMS IN PARTY PLATFORMS

The Democratic Party issued forty-five election platforms from its first in 1840 to 2016, and the Republican Party forty-one platforms since its first in 1856. (Because the COVID-19 pandemic prevented both parties from holding a full national convention in 2020, each party's national committee simply adopted its 2016 platform for the 2020 election campaign.) Although writers tend to link "liberal" with "conservative," the terms have not appeared equally in party platforms. "Conservative" was mentioned only fourteen times in both parties' platforms since 1840, but both parties alluded to "liberal" 126 times in some form. This analysis focuses on the term "liberal."

Once upon a time—indeed, for over a hundred years—Republican Party platforms used "liberal" positively, and Republicans proudly wore the liberal mantle. In 1860, for example, the party favored a policy that "secures to the workingmen liberal wages." In 1864, it favored "a liberal and just" immigration policy. As recently as 1978, the distinguished scholar Samuel Beer noted that Senator Robert Taft, Mr. Republican in the 1940s, "called himself 'liberal' to the end" and that Barry Goldwater was "the first major politician to embrace the name 'conservative.'"[11] Beginning with the second term of Reagan's presidency in 1984, however, the Republican platforms' usage of the root "liberal" dramatically shifted to the dark side.[12] Meanwhile, the forty-four Democratic Party platforms since 1840 staunchly—but not consistently—embraced the liberal label.

Liberal rhetoric in Democratic and Republican platforms over time can be divided into three eras, as shown in figure 4.1. The first era, which extends from the parties' first platforms, might be called "A Century of Consensus." During the 116 years from 1840 to 1956, the Democratic Party's platforms used "liberal" thirty times. During the 100 years from 1856 to 1956, the Republican platforms mentioned "liberal" fourteen times. Both parties throughout this period virtually always used "liberal" in a positive way—in the sense of "free in giving; generous; open-minded"—as listed in the *Oxford University English Dictionary* of 1937.

The second era, which lasted the twenty years from 1960 to 1980, might be deemed "A Period of Adjustment." During this time, both parties shifted to talking about *liberalization* instead of using the word "liberal." Before 1960, "liberalization" had previously occurred only once across the fifty-six platforms of both parties. During the twenty years from 1960 to 1980, Democrats mentioned it thirteen times and Republicans seven. Following the Republican Party's earlier practice, not once during this "Period of Adjustment" did a Republican platform use "liberal" or "liberalization" in a negative way.

The third era, which has lasted a third of a century, began in 1984 and continued through 2016. It might be labeled the "Age of Attack and Avoidance." For the first time in history, the 1984 Republican platform attacked Democratic opponents for being liberals. Since then, Republican platforms repeatedly used the term to deride Democrats. Examples include referring to "liberal experimenters" who "destroyed the sense of community" in 1984, "liberal attacks on everything the American

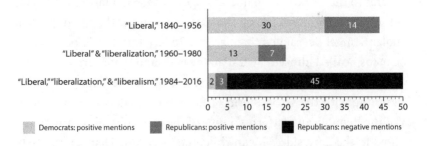

FIGURE 4.1. Number of mentions of "liberal" in party platforms, 1840–2016.

people cherished" in 1988, "the liberal philosophy" that "assaulted the family" in 1992, and "the liberal agenda of litigious lawyers" in 1996. By word count, Republican platform attacks quadrupled from two to eight in 1988 and then almost doubled to fifteen in 1992.

In response, Democrats—who like Republicans had proudly claimed the liberal label before—now avoided it almost entirely in their party platforms, using "liberal" only once from 1980 to 2016. After Republicans began attacking all signs of liberalism, Democrats unilaterally removed the term from their vocabulary. Neither "liberal" nor "liberalism" appeared in the 2016 platform of the Democratic Party. The 2016 Republican platform invoked "liberal" pejoratively only twice and "conservative" approvingly only twice.

The point of this analytical review is to demonstrate that employing ideological labels in contentious discussions of politics is relatively new in American history. Frances Lee's extensive historical analysis of scholarly articles and news stories about congressional politics found that individual members of Congress were not portrayed as liberals or conservatives until the 1960s. My own inquiry into the terms' usage in Democratic and Republican Party platforms found that Republicans did not castigate Democrats as "dirty rotten liberals" until 1984, when Democrats also began avoiding the term in their own platforms. Because the rhetoric of political ideology has permeated recent decades of discussion about American politics, we may think that the world of politics has always revolved about liberal-versus-conservative arguments, thought, and positions.

In fact, national surveys show that voters—and thus party identifiers—do not share any common understanding of the meanings of "liberal" and "conservative." When people were asked to place themselves on a liberal-conservative scale, from one-quarter to one-third declined, saying they "haven't thought much about it."[13] Another survey asking respondents to discuss "the biggest difference between liberal and conservative views" found that 38 percent did not know or gave no answer.[14] Yet party identifiers are ready to align themselves with their party's proclaimed ideologies. Verlan Lewis wrote: "Whatever the Republican Party does (even if it is the opposite of what Republicans did previously) is described as 'conservative,' and whatever the Democratic Party does (even if it is the opposite of what Democrats did previously) is described as 'liberal.' Thus, claims that the Democratic Party moved to the 'left,' or that the Republican Party moved to the 'right' are not helpful because they are tautological."[15]

If both parties' voters have fuzzy conceptions of ideology, both Democratic and Republican party leaders enjoy great latitude in formulating their policies. Such latitude is especially important to Republicans when they gain control of government. Verlan Lewis explains: "Notably, when a new party takes control of government, the members of the party in government will often exercise the powers at their disposal by enacting interventionist policies—even if their party's ideology during the campaign and in the early years of their control of government calls for limited government power and limited intervention."[16] He continues:

> In 2017–2018, with unified control of government, Republican politicians passed legislation that set records for federal spending: topping 1 trillion for the first time in American history. Despite the fact that the US economy had pulled out of the Great Recession, Republicans in control of government decided to increase national government spending levels in real terms and as a percentage of GDP. Based simply on the ideas and attitudes articulated by the Republican Party before assuming control of unified government in 2017, we would have expected federal spending and deficits to decrease. But, knowing what we do about the tendency of almost all politicians to exercise and expand the powers at their disposal, the behavior of President Trump and his Republican Congress was perfectly predictable.[17]

According to Lewis, dominant presidents—for example, Abraham Lincoln, Teddy Roosevelt, Franklin Delano Roosevelt, Ronald Reagan, and Donald Trump—determine party ideology. If they "change their party ideology in ways that justify the actions of their partisans and vilify the actions of their opponents," they can succeed without worrying about departing from established party principles.[18]

IDEOLOGICAL EPOCHS IN AMERICAN PARTIES

How did nineteenth-century historians, writing almost 150 years ago, describe the parties they studied? In 1883, Walter Houghton at Indiana University published *A History of American Politics*.[19] Not once in his comprehensive, 550-page review of every presidential election from 1789 to 1880 did Houghton refer—in any way—to the parties' alignment along a liberal-conservative continuum. In fact, he only used those terms thirty-seven and seventeen times, respectively, and nine of the thirty-seven references to "liberal" were to the Liberal Republicans who held a national convention in 1872.

If the parties' liberal-conservative alignment was not seen in the last quarter of the nineteenth century, perhaps it was visible to political scientists writing in the first third of the twentieth. In 1936, Richard Browne analyzed virtually all U.S. political party platforms to date in his 350-page dissertation. He used the terms "liberal" fourteen times and *never* mentioned "conservative." As argued earlier, only after World War II did observers begin assigning Democrats and Republicans to positions on a left-right, liberal-conservative continuum.

Some contemporary scholars have analyzed historical shifts in American party ideologies without resorting to the liberal-conservative continuum.[20] Most significant is John Gerring's 1998 study *Party Ideologies in America, 1828–1996*. Early in his book, Gerring wrote: "If asked to describe the ideology of the major parties in America, most observers would identify the Republicans as conservative and the Democrats as liberal. Although there is nothing incorrect in this typology, there is surely much that is misleading." Noting "the shortcomings of standard terminology (liberalism, conservatism)," Gerring proposed "a modest reconceptualization of American party ideology along historical lines." He studied "official party platforms as well as an extensive collection of campaign speeches [especially by presidential candidates], letters, and other publications issued by the Whig [the Whigs were the Republicans' predecessors], Republican, and

Democratic parties."[21] He sorted sentences in these documents into content categories (for example, civil rights, small business) and then counted their occurrences.

Gerring subsumed these content categories under broader concepts, such as social order, liberty, equality, tyranny, patriotism, and economic growth. He included the core values of *order, freedom,* and *equality* (discussed in chapter 1) but not *public goods*, which Gerring treated under *welfare*. Gerring searched for changes in the "central dichotomy" confronting the parties at each presidential election year and for changes in the parties' political "themes." Unfortunately, Gerring failed to define "central dichotomy," but it appears to represent a basic clash between political interests or states of affairs. He also failed to define "theme," but that term seems to mean "principle." He summarized his major findings in two tables—one for the Democratic Party from 1828 to 1992 and the other for the Whig/Republican Party from 1828 to 1992.

According to Gerring, Democratic Party principles changed substantially over time. It experienced ideological change over three "epochs" from 1828 to 1992. He called the period from 1828 to 1892 the Democrats' Jeffersonianism epoch, during which the party defended "liberty" against "tyranny." During its populism epoch from 1896 to 1948, the party defended "the people" against "the interests." In the universalism epoch, from 1952 to 1992, Democrats championed "inclusion" over "exclusion." The following text box summarizes Gerring's analysis.[22]

IDEOLOGICAL EPOCHS OF THE DEMOCRATIC PARTY

Persisting theme: equality

Jeffersonianism (1828–1892)
Central dichotomy: liberty versus tyranny
Themes: white supremacy, antistatism, civic republicanism

Populism (1896–1948)
Central dichotomy: the people versus the interests
Themes: egalitarianism, majoritarianism, Christian humanism

Universalism (1952–1992)
Central dichotomy: inclusion versus exclusion
Themes: civil rights, social welfare, redistribution, inclusion
Persisting theme: social order, economic growth, patriotism

In citing "equality" as a "persisting theme" of the Democratic Party, Gerring noted this qualification: "Equal rights were to be extended to all white men, but not to inferior races."[23] One must perform mental gymnastics to reconcile "white supremacy" with "equality" in the first epoch, 1828–1892. The same goes for crediting the party with "egalitarianism" from 1896 to 1948, but Gerring seems to refer "primarily to economic matters" and to a classless society—not to racial matters.[24] After southerners bolted from the party in 1948 and the national Democratic Party became committed to civil rights, it fully embraced the equality principle, without qualifications.

Most scholars credit the Republican Party's founding in 1854 to the threat raised by the Kansas-Nebraska Act, which allowed slavery to expand into free territories. However, Gerring views the Republican Party as a continuation of the Whig Party, itself formed from those who opposed President Andrew Jackson, elected in 1828. As the Whigs lasted only three decades, that difference should not materially affect his analysis. Gerring divides the Whig/Republican history into only two epochs, as shown in the following text box.

**IDEOLOGICAL EPOCHS OF THE
WHIG/REPUBLICAN PARTY**

Persisting theme: social order, economic growth, patriotism

Nationalism (1828–1924)
Central dichotomy: order versus anarchy
Themes: Protestantism, moral reform, mercantilism, free labor, social harmony, statism

Neoliberalism (1928–1992)
Central dichotomy: the individual versus the state
Themes: antistatism, free-market capitalism, right-wing popu-
lism, individualism

According to Gerring, the party's nationalism period lasted from 1828 to 1924, during which Republicans were state builders and economic nationalists who believed that a strong federal government was necessary not only to preserve the union but also to achieve prosperity and preserve the fabric of American society.[25] "During this period, Republicans fought for order over anarchy, and 'statism' was one of its principles."[26] Gerring claimed that the party changed fundamentally in 1928, when Republicans entered its neoliberalism epoch:

> Whereas in the previous century the party had worked to contain the passions of the individual, largely through the actions of an interventionist state, now Republicans reversed this polarity: the individual was to be set free from the machinations of the state. Through Neoliberal eyes, all political measures flowed from the central assumption that government was dangerous and needed to be contained. In economic policy the party adopted the general philosophy of laissez-faire or, more practically, "as little government as possible."[27]

Beginning in 1928, the party championed the individual over the state, and antistatism became a party principle—replacing statism. Concerning "right-wing populism," Gerring describes it as attacking "special privileges, special interests, and various other expressions of elite control."[28] Gerring includes presidential rhetoric in his analysis, and Eisenhower's warning against the "military-industrial complex" exemplifies Republican populism.

Clearly, Gerring's analysis offers a far richer interpretation of American political history than simply calling the Democratic Party "liberal" and the Republican "conservative." He identifies ten principles (themes) that characterize the Democratic Party and ten for the Republican Party—as one of the themes is shared, this totals nineteen different principles across both parties. How well does his study describe the Republican Party today?

FROM THE TWENTIETH TO THE TWENTY-FIRST CENTURY

Gerring exercised personal judgments in reading and categorizing candidates' speeches and party platforms—every platform and hundreds of speeches delivered from 1828 to 1992. Moreover, he reported consulting more than 1,200 texts, "the vast majority speeches by the presidential candidates or their surrogate spokespersons."[29] Just from the parties' platforms, he classified over ten thousand sentences into twenty-four categories plus "unclassifiable."[30] Consequently, Gerring's research cannot be fully replicated—that is, repeated using exactly the same methods. However, his study invites revisiting using only party platforms as a truer indicator of party principles. Would the results be similar?

Given the availability of comparable data on party platforms, could the personal judgments of a researcher conducting a similar content analysis generate similar historical findings for the Democratic and Republican parties? If so, perhaps Gerring's study, which ended at 1992,[31] could be extended to the present. I try to do that in the next chapter only for the Republican Party, using newly collected data on all Republican Party platforms from 1856 to 2016, the last year the Republican Party adopted a new platform.

5

REPUBLICAN PLATFORM
PLANKS SINCE 1856

Both the Democratic and Republican parties' platforms have grown longer over time, especially since the 1970s. Using word counts posted by the American Presidency Project,[1] figure 5.1 plots the number of words in forty-one Republican Party platforms from 1856 to 2016. Beginning in the 1970s, computerized word processing programs probably facilitated writing longer platforms. The increased verbiage also came from longer passages that "pointed with pride" to Republican accomplishments and "viewed with alarm" past and future Democratic dangers. Of course, parties also addressed a larger number of political issues over time.

A century ago, scholars scorned Democratic and Republican party platforms as ambiguous and inconsistent. Writing in 1936, Browne said, "Perhaps the most scathing attack of all levied upon American political parties is the charge that they are too much alike." About Democrats and Republicans, one writer "referred to them as 'Tweedledum and Tweedledee,' two puppets of like character and form, who each four years engage in what is little more than a sham battle."[2] In rebuttal, Browne cited solid research that found "clear-cut party issues dividing the voters" in half of the thirty-two elections from 1796 to 1924.[3] He personally found both parties differing on their platforms' "planks," using a peculiarly American term referring to components of a political platform.[4]

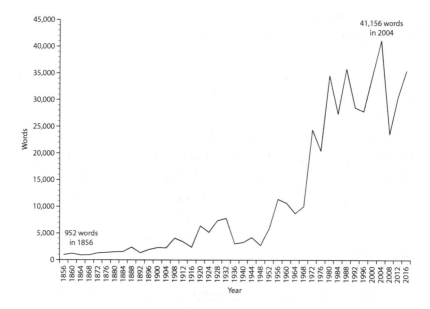

FIGURE 5.1. Increased length of forty-one Republican Party platforms, 1856–2016.

DEFINING AND CATALOGING PLANKS

A platform is a metaphor for announced party principles, and a plank is a metaphor for a platform statement that specifies or supports those principles. Just as "platform" is peculiar to American parties, so is "plank." Robert Harmel's 2018 guide to cross-national research with party manifestos does not mention "plank,"[5] nor does a different guide to the Manifesto Database.[6] Manifesto research focuses on party "pledges." This study looks instead at party planks. Browne identified four types of planks:

1. Specific endorsements or condemnations of specified laws. . . .
2. Proposals which call for action and specify what form the action will take without endorsing a particular law. . . .
3. Proposals which call for legislative or executive action, or both, without stating in any way the form of the action. . . .

4. Expressions of sentiment which do not call for any action, either legislative or executive.[7]

According to Pomper's classification of pledges in Chapter 3, type 1 would be evaluative, types 2 and 3 would be pledges of different specificity, and type 4 just rhetorical.

To find and catalog Republican Party planks, I read through every Republican platform posted on the internet by the American Presidency Project. Admittedly, "reading through" these lengthy files meant looking for positions on issues while skipping over long passages of party rhetoric. I captured relevant platform segments and dropped selected "planks" into a computer database, coding each one for the policy it advocated.

In selecting platform segments as planks, I required, first, that it had action implications and, second, that it implied the party's *position* on the issue. Concerning action implications, I excluded Republican endorsements of past accomplishments, such as praising passage of an act. Concerning the party's position, the party had to indicate a policy stance: "fighting for the farmer" would not qualify. Identifying and cataloging party planks is an uncertain procedure, and other researchers probably would not have identified and cataloged exactly the same 2,722 planks that I did. (See appendix A for an attempt to validate my effort by comparing my party plank analysis with another, earlier study. The Republican planks that I identified are available for inspection and downloading at https://janda.org/GOP.)

The coding categories were constructed in two steps: first laying out the main policy headings and then detailing the specific codes applied to the planks. The main policy headings had eight general categories, organized into two equal-sized groups. The primary group encompassed the four core values of Freedom, Order, Equality, and Public Goods (set forth in chapter 2). Those four values underlie most issues of domestic political conflict. The secondary group also had four general categories— Government, Foreign Policy, Military, and Symbolic. Technically, a Military is a Public Good, but military spending is huge and deserves

TABLE 5.1 Major code headings for classifying party planks

Code Type	General Category	General Category Description
1 - -	Freedom	Policies limiting government
2 - -	Order	Policies restricting citizens' freedom
3 - -	Equality	Policies benefiting disadvantaged people
4 - -	Public Goods	Policies benefiting the public
5 - -	Government	Actions pertaining to the government
6 - -	Military	Actions benefiting the military
7 - -	Foreign Policy	Relations with foreign states
8 - -	Symbolic	Expressions of support, regret

separate treatment. These eight main headings are given in table 5.1, each leading the first digit of a more detailed three-digit scheme.

Table 5.1 outlines the logic of my scheme for classifying Republican Party policies. Within the scheme, each plank was assigned one of 114 three-digit code numbers, presented in table 5.2. The 114 codes are grouped under eight major headings: Freedom, Order, Equality, Public Goods, Government, Military, Foreign Policy, and Symbolic.

Table 5.3 reports frequency and percentage usage of all the major coding categories for all 2,722 Republican planks. Twice as many party planks were assigned to the major code category, Public Goods, than to the next most common major code, Freedom, which was used slightly more often than Foreign Policy and Order. Only 10 percent of Republican planks referenced Equality—fewer than those mentioning Government Reorganization. Only a tiny number of planks fell in the Symbolic category. Chapters in part 3 will discuss planks tagged with detailed codes.

To determine whether and how the Republican Party changed from 1856 to 2016, I divided this distribution into time periods. Gerring contended that the party's principles remained largely intact over two lengthy epochs, changing only once. The change occurred between 1924 and 1928, when it left its nationalism epoch and entered its

TABLE 5.2 All 114 codes for platform planks, 1856 to 2016

Code	Description	Code	Description	Code	Description
1 - -	FREEDOM			6 - -	MILITARY
100	Expression/Privacy	306	Elderly	600	More spending
101	Religion	307	Children	601	Less spending
102	Ethnicity	308	Veterans	602	Navy
103	Immigration	309	LGBTQ	603	Army
104	Education	310	Indigenous	604	Air Force
105	Economy	4 - -	PUBLIC GOODS	605	National Guard
106	Taxation	400	Education	606	Nuclear
107	Trade/Tariff	401	Transportation	607	Missiles
108	Labor	402	Environment	608	Space
109	Agriculture	403	Conservation	609	Intelligence
110	States' rights	404	Welfare	610	Command
111	Transgressions	405	Housing	611	Service
112	Alcohol/Drugs	406	Health	7 - -	FOREIGN POLICY
113	Life/Death	407	Labor	700	World organizations
114	Firearms	408	Communication	701	Europe
115	Lifestyle	409	Agriculture	702	NATO, SEATO, etc.
2 - -	ORDER	410	Energy	703	Asia
200	Expression/Privacy	411	Shipping	704	Americas
201	Religion	412	Merchant Marine	705	Africa
202	Ethnicity	413	Indebtedness	706	Soviet/Russia
203	Immigration	414	Economy	707	China/Taiwan
204	Education	415	Spending/Deficit	708	Middle East
205	Economy	416	Banking and currency	709	Wars post-WW2
206	Taxation	417	Public lands +	710	Foreign aid
207	Trade/Tariff	418	Public lands −	711	Treaties
208	Labor	419	Immigration	712	Monroe Doctrine
209	Agriculture	5 - -	GOVERNMENT	713	Protect citizens
210	National rights	500	Congress	714	Avoid war
211	Transgressions	501	Constitution	715	World leadership
212	Alcohol/Drugs	502	Civil/Postal Service	8 - -	SYMBOLIC
213	Life/Death	503	Expand govt.	800	Presidents

Code	Description	Code	Description	Code	Description
214	Firearms	504	Reorganize govt.	801	Nation
215	Lifestyle	505	Elections: + or −	802	Discrimination
3 - -	EQUALITY	506	Interior	803	Atrocities
300	Nonwhites +	507	New states	804	Politicians
301	Nonwhites −	508	Territories	805	Treaties
302	Women	509	Native populations	806	Political acts
303	Disadvantaged	510	Washington, DC	807	Peace
304	Handicapped	511	Legal	808	Wars
305	Poor	512	Federal courts	809	Other

TABLE 5.3 Distribution of 2,722 planks over
major codes by frequency of usage

Major Heading	Frequency	Percent
4-- Public Goods	862	31
1-- Freedom	439	16
7-- Foreign Policy	402	15
2-- Order	383	14
3-- Equality	260	10
5-- Government	244	9
6-- Military	114	4
8-- Symbolic	18	1
Total	2,722	100%

neoliberalism epoch. An analogy from old-fashioned photography suggests that Gerring used an extremely long shutter speed of nearly one hundred years for his photo. In 1992—sixty-four years later—the party was still in its neoliberalism epoch, according to Gerring. To capture change in Republican principles, I used faster shutter speeds, coding its platforms over shorter intervals.

REDOING GERRING'S ANALYSIS

Gerring's landmark study *Party Ideologies in America* argued that our two major parties, over nearly 170 years, showed more ideological stability than change. The Democratic Party's Jeffersonian epoch lasted sixty-four years (1828–1892), its populism epoch (1896–1948) continued for fifty-two years, and its universalism epoch (1952–1992) ran for forty-four years, to the end of his study. He found the Republican Party even more stable, changing ideological orientations only once. The Republicans' nationalism epoch lasted sixty-eight years (1856–1924), while its neoliberalism epoch was in its sixty-fourth year (1928–1992) when Gerring's research ended.

Writing now in 2021, I believe that the Republican Party in particular has changed in more fundamental ways than Gerring found since the start of its neoliberalism epoch in 1928. Historians, journalists, and politicians write that today's Republican Party is vastly different from what it was during the Eisenhower presidency in the 1950s.[8] While Gerring's study included far more information from candidate speeches than party platforms, I study party change using only party platforms, considering them the most authoritative expression of party principles. Special note will be taken of times when Republican presidential candidates clashed with their party.

One cannot fruitfully analyze each platform separately, for early platforms were short and often contained few planks. To observe changes over time, I divided Republican planks into time periods. Choosing the appropriate period, or shutter speed, for such analysis is problematic. Nevertheless, displaying results for platforms grouped by adjacent eras may show continuities or discontinuities in party principles. All told, I analyzed the Republican Party planks using shorter political "eras" covering twenty-four to twenty-eight years based on (mostly) seven presidential election cycles, as shown in table 5.4.

The last two eras depart from the pattern and deserve some discussion. The 1984–2012 era contains eight elections, not seven, for two reasons. First, the platform in 1984 was under complete control of President Ronald Reagan's forces, so it marked the start of a new era.

TABLE 5.4 Seven platform eras

Eras	Presidential elections	Number of years	Politics of the era
1856–1876	6	24	Began with the Republican Party's origin and ended with the disputed 1876 election, making Hayes president while ending Reconstruction
1880–1904	7	28	Marked an era of Republican dominance during industrialization and ended with Teddy Roosevelt's presidency
1908–1928	6	24	Brought two terms of the Wilson presidency, otherwise Republican dominance until the stock market crash of 1929
1932–1956	7	28	Began with the first of Democrat Franklin Roosevelt's four elections and concluded with Republican Dwight Eisenhower's pair of victories
1960–1980	6	24	Includes two early Democratic wins (Kennedy and Johnson) and ends with Ronald Reagan's first win
1984–2012	8	32	Has eight cycles of presidential elections from Republican Ronald Reagan to Democrat Barack Obama; is the longest era
2016–2020*	2	8	Has only two election cycles, beginning with Republican Donald Trump's election
Totals	42	168	

*Republicans readopted their 2016 platform in 2020, so across these forty-two elections there were forty-one platforms.

Second, the era ended at 2012 to keep it separate from the 2016–2020 President Trump era. Note also that although Trump's era contained two elections, the Republican Party drafted and adopted only one platform, that in 2016. In 2020, because of the pandemic, the party simply readopted its 2016 platform. Table 5.5 compares "eras" and "epochs."

OVERVIEW OF REPUBLICAN PLANKS

Finally we can report the distribution of all 2,722 planks cataloged in forty-one Republican Party platforms since 1856. The distribution is displayed in figure 5.2.

Figure 5.2 documents some systematic changes over time in what the Republican planks covered. Most dramatic is the nearly steady increase in the percentages classified under Freedom. Almost as dramatic is the decline in the Equality category. The steady increase in Foreign Policy planks attests to the United States' increasing prominence in world affairs. Interestingly, the percentage of Military planks has been virtually constant over time. There also has been little change in attention to Government over time, but Symbolic expressions, once common, have virtually disappeared.

Although Republican planks dealing with Foreign Policy have increased markedly over time, they were seldom distinctly partisan. The same is true for planks in the Government and Military categories, and neither party had Symbolic planks after 1900. Consequently, the next graph, figure 5.3, excludes those four major types of planks and only shows how the remaining 1,917 Republican planks are distributed over Public Goods, Freedom, Order, and Equality.

The findings in figure 5.3 are striking. Whereas the Republican Party in its early days focused on Order more than Freedom, it increasingly emphasized Freedom after the 1908–1928 era. That dating strongly supports Gerring's fixing of the party's neoliberalism era at 1928. However, tracking the Order line does not support his argument that Republicans favored "the individual over the state" during its neoliberalism epoch. In fact, during the 1960–1980 era, the party swung sharply back toward Order and continued on that path henceforth. Meanwhile, Republican platforms contained fewer and fewer planks concerning Public Goods and Equality. Something happened in the 1960–1980 era that changed the party. Notably, the party embarked on its "Southern strategy" during that era.

TABLE 5.5 Seven eras for analyzing Republican Party platform planks

Election years	Janda's eras	Republican presidential nominees (elected in capitals)	Gerring's party epochs	
			Republican	Democratic
1856	1856–1876	John C. Fremont	Nationalism	Jeffersonianism
1860		Abraham Lincoln		
1864		Abraham Lincoln		
1868		Ulysses S. Grant		
1872		Ulysses S. Grant		
1876		Rutherford B. Hayes		
1880	1880–1904	James A. Garfield		
1884		James G. Blaine		
1888		Benjamin Harrison		
1892		Benjamin Harrison		
1896		William McKinley		Populism
1900		William McKinley		
1904		Theodore Roosevelt		
1908	1908–1928	William H. Taft		
1912		William H. Taft		
1916		Charles Evans Hughes		
1920		Warren G. Harding		
1924		Calvin Coolidge		
1928		Herbert Hoover	Neoliberalism	
1932	1932–1956	Herbert Hoover		
1936		Alfred M. Landon		
1940		Wendell Willkie		
1944		Thomas E. Dewey		
1948		Thomas E. Dewey		
1952		Dwight Eisenhower		Universalism
1956		Dwight Eisenhower		
1960	1960–1980	Richard Nixon		
1964		Barry Goldwater		
1968		Richard Nixon		

(*continued*)

TABLE 5.5 (continued)

Election years	Janda's eras	Republican presidential nominees (elected in capitals)	Gerring's party epochs	
			Republican	Democratic
1972		Richard Nixon	(Neoliberalism)	(Universalism)
1976		Gerald Ford		
1980		Ronald Reagan		
1984	1984–2012	Ronald Reagan		
1988		George H. W. Bush		
1992		George H. W. Bush		
1996		Robert Dole		
2000		George W. Bush		
2004		George W. Bush		
2008		John McCain		
2012		Mitt Romney		
2016	2016–2020	Donald Trump		
2020		Donald Trump		

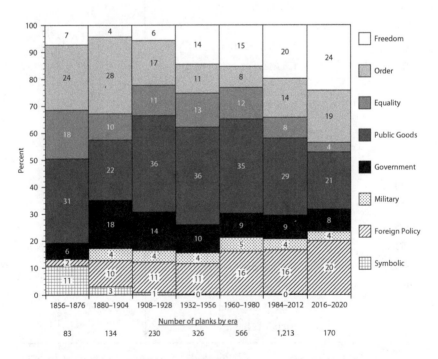

FIGURE 5.2. All 2,722 Republican planks for seven eras and by eight major types.

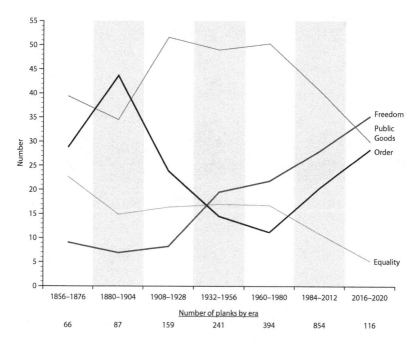

FIGURE 5.3. 1,917 Republican planks for seven eras and by four major types.

Before considering further the politics behind the changes in Republican Party principles since 1928, we should examine in detail some of the party's major principles and how they have changed since the party's founding. Part 3 reviews how platform planks reflect Republican principles over time.

III

PRINCIPLES OF
REPUBLICANISM

6

ORIGINAL PRINCIPLES

When the U.S. Constitution was ratified in 1787, nations across the world still permitted capturing, trading, and using slaves. Some governments moved toward outlawing slavery, but our Founding Fathers sidestepped the controversial practice by not mentioning slavery specifically in the Constitution. However, the document acknowledged and abetted slavery's existence by counting only "three fifths of all other Persons" for congressional representation, by forbidding stopping the "importation" of persons before 1808, and by providing for the return to a state of a "person held to service or labor."

Generally speaking, whites who lived in southern states strongly supported slavery, on which their economy and lifestyle depended. While few northern whites believed that Black slaves were mentally and culturally their equal, many thought that slavery was morally wrong and should be abolished throughout the nation. Abolition, however, posed two serious problems.

The historian Joseph Ellis outlined both problems in his prizewinning book *Founding Fathers*.[1] The first was the financial cost in reimbursing slave owners for their loss. The Constitution's Fifth Amendment said that no "private property be taken for public use, without just compensation," and most northerners conceded that slaves were "private property." Ellis estimated the cost of emancipating the 694,280 slaves counted in the 1790

Census at $170 million; the federal budget at that time was less than $7 million.[2]

The second problem was what to do with so many freed slaves. Some abolitionists favored sending them back to Africa. Others proposed sending them west to new territories. Relatively few thought that former slaves should remain where they were, become American citizens, and live alongside whites—much less mix with them. Abolitionists, nevertheless, firmly opposed extending slavery to territories likely to become states, and they found support in the Free Soil Party, formed from Whigs and antislavery Democrats. In 1848, the Free Soil platform accepted slavery in existing states but prohibited extending the practice beyond them. The party's presidential candidate won only 10 percent of the popular vote and no electoral votes.

REPUBLICANISM'S FINEST HOUR

On January 4, 1854, Congress passed the Kansas-Nebraska Act, a law that increased the chances that slavery would be permitted in new states. Slavery's opponents quickly acted to create a party dedicated to their cause. Two Midwestern towns—Ripon, Wisconsin, and Jackson, Michigan—claim credit for founding the new Republican Party. Ripon's claim lies in a meeting of former Free Soilers, Whigs, and Democrats on March 20, 1854. Jackson boasts that it nominated Republican candidates in a state convention on June 6, 1854. Gatherings in both towns called themselves "Republicans." The eminent historian Lewis Gould said that the name provided two positive links to the past. First, it tied the party to Thomas Jefferson's Democratic-Republican political organization. Second, it related to romantic English and Italian ideas of a "republic"—citizens acting in the political sphere.[3]

The Republican Party's first national convention in 1856 issued a platform based on their antislavery principle, and its text denounced slavery in five places. It was the party's finest hour in its nearly 170-year history. The platform's first paragraph acknowledged "the principles of Washington and Jefferson" and then immediately resolved to maintain "the principles promulgated in the Declaration of Independence."[4] It held to "the self-evident truth, that all men are endowed with the inalienable right to life, liberty, and the pursuit of happiness." It referred to the "barbarism" of slavery and vowed in several places "to prohibit it in the Territories."

In 1856, Republicans effectively fulfilled Edmund Burke's classic definition of a political party and "united for promoting by their joint endeavours the national interest upon some particular principles in which they are all agreed."[5] The party's first presidential nominee, John C. Fremont, won only one-third of the popular vote, but its second nominee, Abraham Lincoln, won on a platform that addressed slavery in five places. After Lincoln's assassination, every Republican platform to 1908 continued to mention slavery at least once, reminding voters of the party's historical legacy. Below, verbatim but with added emphasis, are the passages in Republican Party platforms from 1856 to 1908 mentioning slavery.

1856

Opposed to the repeal of the Missouri Compromise; . . . to the extension of slavery into Free Territory.

Our Republican fathers, when they had abolished slavery in all our National Territory, ordained that no person shall be deprived of life, liberty, or property, without due process of law.

It becomes our duty to maintain this provision of the Constitution against all attempts to violate it for the purpose of establishing slavery in the Territories.

We deny the authority of Congress, of a Territorial Legislation, of any individual, or association of individuals, to give legal existence to slavery in any Territory.

It is both the right and the imperative duty of Congress to prohibit in the Territories those twin relics of barbarism—Polygamy, and slavery.

1860

The new dogma that the Constitution, of its own force, carries *slavery* into any or all of the territories of the United States, is a dangerous political heresy.

Our Republican fathers, when they had abolished *slavery* in all our national territory, ordained that "no persons should be deprived of life, liberty or property without due process of law."

We deny the authority of Congress, of a territorial legislature, or of any individuals, to give legal existence to *slavery* in any territory.

We brand the recent reopening of the African *slave* trade, under the cover of our national flag, aided by perversions of judicial power, as a crime against humanity.

In the recent vetoes, by their Federal Governors, of the acts of the legislatures of Kansas and Nebraska, prohibiting *slavery* in those territories, we find a practical illustration of the boasted Democratic principle of Non-Intervention and Popular Sovereignty.

1864

As *slavery* was the cause, and now constitutes the strength of this Rebellion, and as it must be, always and everywhere, hostile to the principles of Republican Government, justice and the National safety demand its utter and complete extirpation from the soil of the Republic.

We are in favor, furthermore, of such an amendment to the Constitution, . . . as shall terminate and forever prohibit the existence of *Slavery*.

We approve, especially, the Proclamation of Emancipation, and the employment as Union soldiers of men heretofore held in *slavery*.

1872

During eleven years of supremacy [the party] suppressed a gigantic rebellion, emancipated four millions of *slaves*.

1876

When . . . this land was to be purged of human slavery, . . . the Republican party came into power.

1880

[The party] . . . reconstructed the Union of the States, with freedom instead of *slavery* as its corner-stone.

[The party] relieved Congress from the infamous work of hunting fugitive *slaves*, and charged it to see that *slavery* does not exist.

We affirm the belief, avowed in 1876, . . . that *slavery* having perished in the States, its twin brother, polygamy, must die in the territories.

1884

The Republican party, having its birth in a hatred of *slave* labor.

1888

We send fraternal congratulations to our fellow Americans of Brazil upon their great act of emancipation, which completed the abolition of *slavery* throughout the two American continents.

1904

Fifty years ago the Republican party came into existence dedicated among other purposes to the great task of arresting the extension of human *slavery*.

1908

This great historic organization, that destroyed *slavery*, preserved the Union.

By 1912, memories of the Civil War a half-century earlier had faded, and slavery went unmentioned in the Republican platform. However, it recalled "with a sense of veneration and gratitude the name of our first great leader, who was nominated in this city, and whose lofty principles and superb devotion to his country are an inspiration to the party he honored—Abraham Lincoln." Slavery was never mentioned again until 1952, when the party warned against "Communist enslavement," henceforth a staple warning in Republican platforms.

DEMOCRATS' FEDERAL REFUGE

The Democratic platform of 1856 mentioned slavery ten times and defended the practice through legal arguments. Democrats repeatedly sought reference to states' rights under the Constitution. Consider their platform's first resolution: "That Congress has no power under the Constitution, to interfere with or control the domestic institutions of the several States, and that such States are the sole and proper judges of everything appertaining to their own affairs, not prohibited by the Constitution; that all efforts of the abolitionists, or others, made to induce Congress to interfere with questions of *slavery*."

Democrats sought refuge under federalism. Today, the terms "federal" and "national" are used interchangeably—and incorrectly. A federal structure entrusts certain powers to one central government and delegates other powers to provincial governments. So "federal government" includes both national *and* state governments.[6] Taking refuge in federalism's separation of governmental powers, Democrats in 1856 argued that only state governments could rule on the issue of slavery. Republicans in 1856 proposed to contain or end slavery under national powers.

Soon after Lincoln's election in 1860, southern politicians organized to secede from the United States. On February 8, 1861, seven slave states formed the Confederate States of America. A month after Lincoln's March inauguration, secessionist forces in South Carolina attacked U.S.

Fort Sumter, starting the Civil War between twenty northern states and eleven in the south, four others having joined the Confederacy.

In the ensuing Civil War, Republicans in the victorious north were able to fulfill their opposition to slavery, not only preventing slavery from extending to free territories but by ending it in southern states. To their credit, Democrats acknowledged the facts. The Democratic platform of 1868 began by "recognizing the questions of slavery and secession as having been settled for all time to come by the war." Then the party demanded "immediate restoration of all the *States to their rights* in the Union." For decades thereafter, the Democratic Party became known as the "states' rights" party.

Democrats did not mention slavery again until 1952, denouncing "sweatshop slavery at starvation wages." Then in 2000, the Democratic platform proposed creating a commission to "examine the history of slavery." While later Democratic platforms expressed concern about slavery's past and urged study, both parties had laid the once explosive issue to rest.

REPUBLICANS AS A STATES' RIGHTS PARTY

By opposing slavery across U.S. territories, the Republican Party pursued the principle of national Order. Two of the main headings in the 114 codes for Republican platform planks are Order and Freedom (see table 5.1). Under the Order heading, code 210 stands for "National Rights." Under Freedom, code 110 stands for "States' rights." Together, these codes were assigned to sixteen of the 2,722 planks from 1856 to 1928 and to fifty-one from 1932 to 2016. Remember that longer platforms in later years contained many more planks. These sixty-seven planks are distributed by election era, as shown in figure 6.1.

Under the Order heading, code 210 for National Rights was assigned to thirteen Republican planks from 1856 to 1924—for example, to this statement in the 1884 platform: "The people of the United States, in their organized capacity, constitute a Nation and not a mere confederacy of

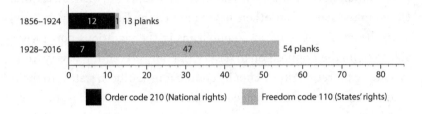

FIGURE 6.1. National rights and states' rights in sixty-seven planks, 1856–1924 vs. 1928–2016.

States." During this early period, the party clearly favored Order imposed by a national government and adopted only one plank recognizing states' rights. In 1868, after the North won the Civil War, the GOP conceded: "The guaranty by Congress of equal suffrage to all loyal men at the South was demanded by every consideration of public safety, of gratitude, and of justice, and must be maintained; while the question of suffrage in all the loyal States properly belongs to the people of those States."

The party did not revisit the sovereignty issue until 1928, after which it reversed itself and favored Freedom and States' Rights (code 110) in forty-seven of fifty-four planks to 2016 as detailed in the following list.

1928   Oppose federal government interfering with state activities
        Favors state over federal regulation
1932   We regard relief problem as one of state and local
          responsibility
1940   Remove waste, discrimination from relief, through
          administration by the states
        Give federal grants-in-aid to states
1944   Avoid federalization of government activities
        Return public employment-office system to the states
        Favor regulation and supervision of the business of
          insurance by the several states
1948   Restore states' rights to submerged lands
1952   Popular education rests upon the local communities and
          the states
        States should order and control their domestic institutions

Favor state rights beneath navigable inland and offshore waters

1956 Opposed to unwarranted growth of centralized Federal power

1960 Leave state and local governments to handle their programs

1964 Channel more Federal grants-in-aid through states

1964 Rely on subordinate levels of government over federal agencies

1968 Strengthen state and local law enforcement and preserve the primacy of state responsibility

States use federal reinsurance against damage and fire caused by riots

1976 Oppose federalizing the welfare system

1980 Replace categorical aid programs with block grants

Favor block grants to states for elementary and secondary education

Pledge to return power to state and local governments

Transfer all welfare functions to the states with tax resources to finance them

1984 Sell surplus public lands

Return programs to states

1988 Favor block grants and revenue sharing

Return power from the federal government to State and local governments

Recognize states' rights in water law

Reduce public land held by government

1992 Not initiate any federal activity that can be conducted better on the State or local level

Seek to reduce the amount of land owned by the government

1996 Smaller, more effective, and less intrusive government

Consolidate federal training programs, transfer to states and local government

Government is too large

Return Medicaid to state management

Unify scattered federal grants to block grants

2000   Raise academic standards through increased local control
   and accountability to parents
  Protect against federal intrusion and bullying
  Turn over to local communities foreclosed and abandoned
   HUD properties
  Give more control to states concerning public lands
2008   Reaffirm traditional state authority over water allocations
2012   Switch to block grants for Medicaid
  Shift training programs to states financed by block grants
2016   Shift regulation from federal government to the states
  Allow states to regulate local insurance markets
  Convey some public lands to the states
  Allow state and local officials to handle criminal justice
  Favor more state and local control over public assistance
   programs

By 1928, the Republican Party began to rival the Democrats in favoring the states over the nation in America's federal form of government. After 1960, Republicans finally eclipsed Democrats in advocating states' rights. The party that began as a champion of national rights had turned into a party of states' rights.

CHANGING STANCES ON EQUALITY

Slavery, of course, denied the equality of human beings. Up to 1952, Republican platform texts were as likely to mention "equality" (twenty-seven times) as Democratic platforms were up to 1948 (thirty-five times). Afterward, Democrats mentioned it twice as often as Republicans (sixty-seven to thirty-two). Moreover, using the word in a party platform is not the same as incorporating the principle in a platform plank that takes an action-oriented position.

Table 5.2 listed all 114 codes applied to 2,722 Republican Party platform planks since 1856. Under the Equality heading, Nonwhite code +300 applied to *positive* steps toward equality for nonwhites, and

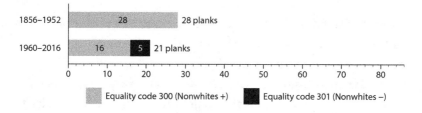

FIGURE 6.2. Positive and negative equality in forty-nine planks, 1856–1952 vs. 1960–2016.

Nonwhite code −301 to *negative* steps—away from equality. Of the 2,722 Republican planks, only 49 took a position on equality concerning nonwhites. Up to 1956, every plank was positive. The first plank against equality for nonwhites came in 1960. The results are given in figure 6.2.

Whereas all twenty-eight Republican planks up to 1952 favored racial equality, almost a quarter of its planks since 1960 objected to enforcing equality. The following list shows the five planks coded negatively since 1960; all dealt with school desegregation and "busing" children to school.

1960   Oppose fixing a target date for school desegregation
1972   Halt immediately all further court-ordered busing
       Oppose busing for racial balance
1976   Oppose forced busing
1980   Condemn forced busing

Despite the party's opposition to busing as a means to desegregate schools, every Republican platform since 1960 boasted of being "the party of Lincoln."

SUMMARY

This initial chapter in part 3, "Principles of Republicanism," begins the detailed, factual analysis of the principles as expressed in forty-one Republican Party platforms over 160 years—from 1856 to 2016. Along with the next seven chapters, it provides the empirical foundation for assessing what Edmund Burke said were the "particular principles" serving the "national interest" on which politicians "agreed" when joining to organize a political party. Part 4 examines when and how the party departed from its historical principles when acting as an electoral Team, a political Tribe, and a personality Cult rather than as a political Party. (These four terms were first described in the introduction to this volume.)

The Republican Party was founded on the principle of containing the spread of slavery in the United States, and it was willing to use the power of the national government to do so. As equality was understood at the time, the Republican Party recognized slaves to be politically equal to their owners. Over time, as equality applied to social relationships between people of color and those born white, the Republican Party backed away from using national power to enforce equality.

According to John Gerring's study of political speeches and party platforms, the nationalism epoch of the Republican Party lasted to 1924. During this period, the "central dichotomy" was *order* versus *anarchy*. The party favored using national authority to impose order. After 1928, Gerring said, the party entered its neoliberalism epoch, during which the central dichotomy was the *individual* versus the *state*. My independent analysis of Republican Party platform planks since 1856 coincides virtually perfectly with Gerring's classification, as shown in table 6.1.

Soon after its founding, the Republican Party controlled both the presidency and Congress, and it wielded national authority as a governing party. Not only did Republicans end slavery across the land, but they

TABLE 6.1 National authority versus states' rights by electoral era

1856–1876	1880–1904	1908–1928	1932–1956	1960–1980	1984–2012	2016–2020
National authority	National authority	National authority				
			States' rights	States' rights	States' rights	States' rights

developed its economy and natural resources. Then after World War II, the Republican Party abandoned its original principle of national government and completely reversed its political orientation, giving states more leeway to govern themselves as they wished. It evolved away from being a national governing party.

7

FINANCING GOVERNMENT

Governments must raise revenue one away or another. One way is to tax people directly, taking a percentage of their income. Another way is to tax people indirectly, for example by taxing goods imported into the country that people consume. Indirect taxation through tariffs is less visible and less likely to arouse voters. Of course, the need for taxes depends on the amount of government spending. During the Republican Party's first fifty years, Republican governments spent government money freely and raised revenue accordingly. Thus, the Republican Party was the original "tax and spend" party. Nevertheless, Republicans were fiscally responsible during the first half of their party's existence.

TARIFFS: A DOUBLE REVERSE

The first major piece of legislation in the 1789 Congress was the Tariff Act.[1] Tariffs on imported goods were the major source of receipts under the old Articles of Confederation, and the Tariff Act was designed to continue the money flow. Tariffs generated 80 to 90 percent of U.S. funds until the Civil War, when an income tax was enacted to bolster finances. The income tax expired in 1872, as spending returned to normal. From

1875 to 1890, tariffs provided more than half the government's cost, with taxes on alcohol and luxuries providing most of the remainder.[2] Republicans, who usually controlled government after the Civil War, kept the tariff high to produce revenue and protect domestic industry. The "protective tariff" became a key party principle, opposed by Democrats, who saw high tariffs as harming consumers and farmers.

The historian Lewis Gould wrote, "One issue on which most Republicans agreed during the Gilded Age was the protective tariff."[3] He continued: "Protection was more than just an economic policy. In the hands of the Republicans, it sounded themes of nationalism and patriotic pride."[4] Although the term "protective tariff" did not appear in Republican platforms until 1900, at the end of the Gilded Age, the concept appeared in the 1888 platform: "We are uncompromisingly in favor of the American system of protection." The 1912 Republican platform praised the tariff as a bedrock party principle: "We reaffirm our belief in a *protective tariff*. The Republican tariff policy has been of the greatest benefit to the country, developing our resources, diversifying our industries, and protecting our workmen against competition with cheaper labor abroad, thus establishing for our wage-earners the American standard of living." A "protective tariff" reflected a desire for economic and political order; "free trade" reflected the opposite: a desire for economic and political freedom.

Republicans did not adopt a specific plank on tariffs until 1872. Eventually, a total of eighty-one Republican planks on "Trade/Tariffs" were coded separately under Order and Freedom headings. Trade/Tariff code 207 under Order favored higher tariffs. Under Freedom, Trade/Tariff code 107 favored freer trade and reciprocal trade agreements. Figure 7.1 shows that up to World War II, Republican platforms almost always backed high, protective tariffs.

After the war, Republicans' views on international trade changed, becoming less protectionist. In 1980, the party reversed its position, becoming a "free trade" party. Its 1980 platform denounced its former bedrock trade principle: "The Republican Party believes that *protectionist tariffs* and quotas are detrimental to our economic well-being." Gould wrote in 2003: "Once the party of the protective tariff, it is now the most reliable ideological proponent of free trade."[5]

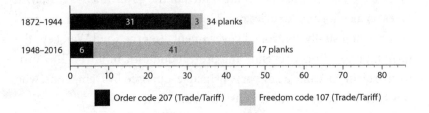

FIGURE 7.1. Tariffs/trade in eighty-one planks, 1872–1944 vs. 1948–2016.

But Gould wrote before Donald Trump influenced the party's 2016 platform. Its section "A Winning Trade Policy" foreshadowed a return to protectionist tariffs: "We need better negotiated trade agreements that put America first. When trade agreements have been carefully negotiated with friendly democracies, they have resulted in millions of new jobs here at home supported by our exports. When those agreements do not adequately protect U.S. interests, U.S. sovereignty, or when they are violated with impunity, they must be rejected."

As the party's presidential candidate, Donald Trump clearly put his personal "America First" stamp on the Republican Party platform. As president, he imposed taxes on imported products to protect American industries. In his acceptance speech to the 2020 Republican convention, Trump said, "We will impose tariffs on any company that leaves America to produce jobs overseas."[6] The "free trade" banner no longer led the Republican parade. Although 56 percent of Republican voters favored free trade in 2015, just 29 percent did by October 2016.[7]

REPUBLICANS INVENT, THEN RESIST, INCOME TAXES

Given Republicans' contemporary antitax rhetoric, Americans might think that Democrats invented the income tax. In truth, a Republican president and Congress imposed the first personal income tax in 1861 to help pay for the Civil War. Another act in 1862 raised the rates, but both acts were rescinded or repealed by 1872.

In 1894, a Democratic Congress and president (Cleveland) revived the Republican income tax, but the Supreme Court declared it unconstitutional in 1895. Early in the twentieth century, progressive Republicans recognized the need for a new and more productive source of revenue, and in 1909 a Republican Congress, supported by a Republican president (Taft) proposed a Sixteenth Amendment to the Constitution allowing an income tax. Democrats controlled Congress and the White House (Wilson) when the Sixteenth Amendment was ratified in 1913. While Democrats did pass the law that year establishing a national income tax, Republicans actually began the practice of taxing personal incomes.

A total of eighty-five Republican planks on "Taxation" were coded separately under the Order and Freedom headings. Over 105 years, from 1864–1960, only four planks addressed taxation. Of those, three actually favored government action to increase revenue (Order Taxation code 206), and they were all before 1960. Beginning with the 1964 Republican platform of nominee Barry Goldwater, taxation attracted seventy-six planks, of which 93 percent were for lower taxes, coded 106 (under Freedom). Figure 7.2 graphs the data.

The 1992 (Dole) and 1980 (Reagan) platforms tied for a high of eleven planks calling for lower taxes. Here are the eleven planks from 1980:

- Favor tax incentives for contributions to cultural organizations
- Cut taxes, increase incentives to save, and stimulate capital investment to create jobs
- Support reductions in personal income tax rates from 14–70 to 10–50 percent
- Achieve lower tax rates for small businesses
- Allow deductions for charitable contributions even if not itemizing
- Call for a reduction in the estate tax burden
- Eliminate estate taxes on inherited farm property between spouses
- Lower tax rates on savings and investment income
- Phase out tax on old oil
- Repeal windfall profits tax for small volume owners
- Simplify and accelerate depreciation schedules

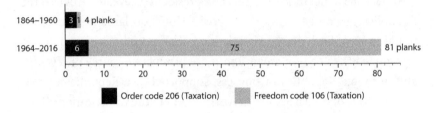

FIGURE 7.2. Taxation in eighty-five planks, 1856–1960 vs. 1964–2016.

Because most citizens prefer lower taxes to higher taxes, Republicans after 1960 deserve some credit for advocating lower taxes. Both parties in a two-party system should be guardians of the public purse, and voters should be free to choose which party fits the country's need for government spending. Having one party restricting available revenue more than the other serves party competition. Republicans also consistently recorded their concern over government spending and budget deficits.

REPUBLICANS DEPLORE, THEN GENERATE, BUDGET DEFICITS

People often confuse the budget deficit with the national debt. The U.S. government operates on an annual estimate of revenue and spending called a fiscal year (FY) that begins on October 1 and ends on September 30. The fiscal year is named for the year it ends. Thus FY2023 ends on September 30, 2023. If spending equals revenue, the budget is said to be "balanced" for that fiscal year. A budget deficit *for that* year results when spending exceeds revenue. A budget surplus occurs in the rare case that revenue exceeds spending. In contrast to the budget deficit, the national debt is the amount accumulated over all years that the government owes to lenders, both foreign and domestic. Republican platforms used the words "national debt" (twenty-one times) and "budget deficit" (nine times), but they were most likely to refer to a "balanced budget" (thirty-five times).

The Spending/Deficit code 415 was assigned to fifty planks under the Public Goods heading. The code was placed under Public Goods because most people view spending in a general way, as a discretionary matter for all sorts of domestic programs. In actuality, most spending is committed to mandatory programs such as Social Security and Medicare. The largest discretionary expenditure is military spending, which has amounted to roughly 15 percent of the entire national budget in recent years.

Because only fourteen of the fifty Republican planks came between 1856 and 1960 and thirty-six occurred after 1960, one might think that the party's concern with spending and the deficit was relatively recent. However, my database contained many fewer planks before 1964 (864) than after that date (1,858). In actuality, 2 percent of Republican planks were coded for Spending/Deficit in each time period. The party seems to have addressed this issue comparably over time. Republican concern about government spending beyond government revenue is admirable, and government spending beyond its income has been a real problem.

There is, however, one aspect of the Spending/Deficit topic that is peculiarly Republican and contrary to reality. Every Republican platform from 1984 to 2016 called for a balanced budget, and "balanced budget" appeared in one-third of the 36 Spending/Deficit planks. In truth, only three presidents have managed to achieve a balanced budget since World War II. Republican Eisenhower generated small budget surpluses in FY1956 and FY1957, and Democrat Johnson produced a small surplus in FY1969. Only Democrat Clinton produced sizable surpluses over four years, from FY1998 to FY2001. Nevertheless, Republicans succeeded in tagging Democrats as the "tax and spend" party. The 1984 Republican platform stated: "Democrats claim deficits are caused by Americans' paying too little in taxes. Nonsense. We categorically reject proposals to increase taxes in a misguided effort to balance the budget. *Tax and spending* increases would reduce incentives for economic activity and threaten the recovery."

In 1992, ironically the year President Clinton was first elected, the Republican platform stated: "Contrary to statist Democrat propaganda, the American people know that the 1980s were a rising tide, a magnificent decade for freedom and entrepreneurial creativity. We are confident that, knowing this, they will never consciously retreat to the bad old days of *tax and spend*." Clinton later succeeded in balancing the budget four years in a row. Nevertheless, Newt Gingrich, who led the party to take over the House of Representatives in 1994, sought to "smash 'tax and spend liberalism' which has dominated our domestic politics for sixty years."[8]

REPUBLICANS: DON'T TAX AND SPEND

If Democrats are the "tax and spend" party, Republicans are the "don't tax and spend" party. That conclusion can be drawn from the U.S. Bureau of the Budget data on budgetary surpluses and deficits.[9] Figure 7.3 plots annual amounts for ten presidential administrations—six Republican and four Democratic—from the first year of their term to the last.[10] FY1954 represents the first budget drawn up by President Eisenhower's administration; FY2021 represents the budget left by the Trump administration.[11] The amounts are expressed in "constant" FY2012 dollars to adjust for inflation.

Three of the four Democratic presidencies in figure 7.3 experienced smaller budgetary deficits than five of the six Republican presidents. Only Eisenhower compares favorably with Clinton, Kennedy/Johnson, and Carter. While President Obama, the fourth Democrat, also had huge deficits, he inherited them from the 2008 economic collapse during George W. Bush's administration. President Obama steadily decreased annual deficits through most of his eight years. Figure 7.3 clearly demonstrates that Republican presidents ran up far larger budget deficits than Democratic presidents in fiscal years since 1954.

DO DEFICITS MATTER?

In 1950, people making over $200,000 paid 91 percent of their earnings above that amount as income tax. The movie star Ronald Reagan's 1965 autobiography said that he quit making pictures for a year after he moved

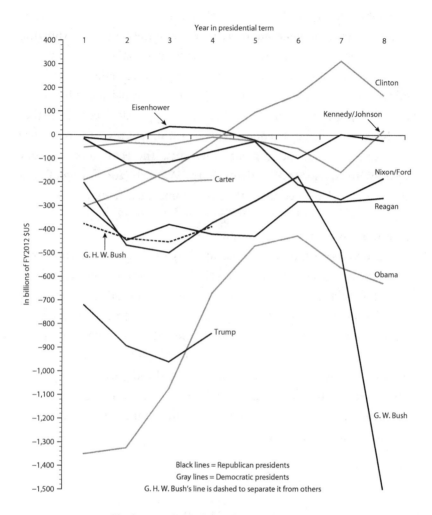

FIGURE 7.3. Annual budget surpluses/deficits by president since 1954.

into that income bracket.[12] The top tax rate was still 70 percent when Reagan was elected president in 1980. In 1981, he signed a bill reducing it to 50 percent. Afterward, Reagan ran substantial budget deficits in every year of his presidency. In 2001, George W. Bush further reduced the top rate to 35 percent. President Obama raised it to 39.6 percent, but President Trump reduced it to 37 percent. The message is clear: Republicans favor low taxes on high incomes.

Republicans argue that such a policy is good for the country. They expect low taxes to generate more revenue in the long run. Allowing wealthy people to keep more of their money enables the rich to invest in productive businesses, which hire more people, who make more money and subsequently pay more in taxes than would be produced by higher taxes on top incomes. This belief fits with "supply-side" economic theory: lower taxes generate enough extra government revenue to balance the budget without making spending cuts. The economist Gregory Mankiw, an advisor to President George W. Bush (2001–2009), found that history failed to confirm the main conjecture of supply-side economics. Mankiw said, "When Reagan cut taxes after he was elected, the result was less tax revenue, not more."[13]

Figure 7.3 shows that the steepest and largest budget deficits occurred during the presidency of Republican G. W. Bush, who invaded Iraq, leading to a long and costly war. Despite the war's initial and increasing costs, President Bush did not propose raising taxes to pay for it. Critics claimed, with justification, that the United States had never fought a major war without designating taxes to pay for it.[14] According to Dick Cheney, Bush's vice president, the accumulated and growing budget deficits posed no problem. Paul O'Neill, the Republican secretary of the Treasury, reported that Cheney said to him: "You know, Paul, Reagan proved deficits don't matter."[15]

SUMMARY

In the nineteenth century, Republicans believed that tariffs would raise sufficient revenue for the government and would protect fledgling domestic industries. By the beginning of the twentieth century, tariffs failed to provide sufficient revenue for government, and Republicans turned to taxing incomes for additional revenue. Table 7.1 encapsulates the changes in party policies.

Unfortunately, Republicans' willingness to adopt the new source of revenue was not matched by a willingness to impose sufficient taxes to avoid perennial debt.

TABLE 7.1 Revenue by tariff versus income tax

1856–1876	1880–1904	1908–1928**	1932–1956*	1960–1980*	1984–2012	2016–2020
Tariff	Tariff	Tariff				
Income tax*		Income tax	Income tax	Income tax	Income tax	Income tax

*Introduced to fund the Civil War.
**Thirteenth Amendment for an income tax ratified in 1913.

TABLE 7.2 Protective tariff versus free trade by eras

1856–1876	1880–1904	1908–1928	1932–1956	1960–1980*	1984–2012	2016–2020
	Protective tariff	Protective tariff	Protective tariff	Protective tariff		Tariff protection
					Free trade	

*The 1980 plank denounced the protective tariff at the end of that era.

At the start of the twentieth century, the United States was exiting a domestic agricultural economy and entering a world of international trade. A protective tariff, which had been the party's bedrock principle, was an "antiquated policy" for that world. The party noted this in its 1988 platform: "Unfortunately, international markets are still restricted by antiquated policies: protective tariffs, quotas, and subsidies." To its credit, the Republican Party scrapped its venerable principle, the protective tariff, in the 1980s. Table 7.2 shows the timing of the shift.

The word "tariff" did not appear in the 2016 Republican Party platform. While it committed the party "to the principles of open markets . . . in which free trade will truly be fair trade for all concerned," the platform also said: "A Republican president will insist on parity in trade and stand ready to implement countervailing duties if other countries refuse to cooperate." When President Trump imposed tariffs on foreign goods to protect American industries, he—in effect—changed Republican policy. The party's orientation had evolved from nationalist to internationalist after World War II and back to nationalist after Trump.

8

ECONOMIC AFFAIRS

Founded in 1854 to prevent slavery from expanding outside the agricultural South, the Republican Party drew its support from the industrial North. After the Civil War ended slavery, the party championed a new issue: economic growth. The celebrated historian Lewis Gould wrote that

> Republicans expanded the power of the national government in the economic sphere. They established a national banking system, imposed an income tax, created a system for dispersing public land in the West, and started a transcontinental railroad. The role of the national government in promoting economic growth went beyond even what the Whigs had contemplated.[1]

Even as the Civil War raged in 1862, a Republican Congress passed the Morrill Act, which provided grants of land to states to finance the establishment of colleges specializing in "agriculture and the mechanic arts."

THE ECONOMY AS A PUBLIC GOOD

Government actions to promote economic growth vary in their political implications. Politicians usually spend money on public goods without much controversy. Although "conservatives" and "liberals" might differ over such government spending, they seldom clash over it. They are more likely to fight furiously over economic policies that promote Order (for example, requiring environmental safeguards) or that serve Freedom (for example, allowing private owners to buy public lands). I categorized the less controversial type of Republican platform planks on the "Economy" under Public Goods code 414. The more controversial fall under Public Goods codes 205 Order and 105 Freedom.

The 2,722 Republican planks divide into two almost equal halves: about 1,350 planks were adopted from 1856 to 1980 and about 1,350 from 1984 to 2016. Only 54 of the 2,722 were coded 414 Economy. Three-quarters of those planks were adopted in the party's first 125 years, from 1856 to 1980, when Republicans were spending for the Public Good in general. Listed in what follows are the very first eight planks after 1856:

1860   Develop industrial interests of the whole country
1868   Administer government with strictest economy
          Improve credit to gain low interest
1872   Promote the industries, prosperity, and growth of the
          whole country
          Secure full protection and the amplest field for capital
          Secure full protection and the amplest field for labor, the
          creator of capital
1876   Promote interests of labor and advance prosperity of
          whole country
1888   Support the fishing industry

These eight Economy planks reflected the party's early intent to serve "the whole country." As the nineteenth century ended and the twentieth century began, Republicans struggled over their connection to business, which came to mean "big" business dominated by corporations, such as the New York Central Railroad (founded 1853), Standard Oil (1870), AT&T (1883), General Electric (1892), U.S. Steel (1901), Ford (1903), and General Motors (1908). Although leaders of these corporations donated heavily to Republicans, the party tried to regulate their commercial activities. Consider these verbatim extracts from Republican platforms:

1872   "We are opposed to further grants of the public lands to corporations and monopolies"

1876   "We reaffirm our opposition to further grants of the public lands to corporations and monopolies"

1880   "No further grants of the public domain should be made to any railway or other corporation"

1884   "The principle of public regulation of railway corporations is a wise and salutary one for the protection of all classes of the people"

1904   "New laws insuring reasonable publicity as to the operations of great corporations"

1916   "The Republican party has long believed in the rigid supervision and strict regulation of the transportation and of the great corporations of the country"

Eventually, Gould said, the party abandoned its belief in the "harmony of workers and capitalists" and replaced it with an economic order where division between capital and labor widened and social conflict became more of a fact of life. It wasn't that the party and its defenders had forsaken their original ideology but that their identification with American business strengthened as the late nineteenth century unfolded.[2]

After the Republican Party became more economically focused on business, fewer general Economy planks appeared in its platforms. Gould noted the increasing "identification of the Republicans with the ambitions and power of the business community in the North and Middle West": "A party that began as an attack on the existing order became an organization that believed in an identity of the interests of capitalists, workers, and farmers. Over time, the commitment to business outweighed the concern for other elements in the economy."

Accordingly, party planks later became more targeted to specific segments of the economy. Here are the last eight planks before 2016:

1996   Committed to resurgence of small business
        Pledge monetary policy to stabilize prices
        Enforce U.S. trade laws

2000   Fight European Community's restrictions of our farm
          products
        Go beyond arguments that pitted bilateral deals against
          global trade rules
        Launch new round of multilateral negotiations

2004   Support making manufacturing a top priority

2012   Favor free trade but fair trade

Increasingly, the party adopted a laissez-faire approach to economic regulation.

AN ORDERLY BUT FREE ECONOMY

Not surprisingly, the Republican Party adopted more planks dealing with economic concerns than any other topic. There is no clear point at which the party's 147 platform planks switched from emphasizing Economic Order (code 205) to Economic Freedom (code 105). Figure 8.1 divides them at 1936–1940. Before 1940, almost 70 percent of 36 Republican planks imposed governmental order of some form on economic activity. Since 1940, over 80 percent of 111 party planks favored less government control.

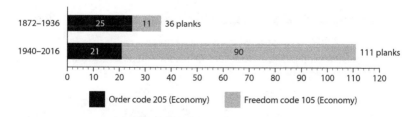

FIGURE 8.1. The economy in 147 planks, 1872–1936 vs. 1940–2016.

The previous section quoted six passages in Republican platforms from 1872 to 1916 on regulating corporations. The same six passages were also coded as party planks and were among the 70 percent in figure 8.1. In what follows are nine examples of planks coded 205 Economy under Order from 1920 to 1936.

1920   Approve existing federal legislation against monopoly and combinations in restraint of trade

1920   Centralize federal agencies for public health

1928   Support railroad regulation through the Interstate Commerce Commission

1928   Prevent monopolies in the control and utilization of natural resources

1932   Strengthen bank supervision

1932   Favor supervision, regulation, and control of interstate public utilities

1936   Enforce laws against monopolies and trusts

1936   Favor federal regulation of the interstate activities of public utilities

1936   Favor federal regulation of marketing securities to protect investors

After 1940, Republicans favored Economic Freedom more than Economic Order, and 81 percent of the party's planks on the economy were tagged with Freedom code 105 Economy. Listed in what follows are the fourteen planks so coded only for the Republican's 2016 platform:

- Eliminate federal grants imposing conditions on state and local governments
- Oppose taking private property for "public purpose" as well as "public use"
- Protect citizens from asset forfeiture
- Allow purchase of health insurance across state lines
- Rein in regulations of the FDA

- Transform the EPA into an independent bipartisan commission, like the Nuclear Regulatory Commission
- Oppose mandatory labeling of genetically modified food
- Oppose rules for producing and marketing milk, meat, poultry, and livestock
- Oppose EPA WOTUS rules concerning water on private property
- Reduce occupational licensing laws
- Remove overregulation of startups and excessive licensing requirements
- Repeal the Dodd-Frank Law
- Require both houses to approve regulations imposing significant costs
- Repeal FATCA, which seizes personal financial information

By the end of the twentieth century, Republican Party platforms embraced unfettered free enterprise.

THE SMALL BUSINESS PARTY

In 1925, President Calvin Coolidge publicly stated, "The chief business of the American people is business." Whatever that statement meant, the Republican president reinforced his party's link to thriving corporations. The stock market crash in 1929 and the Great Depression of the 1930s worked against Republicans campaigning as the party of business.

During World War II, Republicans distanced themselves from corporations by branding themselves as the "small business" party. A journalist who has tracked the term's appearance in digitized books since 1800 found that "the phrase 'small business' didn't come into general use until the latter part of the 19th century. Its usage grew rapidly in two distinct time periods: (1) From 1920 to 1940 and (2) From 1970 until the present."[3]

I conducted a search for "small business" in Republican and Democratic platforms since 1856 to match the journalist's search for the phrase in books since 1800. Both parties used it for the first time in 1940. Since then, Republicans used "small business" 232 times—ninety-eight more times than Democrats. The Republicans mentioned it three times in 1940:

SMALL BUSINESS

The New Deal policy of interference and arbitrary regulation has injured all business, but especially *small business*. We promise to encourage the *small business* man by removing unnecessary bureaucratic regulation and interference.

The phrase was used only once in 1944 and 1948 and four times in 1952, but "small business" has appeared 223 times since 1956. The Republican 2016 platform alone mentioned "small business" thirteen times.

Republicans can and should be proud of their support of small businesses. They were properly worried in their 2016 platform when stating: "More businesses are closing in our country than are starting." That Republican platform attributed this trend to the effect of capital gains and to occupational licensing laws that shut untold millions of potential workers out of entrepreneurial careers. Republicans were less concerned about the actions of "big" business—that giant companies like Amazon and Walmart were forcing small businesses to close. Similarly, national corporations like Home Depot and Lowe's drove out local hardware stores, and Walgreens and CVS drove out local pharmacies. Remaining businesses are more likely to be headed by salaried managers rather than proprietors of small businesses. Some observers fault government and both parties for not invoking antitrust legislation.[4]

SUMMARY

In 1860, before the Civil War, the Republican Party platform addressed the need for adequate revenue "to encourage the development of the

TABLE 8.1 Economic regulation versus deregulation planks by eras

1856–1876	1880–1904	1908–1928	1932–1956*	1960–1980*	1984–2012	2016–2020
Favor regulations	Favor regulations	Favor regulations				
			Oppose regulations	Oppose regulations	Oppose regulations	Oppose regulations

*Up to 1936, 69 percent of economy planks favored regulation; since 1940, 81 percent opposed them. Concerning economic affairs, the Republican Party shifted from its original position of governing to its current antigovernment position. The party evolved from being probusiness with regulations to being probusiness without regulations.

industrial interests of the whole country." After the war, the party's 1872 platform sought additional revenue "to aid in securing remunerative wages to labor, and to promote the industries, prosperity, and growth of the whole country." The Republican Party clearly intended to be a governing party. To that end, it sought to raise additional revenue through taxes on personal income, even proposing a constitutional amendment to ensure the legality of an income tax. Although the Republican Party was firmly aligned with manufacturing interests and corporations, the party regulated large-scale commercial activity through national legislation. Republican president Teddy Roosevelt drew fame for "trust-busting."

In the second half of the twentieth century, Republican Party platforms denigrated economic regulations and extolled free enterprise, cloaked under the mantle of "small business." My independent analysis of Republican platform planks again corresponds with Gerring's characterization of the Republican Party entering an epoch of neoliberalism in 1928, with free-market capitalism as a major theme. The distribution of Republican planks on economic regulation and deregulation is given in table 8.1.

9

LAW AND ORDER

The Republican Party regularly adopted conflicting positions concerning law and order versus personal freedoms. While favoring the death penalty, imprisoning lawbreakers, and forcing women to give birth to unwanted children, many Republican officials opposed requiring people to wear facemasks to prevent against COVID-19 infections. Relatively recently, the party came to oppose regulating citizens' ownership and use of deadly weapons, thus surrendering the government's monopoly of force, which is required to impose law and order.

In the seventeenth century, Thomas Hobbes described life without government as "solitary, poor, nasty, brutish, and short." Formed to protect people against violence from other people, governments sought to "monopolize" violence—to own all instruments of force and to lawfully and exclusively administer force as needed.[1] Early in the twentieth century, the German sociologist Max Weber wrote that "the state is a human community that (successfully) claims the *monopoly of the legitimate use of physical force* within a given territory."[2] A century later, American scholars continue to acknowledge Weber's classic assertion.[3] Others phrase this theme as "the monopoly of violence" or "the monopoly of force."

LAWFUL EXECUTION

Historically, governments legitimately killed citizens convicted of capital crimes, real or imagined. Many governments still do. By one count, fifty-six of almost two hundred countries maintained the death penalty in 2020.[4] No Western European country still allows the practice. The United States stands instead with countries in the Middle East (Iran, Iraq, Saudi Arabia) and Asia (China, Pakistan, North Korea). For a time in the 1970s, the Supreme Court invalidated existing death penalty laws, holding that they violated the Eighth Amendment, which prohibits cruel and unusual punishment in the manner of execution. After some states revised their methods, executions resumed on a limited basis in the 1980s.

The Republican Party took issue with the court's decision in 1972 and has supported executing criminals for major crimes in all platforms since 1980:

1980 "We believe that the *death penalty* serves as an effective deterrent to capital crime and should be applied by the federal government and by states which approve it as an appropriate penalty for certain major crimes."

1984 "The Republican Senate has overwhelmingly passed Administration-backed legislation which would . . . Restore a constitutionally valid federal *death penalty*."

1988 "We will reestablish the *death penalty*."
"Impose the death penalty for drug kingpins and those who kill federal law enforcement agents."

1992 "[Democrats] refuse to enact effective procedures to reinstate the *death penalty* for the most heinous crimes."
"We therefore support the stiffest penalties, including the *death penalty*, for major drug traffickers."

1996 "We believe it is time to revisit the Supreme Court's arbitrary decision of 1977 that protects even the most vicious rapists from the *death penalty*."

2000   "Within proper federal jurisdiction, the Republican
       Congress has enacted legislation for an effective
       deterrent *death penalty.*"

2004   "We support courts having the option to impose the *death
       penalty* in capital murder cases."

2008   "We object to the Court's unwarranted interference in the
       administration of the *death penalty* in this country for
       the benefit of savage criminals whose guilt is not at
       issue."

       "Courts must have the option of imposing the *death
       penalty* in capital murder cases."

2012   "Courts should have the option of imposing the death
       penalty in capital murder cases."

2016   "The constitutionality of the *death penalty* is firmly settled
       by its explicit mention in the Fifth Amendment."

Historically, governments legitimately used force to apprehend and imprison lawbreakers. In the nineteenth century, Republicans did not need to confirm in their platforms that citizens could be punished for transgressing laws. In the twentieth century, however, Republicans frequently went on record against various types of lawbreakers.

Republican planks about social Transgressions fell under Order code 211 and Freedom code 111. The party's first twenty platforms to 1932 contained only six planks on this topic under either code. In 1860, for example, Republicans denounced *lawless invasion by armed forces* in Kansas supporting slavery, which was coded Transgressions 211 under Order. In 1868 and again in 1872 it favored *the removal of the disqualifications and restrictions imposed upon the late rebels*, coded Freedom 111. Then a gap of thirty-six years occurred, from 1932 to 1968, before the party's next Transgression plank. Both codes were used forty times across the next thirteen platforms. Figure 9.1 displays the distribution of Transgression planks for both eras.

Only seven of forty planks since 1968 reflect leniency, most decrying high lawyers' fees in "frivolous" medical malpractice suits. Republicans were quick to punish transgressions in thirty-three of the forty planks

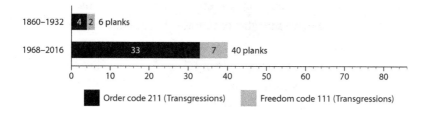

FIGURE 9.1. Social transgressions in forty-six planks, 1860–1932 vs. 1968–2016.

(83 percent) since 1968. These thirty-three planks reflect the party's tough stance on lawbreakers:

1968 Apprehend, prosecute, convict, and punish the overlords
         of organized crime in America
       Pledge an all-out, federal-state-local crusade against crime
1972 Accelerate the drive against organized crime
       Pledge a tireless campaign against crime to restore safety
         to our streets
       Support of local police and law enforcement agencies
1976 Penalize airplane hijacking as terrorism
1984 Make punishment certain and swift
1988 Penalize those who contribute tainted blood
       Emphasize preemptive antiterrorist measures
       Favor tougher laws against drunk driving
       Suspend drivers' licenses for convicted users
1992 Pass tougher state laws against drunken drivers
       Restore severe penalties for heinous crimes; give manda-
         tory sentences to criminals
       Penalize welfare fraud
       Give law enforcement funds to do their job
1996 Condemn desecration of church buildings and arson
       Consider juvenile nocturnal curfews as effective law
         enforcement
       Prevent inmates from government entitlements while in
         prison

Require violent felons to serve 85 percent of terms

Revoke pension rights of public officials convicted of crimes

Support community policing

Tough law enforcement

Tougher standards on statutory rape

2000   Bring individual terrorists to justice

Isolate and punish terrorists and sponsors

Make imprisonment a threat to crime

Punish juvenile offenders; open criminal proceedings to victims

Support a resolute but not impulsive response to terrorism that makes no concessions

2004   Jail time is an effective deterrent to drug use

2008   Call for stronger enforcement and determined prosecution of gang conspiracies

Support mandatory sentencing for gang conspiracy crimes

2012   Support mandatory prison sentences for major crimes

2016   Give mandatory prison time for all serious injuries to law enforcement officers

When it comes to transgressions, the Republican Party favors strong government to impose law and order.

GUN CONTROL

Most governments try to secure a monopoly on violence by limiting lawful access to lethal weapons. Only three countries have constitutions that grant the right to own a gun. They are Mexico, Guatemala, and the United States, and only the United States has no constitutional restrictions.[5] The Second Amendment to the Constitution reads: "A well regulated Militia, being necessary to the security of a free State, the right of the people to keep and bear Arms, shall not be infringed." Nevertheless, throughout most of its history the Republican Party has regulated the use of firearms.

The word "arms" appeared in early Republican platforms concerning the Civil War and in later platforms concerning international rearmament, but it did not appear in the context of personal weapons. Some people owned handguns (often in cities), and many people owned rifles and shotguns (usually outside of cities). Throughout the nineteenth and twentieth centuries, Republican platforms never mentioned the Second Amendment. In 1934, Congress passed a Firearms Act that banned sawed-off shotguns, which were favored by prohibition gangsters. In 1938, the Supreme Court supported the ban, explaining that "the Framers included the Second Amendment to ensure the effectiveness of the military."[6] The National Rifle Association (NRA), founded in 1871 as a recreational group for rifle shooting, had backed the 1934 law.[7]

After President Kennedy's 1963 assassination with a mail-order rifle, Congress passed the Gun Control Act of 1968, also supported by the NRA.[8] The Republican Party apparently accepted this law, for its 1968 platform favored "enactment of legislation to control indiscriminate availability of firearms, safeguarding the right of responsible citizens to collect, own and use firearms for legitimate purposes." That statement launched the first of five Republican planks favoring some degree of gun control.

1968	Control availability of firearms but safeguard gun rights
1972	Prevent criminal access to all weapons, including cheap handguns
1996	Extend point-of-purchase check
2000	Support background checks to ensure that guns do not fall into the hands of criminals
2004	Support the instant background check system

After President Reagan was seriously wounded by a handgun in 1981, the city of Washington, DC, acted to ban handguns. This time the NRA silently opposed the legislation. In 2008, the Supreme Court by a 5–4 vote struck down the DC ban on handguns as violating the right to possess firearms under the Second Amendment. By another 5–4 vote in 2010, it struck down a similar ban in Chicago. This time the NRA actively opposed the Chicago ban.

The Second Amendment was first mentioned in a Republican platform in 2000. It has been mentioned fifteen times in every subsequent platform. Moreover, Republicans produced twenty-two planks since 1972 that opposed gun control or supported gun rights:

1972   Recognize right of owning firearms for legitimate
       purposes
1976   Oppose federal registration of firearms
       Support the right of citizens to keep and bear arms
1980   Oppose registration of firearms
1984   Continue to defend the constitutional right to keep and
       bear arms
1988   Defend right to keep and bear arms
1992   Support right to bear arms
1996   Defend right to keep and bear arms
       Keep guns from convicted felons
2000   Affirm right of individuals to carry arms
       Oppose federal licensing of law-abiding gun owners and
       national gun registration
2004   Oppose federal licensing of gun owners
       Strongly support an individual's right to own guns
2008   Oppose federal licensing of law-abiding gun owners and
       national gun registration
       Support right to keep and bear rams
2012   Support the right to bear arms
       Oppose limiting capacity of clips or magazines
       Oppose registration of gun owners
2016   Defend the right to bear arms
       Support right-to-carry laws
       Oppose frivolous lawsuits against arms manufacturers

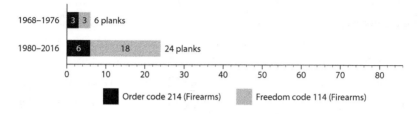

FIGURE 9.2. Gun control in thirty planks, 1968–1978 vs. 1980–201.

Figure 9.2 graphs the number of Republican planks on gun control. The topic was not addressed until 1968. After 1980, planks opposing gun control became common.

Historically, governments sought to maintain their monopoly of violence by restricting citizens from carrying weapons. Swords were once frequent instruments of domestic violence;[9] now firearms are. The Republican Party supported limited forms of firearm control before the 2008 Supreme Court interpreted the Second Amendment to limit control. Since then, gun control has become a highly partisan issue, with Republicans opposing governmental efforts to limit the availability, possession, capabilities, or use of firearms.

FORCING BIRTH

Whether life begins at birth or at conception, as Republicans claim, is debated by physicians, theologians, and philosophers, who take positions on both sides of the question.[10] During its first 116 years, Republican platforms never mentioned abortion. After the Supreme Court's 1973 decision in *Roe v. Wade* held that a state statute outlawing abortion violated a woman's right to privacy, which was implicit in the due process clause of the Constitution, abortion became a central plank in Republican platforms. The party opposed to government now argued that, to protect unborn life, government can force a woman to give birth to a child she does not want.

The 1976 Republican platform mentioned abortion five times, beginning with: "Because of our concern for family values, we affirm . . . a position on abortion that values human life." In all, abortion appeared 118 times from 1976 to 2016. In just eleven platforms during that time period, the party managed to offer these thirty-seven planks relating to abortion:

1976   Favor a continuance of the public dialogue on abortion
Adopt a position that values human life
Support amendment to protect life of unborn children

1980   Favor constitutional amendment to protect life of unborn children

1984   Oppose public revenue for abortions
Support amendment to protect rights of the unborn

1988   Oppose use of public revenue for abortion
Support amendment to protect the unborn

1992   Oppose using public funds for abortion
Oppose school programs on birth control or abortion
Favor amendments to protect the unborn child

1996   Not fund international organizations involved in abortion
Oppose using public funds for abortion
Stop cash payments to unmarried teens with children

2000   Not fund any agency engaged in abortion
Oppose school-based clinics giving referrals or counseling on contraception and abortion
Replace "family planning" programs for teens with increased funding for abstinence education
Favor amendment to protect life of unborn children

2004   Oppose abortion
Oppose funding international organizations engaged in abortion
Ban on human cloning and on the creation of human embryos
Support human life amendment to the constitution

2008   Oppose funding international groups engaged in abortion
        Support a human life amendment

2012   Oppose public funds for abortion
        Oppose funding international organizations that perform
           abortions
        Allow courts to impose the death penalty
        Ban human cloning
        Ban use of body parts from fetuses
        Oppose euthanasia and assisted suicide
        Favor an amendment to protect the unborn

2016   Oppose using public funds for abortion
        Teach abstinence until marriage
        Ban human cloning
        Ban sale of fetal body parts
        Oppose euthanasia and assisted suicide
        Support amendment to protect the unborn

SUMMARY

This chapter discusses three issues—the death penalty, gun control, and abortion—that were not relevant to party politics during what John Gerring called the party's nationalism epoch, which according to him ended in 1924. These issues also did not arise early in his neoliberalism epoch, which began in 1928. In fact, they became controversial and partisan only in the middle of the twentieth century. Moreover, they do not seem to match any of that epoch's themes, which Gerring's listed as "antistatism, free market capitalism, right-wing populism, and individualism."

From the party's beginning, Republicans approved of the death penalty and consistently backed governmental use of force in apprehending, imprisoning, and executing lawbreakers. For most of its existence, the Republican Party endorsed the principle that government should hold the "monopoly of force"—and control over deadly weapons is inherent in monopolizing force. Over the first century of the party's existence, gun control was not a prominent political issue. When it surfaced after President Kennedy's assassination, the party supported gun control to some extent. Heavily lobbied by the NRA, however, the party changed its position. It opposed strengthening controls even after President Reagan was shot. The party today favors weak or no regulations against possessing or using firearms of any type. While life did not become "solitary, poor, nasty, brutish, and short" for every American citizen as a result, it did become unpredictably brutish and short for many.

Since the abortion issue surfaced in the 1970s, the party's platforms have consistently backed governmental efforts to force women to give birth against their will. Republicans view antiabortion laws as preserving life while favoring the death penalty for ending life. Republicans' support of the death penalty and its opposition to gun control and abortion herald a new theme: *cultural defense.* The party that was created in 1854 to overthrow the centuries-old culture of slavery in the southern states had turned a century later into a defender of nineteenth-century cultural norms that clashed with the changing values of the twentieth century.

Just as Republicans judged slavery to be morally wrong in the mid-1800s, citizens in Western nations and many in the United States judged the death penalty to be morally wrong in the mid-twentieth century. Despite the Supreme Court's 2008 decision upholding the Second Amendment as a barrier against gun control, many citizens clamored for such controls in the wake of mass shootings. While religious leaders in the 1970s declared that life begins at conception and viewed abortion as murder, women proclaimed their right to decide whether to have and raise a child. The party that had been born committed to cultural change in the South evolved to one defending traditional culture against change nationwide. Additional evidence comes in the next chapter, "Culture and Order."

10

CULTURE AND ORDER

Sociologists define culture as "the languages, customs, beliefs, rules, arts, knowledge, and collective identities" of a society.[1] "Order," in the phrase "law and order," implies preserving the status quo. That includes maintaining the dominant culture, with force if necessary. To preserve their dominant culture, social conservatives favor government policies that limit immigration and discourage threatening lifestyles. Increasingly since World War II, Republican platforms have reflected the wishes of social conservatives in opposing cultural changes.

IMMIGRATION

Early in U.S. history, Republicans generally welcomed immigration and all types of immigrants. Its 1860 platform resolved: "That the Republican party is opposed to any change in our naturalization laws or any state legislation by which the rights of citizens hitherto accorded to *immigrants* from foreign lands shall be abridged or impaired; and in favor of giving a full and efficient protection to the rights of all classes of citizens, whether native or naturalized, both at home and abroad."

In the 1800s, Republicans usually, but not always, treated immigration as a Public Good, a benefit. The United States had more land than people and needed help from outside to develop its potential for all. After World War I, Republicans turned to restrict immigration, adopting a plank to "regulate immigration and improve immigration laws" in 1924. Afterward, the party's stance softened. Consider these nineteen planks tagged with Public Good code 419, Immigration, before 1900 and after World War II:

1864	Favor liberal and just policy
1868	Favor liberal and just policy
1872	For careful encouragement and protection of voluntary immigration
1876	Protect immigrants
1880	Same protection as to citizens of birth
1884	Same protection as to citizens of birth
1956	Supports providing a haven for oppressed peoples
1960	Judge applicants on their merits
1964	Reunite families and continuation of the "Fair Share" refugee program
1996	Ensure laws reflect America's national interest Set immigration at manageable levels
2000	Emphasize skills Increase number of H-1B visas and expand H-2A programs for farm workers Give priority to spouses and children, not extended family
2004	Enforce the law while welcoming immigrants Support reforming the immigration system to ensure that it is legal, safe, orderly, and humane
2008	Integrate legal immigrants into American life Update the H-1B visa program to gain specialists from abroad
2012	Grant more visas to highly educated

None of these planks raised issues of Freedom versus Order; all aimed to promote immigration as a Public Good.

In truth, however, Republicans saw negative aspects in immigration. Delivering his annual message to Congress in 1903, President Theodore Roosevelt spoke bluntly: "We cannot have too much immigration of the right kind, and we should have none at all of the wrong kind. The need is to devise some system by which undesirable immigrants can be kept out completely, while desirable immigrants are properly distributed throughout the country."[2]

Immigration planks were coded separately under different codes to capture Republican platforms' discriminatory actions. Order code 203 indicated restrictions on immigration, and Freedom code 103 marked welcoming planks. These planks reveal that about one-quarter of Republican planks before 1984 supported immigrants' rights, while none of twenty-nine planks did after 1984.

Here are all seven planks in Republican platforms before 1984 that welcomed immigration:

1860   Oppose abridging immigrant rights
1868   Support immigrant rights
1960   Increase immigration to stimulate growth; abandon use
           of 1920 census guidelines
1968   Support the 1965 act and make it more equitable and
           nondiscriminatory
1972   Support right to emigrate from all countries
           Support the 1965 Immigration Act; nondiscrimination
           against national origins
1980   Recognize citizens from Eastern, Central, and Southern
           Europe and Asian-Americans

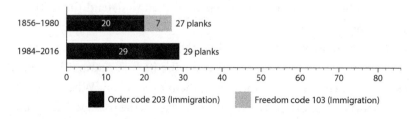

FIGURE 10.1.   Immigration in fifty-six planks, 1856–1980 vs. 1984–2016.

Space does not allow listing all later Republican planks coded under Order that restricted immigration. Every platform after 1984 referred to border control, and the 2016 platform had the most planks, seven:

- Build a wall to secure our borders
- Impose stiffer penalties on illegals who reenter
- Make gang membership a deportable offense
- Make E-Verify mandatory
- Oppose amnesty in any form
- Secure our borders, enforce our immigration laws, and properly screen refugees
- Stop federal funds to sanctuary cities

The party that began welcoming immigrants changed its stance—possibly responding to bad behavior by immigrants, possibly reacting to Republican voters opposed to immigration.

RELIGION

Early American colonialists were overwhelmingly Protestant, as were most immigrants for a few decades after independence. Famine in Ireland in the 1840s caused many Irish Catholics to migrate to the United States. Later in the century, Catholic immigrants came from Central and Southern Europe. Whereas Catholics were only 5 percent of the population in 1850, they were 17 percent by 1906.[3] For many Protestants, the influx of Catholics became a political issue, but "Catholic" did not appear in a Republican platform until 1988, and then to defend the Catholic Church against unfair taxation.

Readers today might be surprised that the Republican Party rarely referred at all to religion in any way during its first century. Not until 1880 did a Republican platform even mention religion. When it did, it was to forbid support of religious schools. Here's the passage: "The Constitution wisely forbids Congress to make any law respecting the establishment of religion, but it is idle to hope that the Nation can be protected against the influence of secret sectarianism while each State is exposed to its domination. We, therefore, recommend that the Constitution be so amended as to lay the same prohibition upon the Legislature of each State, and to forbid the appropriation of public funds to the support of sectarian schools."

The next mention was in 1912. After 1936, virtually every platform endorsed freedom of religion. Readers may be even more surprised that the party never mentioned "God" in its platform until 1908. The next usage was in 1948. Beginning in 1964, "God" became used multiple times in virtually every platform, culminating in ten mentions in 2012 and these fifteen in 2016:

- "The Declaration sets forth the fundamental precepts of American government: That *God* bestows certain inalienable rights on every individual, thus producing human equality."
- "That government exists first and foremost to protect those inalienable rights; that man-made law must be consistent with *God*-given, natural rights."
- "And that if *God*-given, natural, inalienable rights come in conflict with government, court, or human-granted rights."
- "*God*-given, natural, inalienable rights always prevail."
- "That there is a moral law recognized as "the Laws of Nature and of Nature's *God*."
- "It is the solemn compact built upon principles of the Declaration that enshrines our *God*-given individual rights."
- "In a free society, the primary role of government is to protect the *God*-given, inalienable rights of its citizens."
- "Only a Republican president will appoint judges who respect the rule of law expressed within the Constitution and Declaration of Independence, including the inalienable right to life and the laws of nature and nature's *God*."
- "The Free Exercise Clause is both an individual and a collective liberty protecting a right to worship *God* according to the dictates of conscience."
- "Lawful gun ownership enables Americans to exercise their *God*-given right of self-defense."

- "The Republican Party reaffirms the moral obligation to be good stewards of the *God*-given natural beauty and resources of our country."
- "Strong families, depending upon *God* and one another, advance the cause of liberty by lessening the need for government in their daily lives."
- "A young person's ability to succeed in school must be based on his or her *God*-given talent and motivation."

Over all forty-one platforms, Republicans referred to God sixty-one times (plus two for "Godless" communism) versus thirty-five times in Democratic platforms, the first in 1924. Of course, platforms were longer in later years, providing more opportunity for heavenly references. Figure 10.2 reports the number of times per ten thousand words in the platforms.

Today's readers are apt to think of religion playing a larger role in daily life during the nineteenth century, and that is certainly true. Nevertheless, Republican Party platforms over one hundred years ago seldom mentioned religion and never mentioned God before the twentieth century.

Interestingly, the word "Christian" was not used in Republican platforms until 1976, after which it appeared nineteen more times. Throughout the nineteenth century, the U.S. population was overwhelmingly Protestant in religion. In the middle of the twentieth century, Protestants were dominant in the Republican Party, while most Catholics voted Democratic. By the end of the twentieth century, Catholics began moving toward Republicans, while the Democratic Party attracted more non-Christian voters. In turn, Republicans attracted more white Christians,

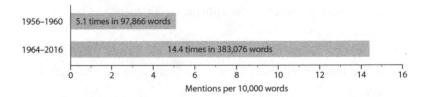

FIGURE 10.2. Mentions of "God" per 10,000 words in Republican platforms, 1956–1960 vs. 1964–2016.

especially Evangelicals committed to a literal interpretation of the Bible.[4] In every election since 1980, "majorities of white Christians—including not just Evangelicals but also mainliners and Catholics—voted for Republican candidates."[5] In the 2016 election, 77 percent of white Evangelical Protestants voted for Donald Trump;[6] the percentage increased to 84 in 2020. In 2016, 64 percent of white Catholics voted for Trump.[7] Even in 2020, 57 percent chose Trump over the practicing Catholic Joe Biden.

WOMEN'S RIGHTS

Sociologists sometimes describe women as carriers of the dominant culture. Traditionally, their role was to marry, raise children, keep house, and feed the family. Women were denied the right to vote in national elections until 1920, and their employment opportunities were drastically limited. For most of its history, the Republican Party's platforms supported women's rights, in the sense of political equality—like equal rights for former slaves. Republican platform planks fall under codes headed 3-- dealing with Equality. Code +302 Women applies to supportive planks, while Women code −302 indicates opposition. From 1856 to 1988, forty of forty-five planks supported women's rights, again meaning political equality. Opposition arose after women clamored in the 1970s for social equality, pushing for an Equal Rights Amendment to the Constitution. All five planks in opposition came after 1988. Figure 10.3 displays the results.

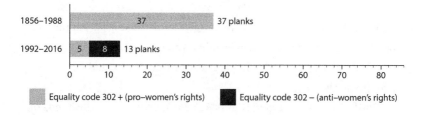

FIGURE 10.3. Women's rights in fifty planks, 1856–1988 vs. 1992–20.

Consider these platform statements:

1872   "The Republican party is mindful of its obligations to the
       loyal *women* of America for their noble devotion to
       the cause of freedom. Their admission to wider fields of
       usefulness is viewed with satisfaction, and the honest
       demand of any class of citizens for additional *rights*
       should be treated with respectful consideration."
1876   "The Republican party recognizes with approval the
       substantial advances recently made toward the estab-
       lishment of equal *rights for women.*"
1896   "The Republican party is mindful of the *rights and
       interests of women*, and believes that they should be
       accorded equal opportunities, equal pay for equal
       work, and protection to the home."

The party's position on the Equal Rights Amendment deserves special attention. In 1923, Congress received a bill for a constitutional amendment that stated, "Equality of rights under the law shall not be denied
or abridged by the United States or by any state on account of sex." It
failed to pass, but the 1940 Republican platform affirmed, "We favor submission by Congress to the States of an amendment to the Constitution
providing for equal rights for men and women." That did not happen.
The party specifically reaffirmed its support of such an amendment in
1948, in 1960, and in 1972—the year that Congress proposed the Equal
Rights Amendment to the Constitution.

Then in 1980, the Republican activist Phyllis Schlafly campaigned vigorously against the Equal Rights Amendment and succeeded in placing
this weak text in the party's platform:

> We acknowledge the legitimate efforts of those who support or
> oppose ratification of the Equal Rights Amendment.
>
> We reaffirm our Party's historic commitment to equal rights and
> equality for women. . . .
>
> Ratification of the Equal Rights Amendment is now in the hands of
> state legislatures, and the issues of the time extension and rescission are

in the courts. The states have a constitutional right to accept or reject a constitutional amendment without federal interference or pressure.

The Christian historian Du Mez said, "It's hard to overstate Schlafly's significance in marshalling the forces of the Religious Right." Years before celebrity pastors entered the fray against women's rights, Schlafly "helped unify white Christians around a rigid and deeply conservative vision of family and nation."[8]

By 1992, Republican platforms spoke against women's equality:

1992 Oppose placing women in combat positions
1996 Exempt women from ground combat areas
2000 Support a reasonable approach to Title IX without affecting men's teams
2004 Favor exempting women from combat
2008 Exempt women from ground combat units

The party's 2012 and 2016 offered no planks on women's rights.

LIFESTYLES

"Lifestyle" refers to the way a person lives, including their marriage and sexual preferences and their consumption of alcohol and other drugs. A total of twenty-seven planks, scattered across time, addressed lifestyle differences. Although early party platforms did not denigrate religions (except for Mormons), they certainly backed some prohibitions related to marriage, alcohol, and drugs.

POLYGAMY

From the beginning, nearly all Americans were Christians, and they believed in the biblical injunction to "be fruitful and multiply," but that applied to monogamous marriages. In the middle of the nineteenth century, some members in the Church of Jesus Christ of Latter-day Saints, commonly called Mormons, practiced polygamy, marrying multiple women. The very first Republican platform in 1856 promised to prohibit the spread of "those twin relics of barbarism—Polygamy, and slavery." Republicans repeated their promise in 1876, 1880, and 1884. Located in the Utah Territory, the Mormon Church officially ended the practice to gain the territory's admission as a state in 1896.

Although Republican platforms condemned polygamy as practiced by Mormons, the party restrained from criticizing their religion, referring to Mormons only twice. And in 2012, the Republican presidential candidate, Mitt Romney, belonged to the Church of Jesus Christ of Latter-day Saints.

SAME-SEX MARRIAGES

"Monogamy" refers to a sexual relationship with one person at a time. Most religions assumed that a monogamous marriage involved spouses of different sexes. When two people of the same sex sought to marry each other, most pastors and priests refused to perform the ceremony. The Republican Party took positions on the issue in 1992 and 2000:

1992   "We oppose any legislation or law which legally recognizes same-sex marriages and allows such couples to adopt children or provide foster care."

2000   "We support the traditional definition of 'marriage' as the legal union of one man and one woman."

In 2004, the first legal same-sex marriage occurred in Massachusetts. Later that year, the Republican platform backed the Defense of Marriage Act and stated: "We urge Congress to use its Article III power to enact this into law, so that activist federal judges cannot force 49 other states to approve and recognize Massachusetts' attempt to redefine marriage." Republican platforms in 2008, 2012, and 2016 urged restoring marriage to a union between a man and a woman, but that ship had sailed a decade earlier.

PROHIBITION

Drunkenness can be considered a negative lifestyle, one with dangerous consequences. Some pious souls also regarded drinking as sinful and sought to prohibit the consumption of alcohol nationwide through a constitutional amendment. Although the amendment passed both chambers of Congress with bipartisan support, only Republicans backed temperance in their party's platforms—in 1888, 1892, and 1896.

The Eighteenth Amendment, ratified in January 1919, prohibited "the manufacture, sale, or transportation of intoxicating liquors" nationwide. In 1933, after more than a decade without legal alcohol but with illegal alcohol and related crime, an amendment repealing Prohibition passed both chambers of Congress with bipartisan support. It was ratified the same year.

SUMMARY

Throughout the nineteenth century, the Republican Party welcomed immigrants (except Asians), but it became more exclusionary in the

TABLE 10.1 Cultural change versus cultural defense

1856–1876*	1880–1904	1908–1928	1932–1956	1960–1980**	1984–2012	2016–2020
Cultural change						
				Cultural defense	Cultural defense	Cultural defense

*Ended slavery.
**1976 opposed gun registration; 1980 endorsed death penalty, opposed abortion and ERA.

twentieth century and increasingly so in the twenty-first. Republican platforms were surprisingly secular in the nineteenth through the middle of the twentieth century. In the later half of the twentieth century, the party firmly embraced religion. Concerning lifestyles, the party successfully opposed polygamy, and it successfully backed the prohibition of alcohol. However, the party backtracked on Prohibition as the nationwide policy produced circumvention and corruption. The Republican Party unsuccessfully opposed same-sex marriages. The pattern is summarized in table 10.1.

11

CONSERVATION AND CONSERVATIVES

The Republican Party once led efforts for conserving public lands for the Public Good. The 1862 Morrill Act granted public lands for colleges devoted to agriculture and mechanic arts. Under President Grant, in 1872 the party established Yellowstone National Park. Under Republican presidents Benjamin Harrison, William McKinley, and Theodore Roosevelt, Congress created Yosemite National Park and Sequoia National Park in 1890, Mount Rainier in 1899, Crater Lake in 1902, Wind Cave in 1903, Mesa Verde in 1906, Glacier in 1910, and Rocky Mountain in 1915—the last four under Roosevelt. In the 1970s, President Nixon backed environmental legislation to protect the water we drink, the air we breathe, and the soil on which we live. However, party platforms did not always employ terms that we use today for protecting the environment.

CONSERVATION

"Conservation" was first mentioned in the 1908 Republican platform, which recognized President Roosevelt for "the conservation of the natural resources of the country."[1] Although Democratic president Woodrow Wilson signed the National Park System into law in 1916, the

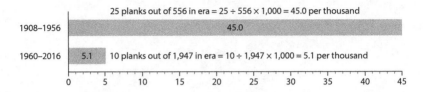

FIGURE 11.1. Number of conservation planks per 1,000 planks in party platforms, 1908–1956 vs. 1960–2016.

official NPS website recognizes Republican president Theodore Roosevelt as the "conservationist president," saying:

> Conservation increasingly became one of Roosevelt's main concerns. After becoming president in 1901, Roosevelt used his authority to protect wildlife and public lands by creating the United States Forest Service (USFS) and establishing 150 national forests, 51 federal bird reserves, 4 national game preserves, 5 national parks, and 18 national monuments by enabling the 1906 American Antiquities Act. During his presidency, Theodore Roosevelt protected approximately 230 million acres of public land.[2]

Only thirty-five Republican platform planks ever called for conservation of natural resources. They were coded 403 under Public Goods. The first one came in 1908; the next forty-eight years to 1956 accounted for twenty-four more. The last fifty-six years since 1960 produced only ten more planks. Figure 11.1 shows the results.

Adjusting for the number of conservation planks per thousand platform planks, we find that Republican platforms were nine times more likely to adopt a conservation plank before 1956 than after 1960.

PUBLIC LANDS

The United States owned vast tracts of land across the nation, mostly in western states. In the mid-1800s, the government granted portions of these "public lands" to railroad companies to promote railroad construction. Private companies benefited, but so did the public. Public lands were also granted to individuals who would settle on the land and farm it. Other individuals sought to profit commercially from the government's generosity. Although "conservation of natural resources" and "disposition of public lands" are closely related, I coded them separately.

Under Public Goods, Public Lands code 417 was for disposing public lands to favor the general public. Code 418 tagged planks that opened public lands to development for private gain. Figure 11.2 reports the coding for twenty-three planks.

The 1860 Republican platform strongly favored settlers over private developers, declaring: "That we protest against any sale or alienation to others of the public lands held by actual settlers, and against any view of the free-homestead policy which regards the settlers as paupers or suppliants for public bounty." That statement underlies the nine Pro-Public code 417 planks adopted to 1960:

1860   Oppose sale of public lands held by settlers
1888   Favor giving public lands to citizens
1892   Favor giving public lands to citizens
1900   Favor giving public lands to citizens
1908   Favor giving public lands to citizens
1912   Favor giving public lands to citizens
1924   Favor constructing roads and trails in national forests for
            their protection and utilization
1928   Favor the construction of roads and trails in our national
            forests
1952   Favor citizens to use public lands

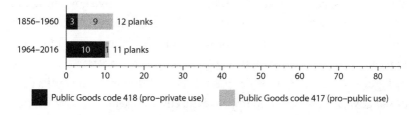

FIGURE 11.2. Disposition of public lands in twenty-three planks, 1856–1960 vs. 1964–2016.

Planks were coded as Pro-Private 418 if they viewed the public lands for "multiple uses." Even "recreational use" meant additional traffic and often granting commercial concessions to provide food, fuel, and accommodations. More damaging was opening them to extracting mineral resources. Here are the ten (of eleven) planks coded 418 since 1964:

1968 Manage public lands to use both as economic resources and recreation
1976 Use public lands for multiple uses
1980 Favor multiple uses of public lands
      Oppose withdrawing federal lands from development
1992 Support multiple uses of public lands
1996 Favor multiple uses of public lands
2000 Support multiple uses of public lands
2012 Make federal lands available for harvesting timber
2016 Encourage ranching on public land
      Support permitting process for mineral production on public lands

THE ENVIRONMENT

During the nineteenth century, no Republican or Democratic platform addressed environmental quality. In fact, none addressed this issue until the middle of the twentieth century, when in 1940 Republicans approved a plank for "the orderly development of reclamation and irrigation." That plank was coded Environment +402 to indicate positive governmental actions on the environment as a Public Good. Environment code −402 was applied to negative actions or actions benefitting private interests. Figure 11.3 shows the distribution of codes by election years.

Figure 11.3 shows that before 1980, almost all Republican planks proposed government action to improve the environment. The 1972 Republican platform alone accounted for fifteen of the twenty-one planks.

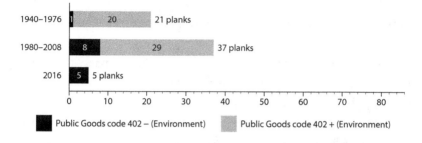

FIGURE 11.3. Environment in sixty-three planks, 1940–1967 vs. 1980–2008 and 2016.

Listed here, they indicate strong government action to improve environmental quality under President Nixon's administration:

1. Conserve and develop water supplies
2. Control dangerous substances
3. Create clean-burning gasoline engines
4. Establish realistic environmental standards
5. Identify and protect endangered wildlife
6. Make containers biodegradable
7. Manage ocean fisheries
8. Pass a federal noise control act
9. Preserve the coastal environment
10. Prohibit dumping of wastes into the oceans, estuaries, and Great
    Lakes;
11. Protect and conserve marine mammals
12. Protect the oceans from pollution
13. Support physical development of urban areas
14. Urge the fair and energetic enforcement of all fire-prevention laws
15. Work with the United Nations on ocean activities

Since 1980, Republican platforms evinced little interest in government
action to improve the environment. Instead, they were concerned with
preserving property rights, as in this ambiguous passage from the 1996
platform: "Because we view the careful development of our country's

natural resources as stewardship of creation, we believe *property rights* must be honored in our efforts to restore, protect, and enhance the environment for the generations to come.''

No environmental planks were coded at all for the party's 2012 platform, which mocked President Obama for elevating " 'climate change' to the level of a 'severe threat' equivalent to foreign aggression. The word 'climate,' in fact, appears in the current President's strategy more often than Al Qaeda, nuclear proliferation, radical Islam, or weapons of mass destruction.''

Figure 11.3 has a third row for these five environmental planks in the Republican Party's 2016 platform:

- Downplay climate change as a national security issue
- Forbid the EPA to regulate carbon dioxide
- Oppose overreach of Endangered Species Act
- Remove provisions of National Environmental Policy Act that drive up transportation costs
- End the legal practice of "sue and settle" (aimed at environmental lawsuits)

All five planks were coded as negative, that is, as being against government regulation.

SUMMARY

Soon after its founding, Republican governments led in the conservation of natural resources. Thanks to their efforts, Americans today enjoy visiting over four hundred sites in a system of national parks, monuments, battlefields, historic sites, and so on covering more than fifty million acres in all fifty states. Under Republican presidents Richard Nixon and George H. W. Bush, the party also passed laws to protect the environment against pollution. Afterward, the party took very few steps

TABLE 11.1 Land steward versus property agent

1856–1876	1880–1904	1908–1928	1932–1956	1960–1980*	1984–2012	2016–2020
Public good	Public good	Public good	Public good	Public good		
					Private benefit	Private benefit

*The 1972 platform had fifteen planks for protecting the environment.

toward conservation or environmental protection and avoided addressing climate change.

After Theodore Roosevelt, only one Republican president, Richard Nixon, stands out as a steward of the land for backing legislation to protect our environment. Other presidents took little notice of conservation or saw economic opportunities in public lands. The gross party trends are reflected in table 11.1.

The party that began as the champion of conservation, using government power to create national parks and protect the environment, evolved into a party that granted economic opportunities to private interests on public lands and that blocked environmental safeguards.

12

ELECTIONS

F rom the beginning, the Republican Party backed democratic principles for electing candidates to public office. A Republican Congress introduced a bill to amend the Constitution in 1869 to expand the electorate. Ratified in 1870 as the Fifteenth Amendment, it stated: "The right of citizens of the United States to vote shall not be denied or abridged by the United States or by any State on account of race, color, or previous condition of servitude." During Reconstruction, Republicans enforced the voting rights of former slaves throughout the South. For decades after the Civil War, Republican platforms barely discussed elections, except occasionally decrying restrictions on Blacks voting in southern states. Then in the 1970s, Republicans reversed their original stance; instead of expanding the electorate, they began to restrict voting.

PLATFORM PLANKS

Only forty of my 2,722 planks in all Republican platforms took a position on the topic of national elections. Planks that favored expanding the electorate and easing the act of voting fit under the Government

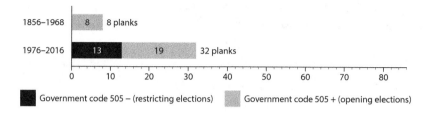

FIGURE 12.1.   Elections in forty planks, 1856–1968 vs. 1976–2016.

heading and were tagged code +505, Opening Elections. Planks restricting the reach of elections or voting got code –505, Restricting Elections. Figure 12.1 shows the distribution of these codes over time.

Here are the eight Republican planks up to 1968 coded as favoring "Open" elections:

1896   Support voting rights
1900   Support voting rights
1904   Support voting rights
1912   Prohibit corporations from contributing funds to federal
       election campaigns
1928   Promise to keep our elections clean, honest, and free from
       taint of any kind
1968   Favor new election reform act to restrain political spending
       Remove unreasonable requirements, residence and
          otherwise, for voting
       Lower age groups should be accorded the right to vote

Here are the thirteen planks since 1976 coded as "Restricted":

1976   Oppose federal postcard registration
1980   Support the repeal of restrictive campaign-spending
       limitations
       Strongly oppose national postcard voter registration
1984   Oppose public funding of campaigns
1988   Oppose public funding of campaigns

1992 Oppose public funding of campaigns
1996 Oppose the Motor-Voter Act
        End taxpayer subsidies for campaigns
2008 Oppose restoration of the franchise to convicted felons
2012 Applaud requiring photo IDs to vote
        Oppose restricting political contributions
2016 Repeal restrictions on campaign contributions
        Support proof of citizenship and voter ID photos to vote

PLATFORM TEXTS

Platform planks come from platform text, and the full text gives us more information than my abbreviated planks. The importance of elections to democratic government and the fissure in the Republican Party over the legitimacy of the 2020 election call for examining all sixty-six mentions of "elections" in the party's platforms since 1856. Not all mentions are relevant: nine were to nongovernment elections (e.g., in unions), nineteen to foreign countries (e.g., Cuba, Iraq), nine to specific elections (e.g., "After the elections of 1994"), five to prospects of elections in American territories (e.g., Guam), and so on. Nevertheless, some passages deserve to be quoted at length. Consider these four ringing endorsements of the role of elections and voting in our democracy, all of which came during the Republican Party's first hundred years.

1888 "We reaffirm our unswerving devotion to the National
        Constitution and the indissoluble Union of the
        States . . . and especially to the supreme and sovereign
        right of every lawful citizen, rich or poor, native or
        foreign born, white or black, to cast one free ballot in
        public elections, and to have that ballot duly counted."
1892 "We demand that every citizen of the United States shall
        be allowed to cast one free and unrestricted ballot in all

public elections, and that such ballot shall be counted and returned as cast; that such laws shall be enacted and enforced as will secure to every citizen, be he rich or poor, native or foreign-born, white or black, this sovereign right, guaranteed by the Constitution."

1928 "There will not be any relaxing of resolute endeavor to keep our elections clean, honest and free from taint of any kind. The improper use of money in governmental and political affairs is a great national evil."

1944 "The payment of any poll tax should not be a condition of voting in Federal elections and we favor immediate submission of a Constitutional amendment for its abolition."

When Republicans objected to the poll tax in 1944, they were still campaigning for Black votes as the "Party of Lincoln." Nevertheless, Republicans' commitment to expanding elections' democratic character extended into the 1960s, when the party called for reforming the Electoral College and favoring congressional representation for Washington, DC, as shown by these statements:

1960 "We favor a change in the Electoral College system to give every voter a fair voice in presidential elections."
"Republicans will continue to work for Congressional representation and self-government for the District of Columbia and also support the constitutional amendment granting suffrage in national elections."

1968 "We propose to reform the Electoral College system, establish a nation-wide, uniform voting period for Presidential elections, and recommend that the states remove unreasonable requirements, residence and otherwise, for voting in Presidential elections. We specifically favor representation in Congress for the District of Columbia."

But the tone and content of Republican platforms changed in the 1980s. Whereas in 1928 the party regarded as "evil" the improper use of money in elections, in 1980, the party said that "restrictive campaign spending limitations somehow created obstacles to local grass roots participation." In 1984, it sought to reverse the federal role in supervising elections:

1980   "We support the repeal of those restrictive campaign spending limitations that tend to create obstacles to local grass roots participation in federal elections. We also oppose the proposed financing of Congressional campaigns with taxpayers' dollars."

1984   "We will remove obstacles to grass-roots participation in federal elections and will reduce, not increase, the federal role."

Republican platforms cited higher voting turnout as evidence of voting fraud. They worried about the integrity of voting by mail yet assured supporters that their mailed-in ballots would be counted. In 2012, the party stated:

We applaud legislation to require photo identification for voting and to prevent election fraud, particularly with regard to registration and absentee ballots.

States or political subdivisions that use all-mail elections cannot ensure the integrity of the ballot.

We affirm that our troops, wherever stationed, be allowed to vote and those votes be counted in the November election and in all elections.

That Republicans sought to limit the ease and frequency of mail-in ballots does not necessarily conflict with democratic values. Those who regard voting as a civic act (as I do) might disparage mail-in ballots as a form of "voting alone." Robert Putnam's classic 2000 book *Bowling Alone: The Collapse and Revival of American Community* used the sport of bowling to illustrate how people were losing social contact with one another. While Americans were bowling as much as they did in the past, fewer were bowling in leagues with others. Over time and nationwide, other voluntary associations were also losing participants at an overall cost to society as people interacted less often with one another.

Similarly, "voting alone" imposes a cost to democracy. Voting alongside neighbors at local polling stations on Election Day engages citizens directly in the democratic process. Few citizens participate otherwise in politics. Of course, citizens must be able to cast absentee ballots when, for good reason, they are unable to vote in person. But encouraging people to vote alone weeks ahead of Election Day directs them away from a shared civic experience of democratic government.

ELECTORAL COLLEGE

Over the last half-century, Republicans reversed their position on the Electoral College. The 1960 Republican platform favored "a change in the Electoral College system to give every voter a fair voice in presidential elections," but the 2012 and 2016 Republican platforms opposed changes to the Electoral College. Here are the platform texts:

2012   "We oppose the National Popular Vote Interstate Compact or any other scheme to abolish or distort the procedures of the Electoral College. We recognize that an unconstitutional effort to impose 'national popular vote' would be a mortal threat to our federal system and a guarantee of corruption as every ballot box in every state would become a chance to steal the presidency."

2016   "Honest Elections and the Electoral College: We oppose the National Popular Vote Interstate Compact and any other scheme to abolish or distort the procedures of the Electoral College."

What caused Republicans to change their position? The simple answer is that Republican presidents George W. Bush and Donald Trump lost the popular vote respectively in 2000 and 2016 but won their elections because each gained a majority of votes in the Electoral College.

A presidential election is not national election but a *federal* election. The president is not chosen by national popular vote but by a majority of the states' electoral votes.[1] Each of the fifty states is entitled to one elector for each of its two senators (one hundred total) and one for each of its House members (435), totaling 535 electoral votes. In addition, the Twenty-Third Amendment awarded three electoral votes (the minimum for any state) to the District of Columbia, even though it elects no voting members of Congress. The total number of electoral votes therefore is 538. The Constitution specifies that a candidate needs a majority of electoral votes, currently 270, to win the presidency. Having an even number of electoral votes creates the possibility of a tie, 269 to 269, throwing the decision to the House of Representatives.

Because every state, regardless of population, has three electoral votes—two for its senators and one for its representative—the electoral vote is biased toward territory, not population. In fact, the smallest fifteen states in population, with a combined population of about 20 million inhabitants, hold fifty-six electoral votes. The state of California, with a population of 40 million, has only fifty-five electoral votes, one fewer. In recent decades, voters in small states have favored Republican presidential candidates. For example, in 2016 Democrat Hillary Clinton won almost three million more popular votes than Republican Donald Trump, but he won a majority of the states' electoral votes, 306 to 232. In effect, Trump won more votes from states in the crucial federal election; Clinton won more votes from citizens in the national election.

In 2000, Republican George W. Bush also became president by winning a bare majority of the electoral vote while losing the popular vote to Democrat Al Gore by a half-million. The Republican Party understands the critical role of the Electoral College in determining its chances of victory in future elections. That factor has also altered its position on admitting new states to the union.

VOTING ON STATEHOOD

In 1856, only thirty-one states formed the United States. Settled territories were clamoring for statehood, so admitting them became a major political issue in the nineteenth century and into the twentieth. In 1959, Alaska and Hawaii became the forty-ninth and fiftieth states. Two codes for platform planks under Government applied to Statehood, code +507 favoring admission and code –507 opposing it. Most of the twenty-six Republican Statehood planks were "omnibus" planks, mentioning multiple territories as candidates for admission. As shown in figure 12.2, up to 1980, all Republican planks favored admission of the territories they named.

As early as 1940, Republican platforms favored statehood as a logical aspiration for the people of Puerto Rico. Concerning the District of Columbia, the Republican position was mixed. At first because of Washington's unique position as the seat of the national government, the party seemed ready to grant home rule and congressional representation but not statehood. Here is the passage that year:

> The principle of self-determination also governs our positions on Puerto Rico and the District of Columbia as it has in past platforms. We again support statehood for Puerto Rico, if that is the people's choice in a referendum, with full recognition within the concept of a multicultural society of the citizens' right to retain their Spanish language and traditions; and support giving the District of Columbia voting representation in the United States Senate and House of Representatives and full home rule over those matters that are purely local.

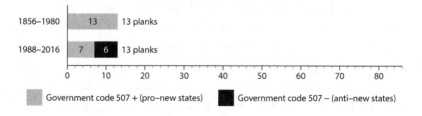

FIGURE 12.2. Statehood in twenty-six planks, 1856–1980 vs. 1988–2016.

Later, Republicans recognized that DC residents were likely to vote for Democrats. In the 1970s, a Democratic Congress sent to the states a District of Columbia Voting Rights Amendment, but it failed ratification by the states. By 1988, Washington, DC, and Puerto Rico were still candidates for statehood and mentioned in thirteen Republican planks, as shown in figure 12.1. The party favored admitting Puerto Rico in seven planks, but opposed Washington, DC, in the other six. Although granting statehood through legislation was the normal procedure, the party's 2016 platform vigorously opposed that method and required a constitutional amendment for Washington, DC: "Statehood for the District can be advanced only by a constitutional amendment. Any other approach would be invalid. A statehood amendment was soundly rejected by the states when last proposed in 1976 and should not be revived."

The 2016 Republican platform spoke very differently about Puerto Rico:

> We support the right of the United States citizens of Puerto Rico to be admitted to the Union as a fully sovereign state. We further recognize the historic significance of the 2012 local referendum in which a 54 percent majority voted to end Puerto Rico's current status as a U.S. territory, and 61 percent chose statehood over options for sovereign nationhood. We support the federally sponsored political status referendum authorized and funded by an Act of Congress in 2014 to ascertain the aspirations of the people of Puerto Rico. Once the 2012 local vote for statehood is ratified, Congress should approve an enabling act with terms for Puerto Rico's future admission as the 51st state of the Union.

Although Puerto Rico's two main political parties are not labeled "Republican" and "Democratic," they align informally with the Republican and Democratic parties on the mainland. The stronger party, aligned with Republicans, favors statehood, which might explain why Republicans supported admission for Puerto Rico. Republicans' opposition to statehood for the District of Columbia lies in DC's voting history. Eligible to vote in presidential elections since 1964, Washington,

DC, has voted ever since for the Democratic presidential nominee. Were DC a state, Democrats in the Senate would almost certainly gain two additional senators.

Although Washington, DC, presently lacks representation in Congress, it possesses three electoral votes awarded through a constitutional amendment. By becoming a state, its three electoral votes would come instead from having two senators and one representative. Because DC's seat would presumably come from a state's loss of a seat following decennial reapportionment, with a Senate of 102 members and the House remaining at 435, the electoral vote would decrease from 538—an even number—to 537.[2] That would eliminate the chance of a tie vote. All citizens should regard avoiding a tie in electoral votes as a Public Good, for it would avoid the political calamity of a constitutionally defined, legitimate tie in a presidential election.

THE 2020 PRESIDENTIAL ELECTION

Although the 2020 presidential election occurred out of context of the Republican platform planks being reviewed in this chapter, party leaders did take positions on the outcome of that election, and their positions deserve to be discussed. After much checking and rechecking by Republican election officials in closely divided states, the 2020 election results showed that Republican president Donald Trump lost both the popular vote and the electoral vote to Democratic challenger Joe Biden. Nevertheless, President Trump denied the results, claimed that the election was illegitimate, and urged his supporters to "stop the steal." On January 6, 2021, as Congress met formally to count the states' electoral votes and certify Joe Biden's election, Trump's supporters stormed the Capitol. Terrified lawmakers fled the mob but reconvened later in the day to confirm Joe Biden's victory.

On January 13, Democrats in the House voted for the second time to impeach President Trump, this time on the charge of "incitement of insurrection." Ten House Republicans joined the impeachment vote, but the Republican Senate failed to convict him. Representative Liz Cheney of Wyoming was one of the ten House Republicans voting for impeachment. At the time, she chaired the House Republican Conference and ranked third in the Republican House leadership.

After President Biden's inauguration, former president Trump continued to deny the 2020 election results, claimed personal leadership of the party, and attacked those who believed in the election's validity. Many Republicans in Congress sided with the former president, as did most of his voters. Representative Cheney did not. She continued to denounce him for failing to accept his election defeat. The evening of May 11, 2021, she delivered these remarks on the House floor: "Today we face a threat America has never seen before. A former president, who provoked a violent attack on this Capitol in an effort to steal the election, has resumed his aggressive effort to convince Americans that the election was stolen from him." Congresswoman Cheney continued:

> The Electoral College has voted. More than 60 state and federal courts, including multiple judges the former president appointed, have rejected his claims. The Trump Department of Justice investigated the former president's claims of widespread fraud and found no evidence to support them. The election is over. That is the rule of law. That is our constitutional process. Those who refuse to accept the rulings of our courts are at war with the Constitution. Our duty is clear. Every one of us who has sworn the oath must act to prevent the unraveling of our democracy.[3]

On May 12, 2021, the House Republican Conference voted to oust Representative Cheney as its chair. The decision was by voice vote and took about fifteen minutes. After the vote, she said: "The party's going to come back stronger, and I'm going to lead the effort to do it."[4]

Later the same day, Republican minority leader Kevin McCarthy, following a meeting with President Biden and others at the White House, said to reporters: "I don't think anybody is questioning the legitimacy of the presidential election."[5] McCarthy was anxious to move the party from the past election to future elections. The previous day, however, the press reported that Republicans had introduced hundreds of voting-restriction bills in forty-eight state legislatures. Nearly 90 percent of the bills were sponsored primarily or entirely by Republicans.[6] Donald Trump, the former president, continued to deny the legitimacy of President Biden's election. A year after the election, polls reported that over half of Trump's supporters believed that Biden's election was invalid.

SUMMARY

When Lincoln promised "government of the people and by the people" in his Gettysburg Address, he invoked two principles in democratic theory: popular sovereignty and majority rule. "Government of the people" did not mean rule *over* the people; it meant that the people rule themselves. "Government by the people" meant that they choose leaders in elections by popular vote. The Republican Party freed slaves after the Civil War, gave them the right to vote, and enforced that right in southern states until after the disputed election of 1876 and the compromise that ended Reconstruction in the South. By the mid-1900s, the party had evolved into one that curtailed the voting rights of slaves' descendants. The party that had pledged to reform the Electoral College became a party that vowed to oppose any change to its procedures. Table 12.1 shows how the Republican Party has evolved over time on elections in American government.

TABLE 12.1 Open elections versus restricted elections

1856–1876	1880–1904	1908–1928	1932–1956	1960–1980*	1984–2012**	2016–2020
Open elections	Open elections	Open elections	Open elections			
				Restricted elections	Restricted elections	Restricted elections

*In 1976 opposed mail registration.
**In 2012 required voter ID.

Unlike most countries in the world, our federal government—nation and states—elects most national, state, and local officials every two years, more frequently than anywhere else. As a result, American voters become bored, confused, and have lower turnout rates than anywhere else. The United States does not have a problem of too many people voting but of too few voting.

Whether voting turnout is high or low matters little if candidates do not respect the election results. Democratic government cannot succeed if citizens lack confidence in the electoral processes that determine the peaceful transfer of power between outgoing and incoming officeholders. President Trump's refusal to accept his defeat in the 2020 presidential election is certain to stain party politics and democratic government in the future.

13

EVOLVING TO ETHNOCENTRISM

The Republican Party is almost 170 years old. Political parties, like people, change over time. So it is not surprising that the Republican Party today does not hold the same political positions that it did when it was founded in 1854. What is surprising is that the party has actually reversed its original principles. Founded to govern the nation according to socially and economically progressive principles, the Republican Party eventually morphed into a reactionary movement aiming to turn back the cultural clock. In practical political terms, the party that began favoring national government over states' rights now distrusts national authority and defends states' rights. The Republicans' reversal on its founding principle and its shifts on other policies did not occur through revolutionary convulsion but evolved sporadically over time. This book documents that evolutionary process through a detailed study of the party's platform planks.

John Gerring also examined party platforms, but his book, *Party Ideologies in America, 1828–1996*, relied more heavily on hundreds of party leaders' speeches. Our studies overlap, but mine produces new information by analyzing party platforms in more detail and by extending the analysis to the present. Our findings about the Republican Party are mutually reinforcing in that they agree on most conclusions about the party's ideological posture into the 1920s.

As described in chapter 5, Gerring contended that the Republican Party experienced two major epochs of governing behavior, dramatically changing only once. Up to the election of 1924, Gerring said that the party was in its "nationalism" epoch, distinguished by what he called a "central dichotomy" pitting order against anarchy. As detailed more below, my findings substantiate his description. In 1928, Republicans entered a "neoliberalism" epoch, with the central dichotomy becoming the individual versus the state.

Gerring and I also agree on his characterization of the party's neoliberalism epoch. We differ in how long that epoch lasted. Gerring's formal research ended in 1992, but he held that the neoliberalism epoch lasted up to 1996. I argue that the party changed fundamentally in the 1960s. In that decade, Republicans entered what I call its ethnocentrism epoch, with the central dichotomy becoming *white Christians* versus *Others*. To support my claim, this chapter reviews the evidence presented in part 3 and then describes the Republican Party's new post-1960s epoch.

RECAPPING THE PRINCIPLES IN THE PLATFORM PLANKS

The preceding chapters analyzed hundreds of planks in forty-one Republican platforms since 1856, thus documenting the party's major principles throughout its history. (Appendix B covers the content of the rest of the 2,722 planks.) The summaries from the preceding chapters warrant restatement for convenient review.

CHAPTER 6: ORIGINAL PRINCIPLES

The Republican Party was founded on the principle of containing the spread of slavery in the United States, and its leaders were willing to use the power of the national government to do so. As equality was understood at the time, the Republican Party recognized slaves to be politically equal to their owners. Over time, as equality applied to social relationships between people of color and those born white, the Republican Party backed away from using national power to enforce social equality.

CHAPTER 7: FINANCING GOVERNMENT

In the nineteenth century, Republicans believed that tariffs would raise sufficient revenue for the government and that tariffs would protect fledgling domestic industries. At the start of the twentieth century, the United States was exiting a domestic agricultural economy and entering a world of international trade. A protective tariff, which had been the party's bedrock principle, was an "antiquated policy" for the new century. The party noted this in its 1988 platform: "Unfortunately, international markets are still restricted by antiquated policies: protective tariffs, quotas, and subsidies." To its credit, the Republican Party scrapped its venerable principle, the protective tariff, in the 1980s.

CHAPTER 8: ECONOMIC AFFAIRS

In 1860, before the Civil War, the Republican Party platform addressed the need for adequate revenue "to encourage the development of the industrial interests of the whole country." After the war, the party's 1872 platform sought additional revenue "to aid in securing remunerative wages to labor, and to promote the industries, prosperity, and growth of the whole country." The Republican Party clearly intended to be a governing party. To that end, it sought to raise additional revenue through taxes on personal income, even proposing a constitutional amendment to ensure the legality of an income tax. Although the Republican Party was firmly aligned with manufacturing interests and corporations, the party regulated their commercial activities through national legislation. Republican president Teddy Roosevelt drew fame for "trust-busting."

In the second half of the twentieth century, Republican Party platforms denigrated economic regulations and extolled free enterprise, cloaked under the mantle of the term "small business." My independent analysis of Republican platform planks again corresponds with Gerring's characterization of the Republican Party entering an epoch of neoliberalism in 1928, with free-market capitalism as a major theme.

CHAPTER 9: LAW AND ORDER

For most of its existence, the Republican Party endorsed the principle that government should hold the "monopoly of force." President Lincoln conscripted an army to prevent the attempted secession of southern states from the Union. From the beginning, Republicans approved of the death penalty. Since 1856, Republican platforms have consistently backed governmental use of force in apprehending, imprisoning, and executing lawbreakers.

Control over deadly weapons is inherent in monopolizing force. Over the first century of the party's existence, gun control was not a prominent political issue. When the topic surfaced after President Kennedy's assassination, the party supported it to some extent. Heavily lobbied by the NRA, the party changed its position. It opposed strengthening gun controls even after President Reagan was shot. While life did not become "solitary, poor, nasty, brutish, and short" for all American citizens as a result, the proliferation of handguns and assault rifles meant that life did become unpredictably brutish and short for many.

Since the abortion issue surfaced in the 1970s, the party's platforms consistently backed governmental efforts to oppose surgical abortions. Laws against abortions empower the government to force a woman to give birth, which Republicans view as preserving life. In sum, the party today backs strong rules against lawbreakers and against women who do not want to give birth. The party favors weak or no regulations against possessing or using firearms of any type.

CHAPTER 10: CULTURE AND ORDER

Throughout the nineteenth century, the Republican Party welcomed immigrants (except Asians), but its immigration policy became more exclusionary in the twentieth century and increasingly so in the twenty-first. Regarding religion, Republican platforms were surprisingly secular in the nineteenth century and to the middle of the twentieth. The party became decidedly religious in the twenty-first century. Concerning lifestyles, the party successfully opposed polygamy, it unsuccessfully opposed same-sex marriages, and it successfully backed Prohibition. However, the party backtracked on Prohibition because the nationwide ban on alcohol produced circumvention and corruption.

CHAPTER 11: CONSERVATION AND CONSERVATIVES

Soon after its founding, Republican governments led in the conservation of natural resources. Thanks to their efforts, Americans today enjoy visiting over four hundred sites in a system of national parks, monuments, battlefields, historic sites, and so on, covering more than 50 million acres in all fifty states. Under Republican presidents Richard Nixon and George H. W. Bush, the party also passed laws to protect the environment against pollution. Afterward, the party took few steps toward conservation or environmental protection and avoided confronting issues in climate change.

After Theodore Roosevelt, only one Republican president, Richard Nixon, stands out as a steward of the land for backing legislation to protect our environment. Others took little notice of conservation or saw public lands as opportunities for exploitation and profit.

CHAPTER 12: ELECTIONS

The Republican Party freed slaves after the Civil War, gave them the right to vote, and in the mid-1800s enforced that right in southern states. By the mid-1900s, however, it had evolved into a party that curtailed the voting rights of slaves' descendants. The party that had pledged to reform the Electoral College became a party that vowed to oppose any change to its procedures. In 2020, Republican officeholders became the first to challenge the outcome of a presidential election won by a candidate with clear majorities in both the popular and Electoral College vote.

ENTERING A NEW EPOCH: ETHNOCENTRISM

From its beginning and for most of its history, the Republican Party was a party of national government. It imposed political equality on the southern states. The party raised and spent national funds on public goods. It funded building a railroad linking the continent's coasts, created national parks, and even supported digging a canal across the Isthmus of Panama for public benefit. Republicans regulated interstate commerce and broke up monopolistic trusts. Republicans also favored a constitutional amendment granting equal rights to women and backed some measures for gun control. In addition, Republicans initiated the tax on personal incomes to raise government revenue.

As reported in chapter 4, John Gerring argued that the "nationalism" epoch in Republican history lasted to 1924, during which, according to Gerring, Republican principles centered on "order versus anarchy." Its major themes were "Protestantism, moral reform, mercantilism, free labor, social harmony, and statism." Gerring fixed the start of the party's "neoliberalism" epoch in 1928.

Authors often have problems convincing readers what scholars see emerging from their extensive research. Readers may not see as clearly as I do the evolution in Republican politics, which has extended over a century. Small changes that happen at different times in the same direction can culminate in a major shift in a party's orientation. The timeline in figure 13.1 may help in picturing the shift. It draws lines from Republican Party platform reversals, named for the new policy, to specific years

FIGURE 13.1. Timeline of changes in Republican platforms since 1924.

when they occurred. It depicts twelve significant changes in Republican platforms since 1924.

Gerring fixed 1928 as the start of his new "neoliberalism" epoch, during which party principles centered on "the individual versus the state." His epoch's major themes were "anti-statism, free market capitalism, right-wing populism, and individualism." Figure 13.1 supports Gerring's classification and themes. It shows that the Republican platform backed states' rights in 1928 and opposed economic regulations in 1940. The shift in 1960 from favoring racial equality to opposing a date to end school desegregation meshes with the theme of right-wing populism. Opposing firearms registration in 1976 aligns with individualism. Gerring's right-wing-populism theme could embrace other post-1960 changes: the antiabortion amendment, abandoning the ERA, and restricting immigration. All this evidence conforms with Gerring's neoliberalism epoch.

The flurry of changes, however, suggests more than a simple extension of neoliberalism. I disagree with Gerring when he writes, "'Radicals' like Barry Goldwater and Ronald Reagan adhered to the same general precepts as their more moderate colleagues" and should be regarded as "the continuation of an older, more established ideological tradition."[1] I contend that Goldwater reversed the party's principles and that Reagan continued the turnaround. Others have argued similarly. The noted historian Heather Cox Richardson wrote: "From 1964 to 1980, Movement Conservatives took over the Republican Party. It was not an obvious or inevitable outcome."[2] The scholar and Republican advisor Geoffrey Kabaservice blamed a party that "continues to reject its own heritage and forgets the hard lessons of the 1960s," when "right-wing activists" nominated Barry Goldwater, "an extreme presidential candidate."[3]

In or about 1964 the party entered a new epoch (using Gerring's term) that I will call *ethnocentrism*. Its central dichotomy (again using Gerring's terminology) became white Christians versus others. Ethnocentrism's themes are *social order, Christianity, anti-intellectualism*, and *antigovernment*. These themes, salient in Republican politics since the 1960s, require separate discussions.

SOCIAL ORDER

Social changes in the 1960s severely threatened the social order. Expansion of civil rights for Blacks was just one of several perceived fears. The religious right blamed "secular humanism" for undermining traditional roles of men and women in marriage, the family, employment, and society; traditional status arrangements between whites and people of color; and traditional lifestyles and norms of expression. As the new Christian alignment crusaded "against secular humanists and "enemies of 'traditional values,'" the religious right's influence grew within the Republican Party.[4]

CHRISTIANITY

Gerring cited "Protestantism" as a Republican theme during the party's nationalism era. Protestantism involved piety, of course, but he meant adhering to the Protestant ethic of hard work, thrift, efficiency, and morality in worldly callings.[5] People inclined to that ethic gravitated to the Republican Party. Not until the end of the nineteenth century did Protestantism suggest electoral support from a religious grouping. In that sense, Republican supporters were also overwhelmingly Protestant.

Gerring did not include Protestantism as a theme in the party's later neoliberalism epoch. Nevertheless, religion was a source of partisan

division, spiking in two notable elections. In 1928, Democrats nominated the Catholic Al Smith as their presidential candidate and lost, as
Protestants voted overwhelmingly for Republican Herbert Hoover. In
1960, Democrats nominated another Catholic, John F. Kennedy, but
enough Protestants voted Democratic to elect him. Soon after Kennedy's assassination in 1963, however, many devout Catholics were drawn
to religious appeals of groups aligned with the Republican Party.

As religious precepts became more important than Christian denom-
inations, Christianity—not just Protestantism—became a Republican
theme in the 1960s, when the party turned toward ethnocentrism. David
Bennett, a historian of the far right in American politics, quoted the
Evangelical Protestant Jerry Falwell as saying, "Catholics in this country do not differ with the views of the moral majority. . . . Pope John is
on our side and the people are on our side. . . . Evangelicals, fundamen-
talists, conservative Catholics and Mormons are all working together
now."[6] United under the umbrella of "Evangelical Christians,"[7] they
could combat secular and competing values held by growing ranks of
nonbelievers and non-Christians.

Although the South was historically Protestant and even anti-
Catholic, the historians Earl and Merle Black, in *The Rise of Southern
Republicans*, held: "The southern white conservative religious movement
is composed primarily of evangelical Protestants and sizable numbers
of conservative Catholics, who believe that secular forces are undermining their way of life and who seek to advance their beliefs, values, and
interests through partisan politics."[8]

ANTI-INTELLECTUALISM

Defined as a "social attitude that systematically denigrates science-based
facts, authority of the intellectual 'elite,' and the pursuit of theory and
knowledge,"[9] anti-intellectualism is not new to American politics. In
1963, the historian Richard Hofstadter won a Pulitzer Prize for his *Anti-
Intellectualism in American Life*.[10] Intellectualism overlaps with secular
humanism, but anti-intellectualism is much broader than opposition to

secular humanism, which is concerned mainly with cultural traditions. Anti-intellectualism underpins the distrust of policy experts, denial of climate change, suspicion of vaccinations, opposition to wearing face-masks to control spreading airborne viruses, and so on. Bennett wrote that academic elites "are responsible for the very programs the New Right rejects: antipoverty, school busing, and consumer protection."[11]

Denying the advice of medical experts in combating the COVID-19 virus may have cost thousands of lives. Perhaps an even more serious consequence of Republicans' anti-intellectualism comes in their denial of climate change. A 2020 Pew survey found Republican identifiers less likely than Democrats to blame human activity (22 to 72 percent) and less likely (35 to 89 percent) to say the government is doing too little to reduce the effects of climate change.[12] Republican activists are beginning to recognize the party's position as "a political liability."[13]

ANTIGOVERNMENT

This theme differs significantly from Gerring's antistatism. According to Gerring, statism characterized the Republican Party during its nation-alism epoch, which ended in 1924. The party embraced antistatism in the following neoliberalism period. He wrote: "The turn from statism to antistatism was accompanied by a parallel shift in political style within the Republican party. Whereas earlier Whig-Republicans had upheld a stately, nineteenth-century vision of politics in which a tacit division between leaders and followers was observed, modern Repub-licans adopted a strident populism. . . . To the 'pressure of groups' rep-resented by the Democratic party, Republicans counterposed 'the con-science of the individual.' "[14]

In the creed of antistatism, certain key words—among them *commu-nity, participation, local, state, the personal element, voluntary associ-ations, citizens, the people, private*, and, perhaps most prominently, *family* —gained talismanic status.[15]

"Statism" does not suggest government domination over people, and "antistatism" does not denote people's hostility to government. During the party's ethnocentrism epoch, however, hostility toward government became widespread among Republican activists. In 1964, Barry Goldwater laid the basis for that hostility in accepting the Republican presidential nomination, saying: "And this party, with its every action, every word, every breath, and every heartbeat, has but a single resolve, and that is freedom—freedom made orderly for this nation by our constitutional government; freedom under a government limited by laws of nature and of nature's God; I would remind you that extremism in the defense of liberty is no vice. And let me remind you also that moderation in the pursuit of justice is no virtue." In effect, Goldwater was encouraging his audience to aggressively oppose governmental rules and laws that, in their view, contradicted those made by nature or God. In *At War with Government*, Amy Fried and Douglas Harris wrote, "Increasingly since Barry Goldwater's 1964 presidential candidacy, the modern Republican Party is, at least theoretically, antigovernment."[16]

By the 1980s, Republican office holders spoke more explicitly against government, especially the national government. In his 1981 inaugural address, Republican president Ronald Reagan said, "In this present crisis, government is not the solution to our problem, government *is* the problem." In 1994, the House Republicans' "Contract with America" promised "the end of government that is too big, too intrusive, and too easy with the public's money." In 2016, Republican presidential nominee Donald Trump promised to dismantle the "deep state" of career civil servants that silently controlled the government in Washington.

David Bennett begins his book *The Party of Fear: From Nativist Movements to the New Right in American History* by citing a bumper sticker sold in Missouri: "I Love My Country, but I Fear My Government," and then quoting a Michigan militia commander interviewed on television: "It is not anger we feel, it is fear, 'fear' of the federal government."[17] Fear of government fed distrust of government, bureaucracy, and—in 2020—state-run elections.

Responding to President Trump's cry to "stop the steal" of the 2020 election he lost to Democrat Joe Biden, thousands of Trump's supporters stormed the U.S. Capitol on January 6, 2021, to prevent the lawful counting of state electoral votes certifying Biden's election. On July 1, 2021, the U.S. House of Representatives established a Select Committee to Investigate the January 6th Attack on the United States Capitol, contending that the insurrectionists attempted to impede Congress's constitutional mandate to validate the presidential election. A majority of Republican members opposed the committee's creation and investigation.

Over 150 years earlier, at another troubled time in American history, President Abraham Lincoln gave what became known as his 1863 Gettysburg Address, concluding with hopeful words for a war-torn nation. He hoped that it "shall have a new birth of freedom—and that government of the people, by the people, for the people, shall not perish from the earth." Lincoln did not coin that phraseology. The theologian John Wycliffe wrote hundred of years earlier that the English translation of the Bible was "for the government of the people, for the people, and by the people."[18] Most observers interpret Lincoln's adaptation as a homespun but useful expression of two major aspects of democratic theory: *procedure* (government of and by the people) and *substance* (government for the people).[19]

That interpretation is certainly true, but Lincoln's words can also be understood as an endorsement of *government* itself. Lincoln equated government with community. People who governed themselves constituted a community and served their own interests. That was the essence of democracy. In Lincoln's world, government was *for* the people, so being antigovernment was acting against the popular interest. In the present world, antigovernment attitudes, not simply antistatism, characterize the Republican Party. I hold that this ethnocentrism era started in 1964, with Barry Goldwater's acceptance speech at the Republican nominating convention. Part 4 examines the conditions that led to Goldwater's nomination and to the party's continuing along the path he cleared.

SUMMARY

Party platforms and planks only reflect Republican principles. As described in chapter 3, American party platforms emerge from a decentralized process. Hundreds of party activists have a hand in writing every Republican platform. Activists debate at length over what to include and how to word it. At the end of the process, every Republican platform reflects Republican activists' basic values and even where their values conflict. However, some contributors have more influence than others in shaping the final product. Frontrunners for the party's presidential nomination have more say in its content, and Republican presidents running for reelection can control what gets included and omitted from the platform.

At times, however, party activists far below incumbent presidents or potential nominees significantly affected individual platform planks. In 1980, the Republican activist Phyllis Schlafly's campaign against the Equal Rights Amendment kept the party from endorsing the ERA. In 1948, freshman senator Hubert Humphrey engineered the Democratic Party's acceptance of an historic civil rights plank. Neither of these efforts, however, would have been accepted if opposed by a majority of delegates at the parties' conventions.

Party platforms and planks at given times only reflect party principles at those times. To fully understand how platforms, planks, and principles originate and perpetuate, one must consider the politics and politicians of the times. Sometimes Republicans redesigned their platforms to win national elections. Democrats did too. Part 4 considers how Republicans have functioned as an electoral team to win elections, as a political tribe for group identity, and as a personality cult loyal to Donald Trump.

IV

REPUBLICANS AS TEAM, TRIBE, AND CULT

14

ELECTORAL TEAMS

The preceding chapter ended part 3 by reviewing planks adopted in all forty-one Republican platforms since 1856. It showed that the GOP governed in socially and economically progressive ways for much of its history. This chapter begins part 4, which considers Republicans acting not as a party organization but alternatively as an *electoral team*, a *political tribe*, and a *personality cult*. It begins with electoral teams.

Two distinct Republican entities are involved in presidential elections: a single *party organization* and multiple *electoral teams*. The Republican *Party* has endured across elections; Republican *electoral teams* are temporary, formed to contest individual elections. *Party* fits Edmund Burke's view of politicians "united for promoting by their joint endeavours the national interest upon some particular principles in which they are all agreed."[1] *Team* fits Anthony Downs's description of organizations "seeking to control the governing apparatus by gaining office in a duly constituted election."[2] Different Republican electoral teams arose to contest each of the forty-two presidential elections since 1856. In the process, they sometimes influenced the direction of the party platform, often affecting its planks' content and wording and even altering the party's basic principles. Nevertheless, electoral teams came and went.

The Republican National Committee (RNC), which supposedly heads the entire party organization, is virtually never part of a presidential electoral team. The RNC functions mainly as a party bureaucracy, keeping records, setting dates for the party convention, making local arrangements, and so on. That is true for the Democratic Party too. Both national committees are described well by the title of a book about their activities, *Politics Without Power*.[3] Independently of the RNC, Republican presidential aspirants attract politically savvy advisers to plan winning the party's nomination for the next presidential election. The successful party nominees then attract other experienced politicians, sometimes from the teams of their defeated primary opponents, to plan for winning office.

Almost all presidential nominees and their electoral teams tinker with the party platform, but few have the desire or the power to change party principles. Although Dwight Eisenhower's electoral victories in 1952 and 1956 returned Republicans to the presidency after two decades of losses, he and his team failed to instill "Modern Republicanism" in the party so that it embraced government's role in providing social services.[4] Barry Goldwater and Ronald Reagan were two presidential nominees who did change party principles in significant ways. So did Donald Trump.

REPUBLICAN DOMINANCE TO 1928

Electoral teams were not needed in the mid-1800s. A noted historian wrote that even "putting a party organization together was relatively easily done once a sufficient number of like-minded men agree to act in concert."[5] Although Horace Greeley, editor of the *New York Tribune*, backed Abraham Lincoln for the 1860 Republican nomination and Lincoln had numerous advisers, historians agree that Lincoln supervised his own nomination and election campaigns.[6]

By 1896, candidates' circles of political consultants had enlarged, but they still did not constitute an electoral team. Although some writers have placed the Ohio industrialist Mark Hanna behind the electoral success of Republican president William McKinley, the party historian Lewis L. Gould said that Hanna "neither made the key decisions nor set the overall strategy."[7]

Warren Harding's getting the 1920 Republican presidential nomination and then winning election provides an early example of a team effort. After two terms of Democrat Woodrow Wilson's presidency, Republican leaders fused their personal ambitions with a desire to recapture the presidency. Elected in 1912 and reelected in 1916, Wilson and his party were unpopular in 1920. Observers at the time believed any Republican candidate could win against any Democrat. However, top-level Republican activists failed to agree on the lucky nominee. A prominent Ohio Republican, Harry M. Daugherty, promoted Ohio senator Warren Harding, himself lukewarm to the prospect.[8] In a fabled "smoke-filled" Chicago hotel room, Republican leaders compromised on Harding as their candidate.

More to the point, Harding's general election campaign was supervised by a small electoral team assembled by Daugherty and managed by the Indiana Republican activist Will Hays, who employed Albert Lasker's advertising skills.[9] The team planned a "front porch" campaign, with Harding staying in Marion, Ohio, and saying as little of substance as possible. Hays and Daugherty employed party workers to deliver speeches, canvass voters, and mount "a massive publicity program, involving parades, billboards, magazine advertisements, motion pictures, newspaper statements, phonograph appeals, posters, telephone conferences, Girl Scout babysitters, and motor corps to carry voters to the polls." One scholar wrote: "The Republican campaign was so thoroughly planned and executed that it stands as a model of smoothness and efficiency."[10]

As expected, the electorate voted overwhelmingly for the 1920 Republican ticket of Warren Harding and his running mate, Calvin Coolidge, over the Democratic ticket of James Cox and Franklin Delano Roosevelt. Republicans won over 60 percent of the popular vote, more than 75 percent of the electoral vote, and carried almost every northern state despite losing almost every southern state. Republicans easily captured the presidency again in 1924 and 1928, getting over 70 percent of the electoral vote both times. After losing to the Democrats and Woodrow Wilson in 1912 and 1916, Republicans had reestablished their dominance of the electorate.

In eighteen presidential elections from 1860 to 1928, Republicans lost to only two Democratic candidates: Grover Cleveland in 1884 and 1892

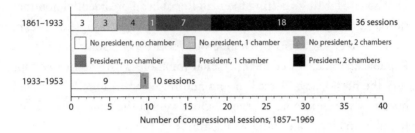

FIGURE 14.1. Republican control of the presidency and Congress, 1861–1953.

and Woodrow Wilson. That is, Republicans outscored Democrats fourteen to four in presidential victories across that period. Republicans also won most of the House and Senate elections from 1860 to 1930. In fact, Republican presidents enjoyed having party majorities in both chambers in almost two-thirds of the thirty-six congressional sessions. Only once did a Republican president (Rutherford Hayes, 1879–1881) face a Democratic Congress. As portrayed in figure 14.1, Republicans held the presidency for more than 70 percent of all thirty-six congressional sessions up to 1952. Moreover, Republicans controlled the presidency and *both* houses of Congress for half the sessions.

Republican electoral fortunes, however, changed dramatically after Democrat Franklin Delano Roosevelt's victory in 1932. For the next twenty years, Republicans failed to elect a president and controlled Congress only once (1947–1949), during Democrat Harry Truman's presidency. The string of losses in federal elections was a blow to a proud party that had dominated national government since its founding.

LOSING AND REGAINING STATUS

To Republican leaders in business, communications, and society across the United States, politics in the 1940s had turned upside down. Their venerable Republican Party—the Grand Old Party, the party that had saved the Union and freed the slaves—had lost its rightful dominance to what they saw as a disloyal, treasonous party: Democrats had tried to secede from the United States of America in the 1860s and enacted their accursed socialist and anti-American "New Deal" in the 1930s.[11] Although 60 percent of the country's newspapers (owned by wealthy publishers and run by conservative editors) endorsed Republican presidential nominees (versus 20 percent for Democratic nominees),[12] the GOP lost the 1940, 1944, and 1948 elections.

Republicans strived to field a winning team in every election during the 1940s. In 1940, they declined to nominate "Mr. Republican," Ohio senator Robert Taft, son of a former president, isolationist, and leader of the party's conservative wing. Instead, they nominated Wendell Willkie, a New York lawyer, internationalist, and former Democrat. Again in 1944, Republicans chose the popular New York governor Thomas Dewey, leader of the party's moderate wing, over Senator Taft, a frontrunner before the convention. In 1948, the party again chose Dewey over Senator Taft. In 1952, "Mr. Republican" Taft lost his party's nomination once more to a party newcomer and avowed internationalist. This time Republicans were sure they had found a winning candidate: the former five-star general and World War II hero Dwight David Eisenhower.

Gould writes: "For the fourth time in succession, the Republicans had turned to the candidate with the best perceived chance of victory in the autumn instead of the politician who reflected the real philosophy of the party."[13] This time, the Republican electoral team finally succeeded. Their 1952 ticket of General Eisenhower and Senator Richard Nixon, a vociferous anticommunist, won a resounding victory. Reelecting Eisenhower in 1956 by an even larger margin, the team also managed to win four states in the old Confederacy: Florida, Louisiana, Texas, and Virginia.

Heading into the 1960 election, most Republicans regarded Vice President Nixon as Eisenhower's heir-apparent, although the president personally never took to him. Nixon's main challenger was thought to be Nelson Rockefeller, of the party's eastern, liberal wing, while many party conservatives favored a long-shot: Arizona senator Barry Goldwater. Led by Leonard Hall and Robert H. Finch, Nixon's electoral team headed off

Nelson Rockefeller's convention challenge.[14] Lacking a formal opponent—both Rockefeller and Goldwater declining to oppose him—Nixon was nominated in 1960 by a vote of 1,321 votes to 10.

Nixon's convention vote was larger than it was enthusiastic. Delegates conceded that he had earned points for being vice president and for dutifully serving the party organization. They also granted that Nixon was thoroughly anticommunist, but many doubted that he was sufficiently conservative. Fervent conservatives wanted Senator Barry Goldwater, whose new book, *The Conscience of a Conservative*, devoted chapters to defending states' rights, opposing civil rights, attacking unions, favoring low taxes, and disdaining welfare.[15] Goldwater got all ten votes against Nixon at the 1960 convention.

Goldwater's name had actually been placed before the 1960 convention, but he withdrew from nomination in a stirring speech, which ended: "Let's grow up, conservatives. If we want to take this Party back, and I think we can someday, let's get to work." Gould comments: "Goldwater did not say from whom the Republican Party should be reclaimed, but he meant Rockefeller and by extension Richard Nixon. For Goldwater the task was to make a conservative political party even more conservative."[16]

Flush with the success of winning the last two presidential elections, Republicans looked forward to winning votes in southern states, an opportunity handed them in 1948 by northern Democrats who chose to act as a *party*, supporting a principle, and not as a *team*, seeking to maximize votes. They passed a civil rights plank, losing southern votes.

DEMOCRATS SURRENDER THE SOUTH

Republicans had closed the door to campaigning for southern votes in 1877 when they compromised over the disputed 1876 election. Although Democrat Samuel Tilden led Republican Rutherford Hayes slightly in popular votes, unresolved differences in the electoral vote count produced no president by March 1877. To settle the dispute, Hayes "made it clear that he would not continue to support Republican regimes in the South with military power."[17] Hayes became president, and Gould's history of the GOP says: "Although the outcome in 1877 did not signify complete Republican abandonment of black Americans, it did mark an important turning point in the nation's approach to race. Over the next quarter of a century, the South became less Republican and more segregated. Civil rights would not return to the region for seventy-five years."[18] By sending delegates from southern states to the National Republican Convention, the party maintained an organizational skeleton in all southern states for the following seventy-five years. That perpetuated the helpful fiction that the Republican Party was a national party.

In the South, few Blacks could vote after Reconstruction ended, but most were personally loyal to the "party of Lincoln." In the North, black migrants to urban areas retained that loyalty, and Wilson's segregationist policies provided no reason to change. Northern Blacks were entitled to vote, however, and Republicans saw a chance to court them in the 1920 election. Gould notes the opportunity and the danger: "The dilemma was that the policies that spoke to one group alienated the other. If Republicans such as Harding promised to support measures in Congress to stamp out lynching, they risked the wrath of southern whites who would flow back toward their Democratic home."[19]

As long as northern Democrats allowed southern Democrats to practice racial politics at home, Republicans had little chance to crack what was popularly called the "Solid South" through the 1950s. *The Rise of Southern Republicans* explains the phrase "Solid South": "It is easy to forget how thoroughly the Democratic Party once dominated southern congressional elections. In 1950 there were no Republican senators from the South and only 2 Republican representatives out of 105 in the southern House delegation."[20] Then in 1948, the Democrats opened the door to the South that the Republicans had closed in 1877.

Since the end of the Civil War, southern delegates to the National Democratic Convention had managed to keep the words "civil rights" out of the Democratic platform. Once again in 1948, the draft platform submitted to the convention failed to mention the topic. Hubert Humphrey, then the young mayor of Minneapolis, rejected advice against fighting for a civil rights plank on the convention floor. To general surprise, he won. The 1948 convention approved this simple statement, which amounted to a monumental shift in Democratic Party policy: "We again state our belief that racial and religious minorities must have the right to live, the right to work, the right to vote, the full and equal protection of the laws, on a basis of equality with all citizens as guaranteed by the Constitution." As mild as that statement seems today, Humphrey's biographer Arnold Offner reports that after the convention reconvened in the evening, "Handy Ellis, chair of the Alabama delegation announced, 'We bid you goodbye,' whereupon half of its delegation and all of Mississippi's walked out of the convention, intent to form a new party."[21]

A States' Rights Party was indeed formed to contest the 1948 election. Naming South Carolina governor Strom Thurmond as its presidential candidate, the party won thirty-nine electoral votes from four southern states: South Carolina, Alabama, Louisiana, and Mississippi. All four states, however, swung back to the Democrats in 1952, and all but Louisiana voted Democratic for president in 1956. President Eisenhower discouraged white southerners from voting for Republicans after he signed the 1957 Voting Rights Act and then employed the Arkansas National Guard to support the integration of Little Rock's schools.

An event during the 1960 election campaign between Republican Richard Nixon and Democrat John Kennedy changed the party preferences of many whites in the South and Blacks everywhere. In October, Dr. Martin Luther King Jr. was arrested in Georgia for participating in a sit-in and sentenced to four months of hard labor. Both candidates learned of King's arrest while campaigning. Nixon avoided taking a stand on his imprisonment; Kennedy did not. Theodore White's *The Making of the President 1960* described John F. Kennedy's role in releasing King from jail. Kennedy's action won over Martin Luther King Sr., "who had come out for Nixon a few weeks earlier on religious grounds."[22] This arguably won enough Black votes to gain Kennedy victory in an election with a razor-thin margin. Kennedy's action helped Democrats with the Black electorate, while Nixon's inaction helped Republicans reconnect with the southern white electorate.

Vice President Lyndon Johnson, a Democrat and southerner, became president after John F. Kennedy's assassination and vowed to complete his predecessor's civil rights agenda. That included passing the 1964 Civil Rights Act, which ended segregation in public places and banned employment discrimination on the basis of race, color, religion, sex, or national origin. President Johnson understood the far-reaching consequences of that legislation and after signing reportedly said, "I think we have just delivered the South to the Republican party for a long time to come."[23] Two weeks after the bill's passage, the Republican Party convened to nominate its 1964 presidential candidate.

Senator Barry Goldwater arrived at the 1964 Republican National Convention fresh from voting conspicuously against the Civil Rights Bill. His conservative forces managed to "take back" the party in a bitterly divided convention. Goldwater won handily with 883 votes out of 1,308 (67 percent). The remaining third split among seven other less conservative candidates. Pennsylvania governor William Scranton led with 214 votes, followed by Nelson Rockefeller with 114.

THE ETHNOCENTRISM ERA BEGINS

"The 1964 election constituted a Rubicon for the Republican Party; and its crossing marked off an era."[24] So claimed Kevin Phillips in his 1969 book *The Emerging Republican Majority*, which focused on the South as "an important presidential base of the Republican Party."[25] Dedicated to President Richard M. Nixon and Attorney General John N. Mitchell, Phillips' 480+-page book, with 143 charts and forty-seven maps, was not a fanciful puff piece. Nevertheless, it was widely pooh-poohed by academics and journalists at the time.

A review by Nelson Polsby, a highly respected political scientist, stated:

> The apparent purpose of this weighty volume is to demonstrate that the "research directors, associate professors, social workers, educational consultants, urbanologists, development planners, journalists, brotherhood executives, foundation staffers, communications specialists, culture vendors, pornography merchants, poverty theorists, and so

forth"—whom Phillips identifies as the main beneficiaries of the New Deal era—are numerically too few to elect a president in the near future.[26]

Warren Weaver Jr., a political reporter for the *New York Times*, referred to the book as a "tract" that was "clumsily written, highly tendentious, full of questionable charts, and a few egregious mistakes."[27] Weaver also said: "It is not a little depressing to read a serious 480-page book on politics based largely on the theory that deep divisive conflicts between black and white, Catholic and Protestant, Jew and Irishman, East and South are immutable, that such differences cannot be harmonized and that the politician should thus simply plan upon them to his own advantage." What is depressing today is how relevant Kevin Phillips's analysis, a half-century ago, is to contemporary politics.

By nominating a true conservative in 1964, Goldwater Republicans acted more like a *political party* than just an *electoral team*. That judgment matches Aaron Wildavsky's 1965 analysis based on 150 interviews with Goldwater convention delegates at the San Francisco Cow Palace Arena.[28] Instead of political "professionals" oriented toward winning elections, according to Wildavsky, they were "purists," given their emphasis "on what they believe 'deep down inside'; their rejection of compromise; their lack of orientation toward winning; their stress on the style and purity of decision—integrity, consistency, adherence to internal norms."[29]

Rockefeller Republicans and Rockefeller himself believed that the party was embarking on a "program based on racism and sectionalism" that was "fantastically short-sighted."[30] In contrast, Goldwater's supporters thought that they would win the election by turning out new voters. The conservative reporter Stewart Alsop wrote that if Goldwater lost, "the notion that the Republican Party is the minority party because it is not conservative enough would be exposed as a myth." Alsop himself had his doubts about Goldwater's chances, titling his August 1963 *Saturday Evening Post* article "Can Goldwater Win in '64?" It noted that Goldwater's "candidacy is squarely based on the assumption that he could carry the South and, in so doing, defeat John F. Kennedy." Alsop summarized Goldwater's reasoning: "The industrial East is lost anyway, sure to support Kennedy. So is the northern Negro vote, overwhelmingly Democratic. Therefore, in Goldwater's words, the Republicans should 'stop trying to outbid the Democrats for the Negro vote.'"[31]

The Goldwater campaign did not invent what was called the Republicans' "Southern Strategy." In some detail, the political scientist Daniel Galvin fixed its origin in "Operation Dixie," started by Dwight Eisenhower soon after his 1952 election.[32] Eisenhower's efforts, however, were aimed at starting and funding state party organizations, not at targeting and converting voters through racial appeals. Operation Dixie's organizational efforts continued into 1964.

Northern "establishment" Republicans largely shunned Goldwater's 1964 campaign. America's newspaper publishers and editors, who typically endorsed Republican presidential candidates, backed Democrat Johnson over Republican Goldwater 42 to 35 percent.[33] For his campaign manager, Goldwater chose the relatively inexperienced Denison Kitchel, a personal friend. Kitchel's aides, Dean Burch and Richard Kleindheist, were politically attuned but also Goldwater loyalists.[34] Without consulting at length with his team, Goldwater chose as his running mate William Miller, chairman of the Republican National Committee. Miller lived in New York, a state Goldwater could not hope to win even by choosing him, and Miller was obliged to resign from the RNC, underscoring the difference between a *party organization* and an *electoral team*.

Goldwater's "team of amateurs" did well only in mobilizing friendly southern voters. A member of the press pool reported on a rally in Montgomery, Alabama: "Some unsung Alabama Republican impresario had hit upon an idea of breathtaking simplicity: to show the country the 'lily-white' character of Republicanism in Dixie by planting the bowl with a great field of white lilies—living lilies, in perfect bloom and gorgeously arrayed." He also said:

These were not really political rallies—they were revels, they were pageants, they were celebrations. The aim of the revellers was not so much to advance a candidacy or a cause as to dramatize a mood, and the mood was a kind of joyful defiance, or defiant joy. By coming South, Barry Goldwater had made it possible for great numbers of unapologetic white supremacists to hold great carnivals of white supremacy.[35]

Gould agreed that Republicans nominated Goldwater more for his principles than his electability: "In other years at other Republican conventions, unity had been the theme after the nominee was chosen. Conservatives had been made to swallow Wendell Willkie, Thomas E. Dewey twice, Dwight D. Eisenhower twice, and then Richard Nixon. Even when Eisenhower had led them to victory, winning seemed to come at the price of principle."[36]

Now principle trumped winning. Two polls taken a month before the 1964 Republican Convention showed only 20 percent of respondents for Barry Goldwater and more than 70 percent for President Lyndon Johnson. Two July polls revealed a light gain for Goldwater, now trailing only 30 percent to 60 percent.[37] Little changed before the November election, which Johnson won 61 to 39 percent. Although Goldwater lost in a landslide to Democrat Lyndon Johnson, the 1964 election marked the beginning of the Republican Party's ethnocentrism era and the end of the neoliberalism epoch that Gerring identified beginning in 1928. The maps in figures 14.2 and 14.3 show that Republicans dominated everywhere but the South in the 1928 elections; in 1964, they won only in the South.

The 1964 election marked the end of the Republicans' neoliberalism epoch and the start of what I call its ethnocentrism era not because the electorate reversed its voting patterns but because the party reversed its principles. The 1960 Republican Party platform contained fourteen paragraphs on "civil rights," including a pledge "to guarantee the right to vote to all citizens in all areas of the country." The party's 1964 platform, drafted before Goldwater won the nomination, devoted only five lines to the defense of civil rights. The party's 1968 platform did not even mention civil rights. In 1964, the Republican Party contradicted its founding principle, political equality among the races—abandoning its origin and entering its ethnocentrism era.

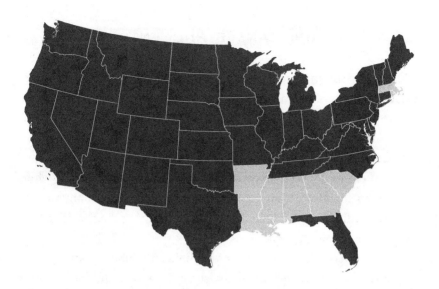

FIGURE 14.2. Republican electoral votes, 1928.

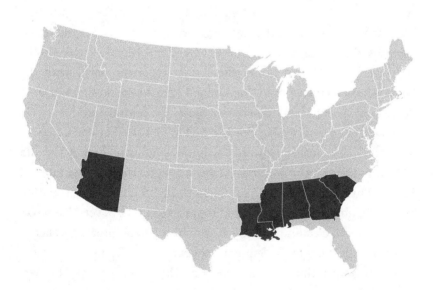

FIGURE 14.3. Republican electoral votes, 1964.

REPUBLICANS' ETHNOCENTRISM

"Ethnocentrism" in sociology means believing that one's cultural norms, values, ideology, customs, and traditions are superior to those of other cultures. Sociologists grant that most people are ethnocentric to some degree, depending on their life experiences. From colonial times to the 1960s, Americans were overwhelmingly white and Christian, and government ethnocentrically favored their race and religion. Today, white Christians constitute a minority of the population, but many in that minority still want government to continue favoring their racial prejudices and religious precepts.

Ethnocentrism in the context of Republican politics means appealing to the norms, values, ideology, customs, and traditions of white Christians rather than seeking votes from the general public. Of course, each political party caters to certain groups of voters. The legendary "Roosevelt coalition" drew votes from blue-collar workers, Catholics, Jews, urban dwellers, southerners, and northern Blacks. Assembled in the 1930s, this coalition still worked for Democrats up to the 1960s. Robert Axelrod contrasted Roosevelt's "coalition of the poor" with the Republicans' coalition of the "nonpoor": "Whites, nonunion families, Protestants, Northerners, and those outside the central cities."[38]

In 1968, the prospective candidate Richard Nixon reoriented Republicans' Southern Strategy toward partisan realignment, hoping to build a "New Majority" for the party. Nixon was not a racist in the mold of Strom Thurmond and other prominent southern politicians. Thirsting for the Republican nomination and the presidency, however, Nixon was open to a racial electoral strategy. By promising to nominate strict constructionist justices to the Supreme Court and by offering other assurances, Nixon got Thurmond's support for the nomination and the services of Harry Dent, Thurmond's aide, in crafting a strategy to carry southern states in the election and to win votes from northern whites who had been inclined to vote Democratic.[39]

For Nixon, the new strategy was not to reimpose white supremacy and not just to win the South. It was to develop a way to win the presidency by catering to population movements in the electorate from the Northeast to the South and West. Kevin Phillips, who worked on Nixon's 1968 campaign, dispassionately explained the strategy in his 1969 book *The Emerging Republican Majority*: "The Republican future is also greatly aided by demographic trends not only internally shaping the Northeast but diminishing the region's national influence. Chart 142 [one of 143 charts] shows how the voting power of the big Northeastern cities diminishes as population shifts to suburbia, local and distant."[40]

Phillips granted that "that the new populist coalition includes very few Negroes,"[41] but he said that appealing to white voters fit with hallowed political traditions:

> Ethnic polarization is a longstanding hallmark of American politics, not an unprecedented and menacing development of 1968. As illustrated throughout this book, ethnic and cultural division has so often shaped American politics that, given the immense midcentury impact of Negro enfranchisement and integration, reaction to this change almost inevitably had to result in political realignment.[42]

Phillips wrote on his last page of text: "Now it is Richard Nixon's turn to build a new era on the immense middle-class impetus of Sun Belt and suburbia."[43]

As president, Richard Nixon did not fulfill conservatives' dreams. He imposed regulations on environmental pollution, offending economic libertarians. He recognized "Red China," offending anticommunists and isolationists. Moreover, he failed to connect with Protestant and Catholic religious groups and advance their traditionalist agendas. He even signed the law (Title IX) banning gender discrimination in education. Nixon campaigned for the white vote, not the religious vote.

During Nixon's campaign and his presidency, 80 percent of the electorate was white and Christian, divided 55 percent Protestant and 25 percent Catholic. Campaigning for the white vote thus implied campaigning for the Christian vote, except that religion then was not tied closely to public policy. In 1973, the Supreme Court's *Roe v. Wade* decision, which legalized abortion, changed the politics, but not immediately. The 1976

Republican platform had said, "The question of abortion is one of the most difficult and controversial of our time," and avoided taking a position either way. The same platform reaffirmed the party's "support for ratification of the Equal Rights Amendment. Our Party was the first national party to endorse the E.R.A. in 1940. We continue to believe its ratification is essential to insure [sic] equal rights for all Americans."

Ronald Reagan's 1980 presidential campaign was chaired by Paul Laxalt, structured by the political consultant and pollster Richard Wirthlin and advised by Stuart Spencer. Reagan's election consolidated the link between Republican conservatives and the religious right. In *The God Strategy*, Domke and Coe wrote that "a new religious politics was born" on July 17, 1980. At the end of Ronald Reagan's speech accepting the Republican presidential nomination, he paused and seemed to depart from his prepared remarks. He spoke about a "Divine Providence" and then cautiously asked thousands of enraptured but subdued convention delegates, "Can we begin our crusade joined together in a moment of silent prayer?" Heads bowed, the auditorium hushed, and Reagan concluded, "God bless America."[44]

Some observers suspected that Reagan's performance "was deliberately and carefully crafted in cooperation with his campaign team."[45] For a presidential candidate to say "God bless America" was certainly novel then. A study of 229 major presidential speeches from Roosevelt in 1933 to Carter in 1981 found only one previous usage of the phrase by a president: Richard Nixon ended with it in 1973, trying to control damage from the Watergate scandal. Then from Reagan's 1981 inauguration to 2008, forty-nine of 129 presidential speeches concluded with "God bless America."[46]

Reagan also advocated policies dear to the evangelical movement, such as the tax-exempt status of private schools.[47] His 1980 Republican platform was modified to address the concerns of evangelical Protestants and Catholics across the country who opposed abortion and the Equal Rights Amendment, which threatened women's fulfilling their traditional roles in society.[48] Although white Protestants and Catholics had already declined to about 70 percent of the electorate, they constituted an important constituency. The 1980 Republican platform now endorsed "a constitutional amendment to restore protection of the right to life for unborn children." It also backed away from supporting the ERA, simply noting, "Ratification of the Equal Rights Amendment is now in the hands of state legislatures," without recommending ratification. In contrast, the Democrats in 1980 strongly favored a woman's "right to choose" and the ERA. Evangelical preachers, such as Jerry Falwell, Jimmy Swaggart, and Pat Robertson, praised the divorced and remarried Hollywood actor.[49]

Like Goldwater and Nixon before him, Ronald Reagan appealed to white voters without using racial rhetoric. He, like Goldwater and Nixon, spoke in a code that whites understood. Reagan favored "law and order"; he criticized "welfare queens." When he told a crowd in Neshoba County, Mississippi, "I believe in states' rights," they understood he was on their side.[50] When he said in his 1981 inaugural address, "Government is not the solution to our problem, government is the problem," everyone understood that the Republican Party was no longer the party of Lincoln. A history of Ronald Reagan and the New Right from 1977 to 1984 held, "What Franklin Roosevelt had been to liberalism in the 1930s, Reagan was to conservatism in the 1980s. The Republican Party became the vehicle for the growing conservative movement."[51]

SUMMARY

Party organizations do not monopolize the power to change party principles. Presidential electoral teams, even losing teams, can also change the party's direction. The Republican Party's neoliberalism epoch ended in 1960, and its ethnocentrism era began with the defeat of Barry Goldwater, who strikingly lost the 1964 election. By nominating Goldwater as its presidential candidate, the party embraced Goldwater's libertarian, antigovernment stance and his ethnocentric campaign strategy to appeal for votes from white southerners. That meant turning against the

descendants of former slaves, whom the party had freed a century earlier, and, by extension, meant appealing to the racial prejudices of many
white northerners. While many analysts argue that Ronald Reagan ush-
ered the party into a different era, Goldwater had already done that earlier. Writing in 1965, Wildavsky held that "the Goldwater movement is
not a temporary aberration, but represents a profound current within
the Republican Party."[52]

Losing in 1964 by a landslide, Goldwater could not carry through on
the party's new course. Richard Nixon stuck to Goldwater's Southern
Strategy in 1968 and—in part aided by the tragedy of the Vietnam War
and upheavals in the Democratic Party—succeeded in winning the election and cementing the party's ethnocentrism. Nixon, however, did not
share Goldwater's libertarian views, and Nixon backed government
regulations opposed by party conservatives. Nixon's personal flaws led
to his resignation from the presidency, which freed the party to return
to its antigovernment direction.

Ronald Reagan's election in 1980 and his landslide victory in 1984
allowed the party to proceed on the course set by Goldwater in 1964. The
new Republican president viewed government as a problem, not as a
solution, and appealed openly to Christians and covertly to whites. The
preeminent scholar of the Republican Party wrote:

> The GOP by the 1980s had detached itself from most of its history. There
> were occasional references at party gatherings to Abraham Lincoln, a
> quotation or two from Dwight D. Eisenhower, and respectful comments
> about Gerald Ford. Theodore Roosevelt had vanished from the Repub-
> lican record, as had the executives of the 1920s and Richard Nixon. The
> ideological turmoil that had marked the 1940s with Wendell Willkie
> and Thomas E. Dewey had not left even faint traces. Moderate Repub-
> licans had disappeared as if they had never been a force in party affairs;
> for the moment, conservatism among Republicans dominated all that
> came before it.[53]

Goldwater and Reagan epitomize the Republicans' ethnocentric era,
which cultivated the existence of *political tribes*—both Republican and

Democratic—which will be described in the next chapter. In 2016, the Republican *Party*—the organization concerned with *principles*— concluded that demographic changes were working against its ethno-centric orientation and laid out plans as an electoral *team* to increase the size of its political tent. Enter presidential aspirant Donald Trump, who had other ideas. That story is told in chapter 16.

15

THE POLITICAL TRIBE

Whereas parties' electoral teams come and go, their social bases endure. Losing electoral teams dissolve, and others soon form for the "next game," but loyal party voters remain to suffer after each defeat. Those sharing a social trait may—like a tribe—bond over their partisanship, commiserating after electoral defeats and celebrating after victories. More than two decades ago, scholars found partisans in both political parties exhibiting such tribal behavior.[1] In academic terms, partisan voters were reflecting their "social identity," which refers to *"an individual's self-image* that derive[s] from the social categories to which he perceives himself [*sic*] as belonging."[2] As applied to politics, social identity theory suggests that some people identify with parties less for their political policies than for their social draw.[3] Several studies have likened such partisan acts to tribal behavior,[4] the key feature of which is "loyalty to their group."[5] Voting for the tribe regardless of policies or issues is not confined to Republicans. Democrats exhibit social identity too. Tribal behavior reinforces voting choice.

Before proceeding further, we must separate social identity theory from the popular and emotionally charged term "identity politics." Bernstein says: "The term identity politics is widely used throughout the social sciences and the humanities to describe phenomena as diverse as multiculturalism, the women's movement, civil rights, lesbian and gay movements, separatist movements in Canada and Spain, and violent ethnic and nationalist conflict in postcolonial Africa and Asia, as well as in the formerly communist countries of Eastern Europe."[6]

Whereas "identity politics" is commonly associated with political demands to grant rights to disadvantaged peoples,[7] "social identity" refers instead to an individual's emotional attachment to a social world, "a sense of shared identity with a particular group."[8] Huddy, Mason, and Aaroe state:

> A social identity involves a subjective sense of belonging to a group that is internalized to varying degrees, resulting in individual differences in identity strength, a desire to positively distinguish the group from others, and the development of ingroup bias. Moreover, once identified with a group or, in this instance, a political party, members are motivated to protect and advance the party's status and electoral dominance as a way to maintain their party's positive distinctiveness.[9]

Identifying with a political party provides some voters with a sense of fitting into a socially desirable group of like-minded citizens.

SOCIAL IDENTITY AND POLITICAL PARTISANS

In every presidential election from 1952 to 2020, the American National Election Studies (ANES) asked a national sample of voters, "*Generally speaking, do you usually think of yourself as a Republican, a Democrat, an independent, or what?*"[10] The voters' answers reflected their political self-images. Figure 15.1 displays how American voters have described themselves from the 1952 presidential election to 2020. Those who thought of themselves as Republicans fluctuated around 25 percent over the years, while Democratic identifications declined from almost 50 percent to under 40 percent. Independents (those lacking a partisan identity) grew from about 20 to 35 percent of the electorate.[11]

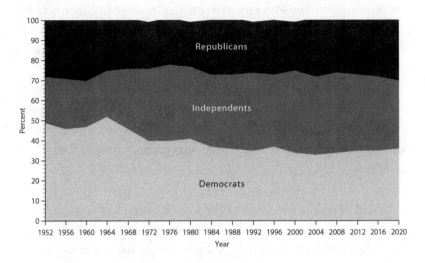

FIGURE 15.1. Party identification of American voters, 1952–2020.

Researchers who devised the measure of partisan identification distinguished between party identity (a psychological state) and voting choice (a physical behavior).[12] People could think of themselves as belonging to one party while defecting to vote for another party because of its candidates or policies. That theoretical distinction held in practice for half a century, but it collapsed in 2000. As portrayed in figure 15.2, for six consecutive elections since 2000, over 90 percent of all Republican identifiers voted for Republican presidential candidates, while over 90 percent of all Democratic identifiers voted for Democratic presidential candidates.[13]

The extraordinary change in voting behavior demonstrated in figure 15.2 suggests that most voters' social identity and party loyalty dictated their candidate choices. Since 2000, voters in both parties have consistently behaved as members of a tribe, uncritically loyal to tribal leaders, rather than as discerning citizens deciding on candidates' qualifications.

Consider the Republican vote in the 2020 presidential election. On December 18, 2019, President Donald Trump was impeached by the House of Representatives, controlled by Democrats, for abuse of power

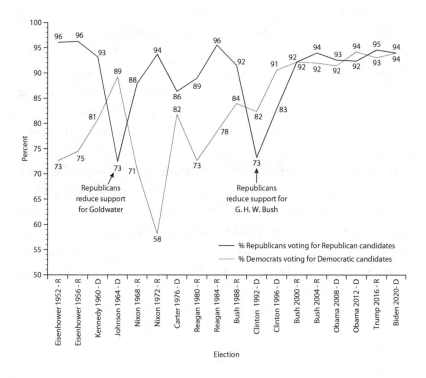

FIGURE 15.2. Presidential vote by party identification, 1952–2020.

Source: Data from 1952–2016 ANES surveys and exit polls for 2020.

and obstruction of Congress. Although Senator Mitt Romney, the 2012 Republican presidential nominee, voted for Trump's conviction, the Republican-controlled Senate voted against conviction. The nation's major dailies (usually Republican) endorsed Trump's Democratic opponent in 2020 by a ratio of forty-seven to seven,[14] and a long list of former Republican officeholders came out against Trump's reelection.[15] Still, more than 90 percent of Republicans voted in 2020 for a discredited president seeking reelection.

Since 2000, both Democratic and Republican partisans have voted for "their" candidates over 90 percent of the time. Moreover, Republican and Democratic partisans now share similar negative opinions of those in the other party. Since the 1978 congressional election, the ANES survey began asking about respondents' "feelings" toward members of other groups using a "feeling thermometer." Given a card with the image of a thermometer, respondents were asked how "cold" or "warm" they felt toward those groups according to degrees on the thermometer. For example, picking 100 degrees meant "very warm," 50 meant "no feeling at all," and 0 meant "very cold."[16] Figure 15.3 reports the mean temperatures of Republicans toward Democrats and vice versa in surveys to 2020.[17]

In the late 1970s, Republicans and Democrats both rated the opposite party at about 50 degrees, harboring neither negative nor positive feelings. By 2000, both partisans' feelings toward opponents' parties had fluctuated, following a downward slope, and then plummeted pretty steadily. Now both parties' followers, on average, feel "quite cold" to the opposition. In 2019, the Pew Research Center reported results from a

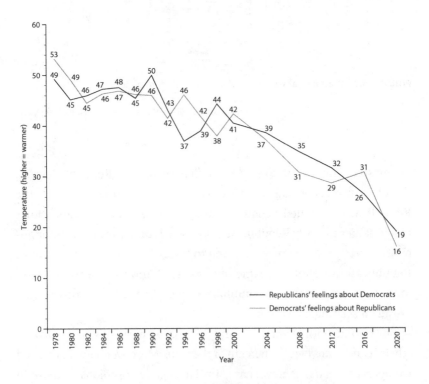

FIGURE 15.3. Mean temperatures of partisans' feelings toward opponents.

panel survey of over ten thousand people interviewed from 2014 to 2018: "Three years ago, Pew Research Center found that the 2016 presidential campaign was 'unfolding against a backdrop of intense partisan division and animosity.' Today, the level of division and animosity— including negative sentiments among partisans toward the members of the opposing party—has only deepened."[18]

Page after page listed how negatively the two social tribes viewed each other. Here are some examples:

- 55 percent of Republicans say Democrats are "more immoral" when compared with other Americans; 47 percent of Democrats say the same about Republicans.
- Republicans are more likely than Democrats to ascribe negative characteristics to people in the opposing party, with one exception: 75 percent of Democrats say Republicans are "more closed-minded" than other Americans, while 64 percent of Republicans say the same about Democrats.
- Republicans are substantially more likely (63 percent) to characterize Democrats as more unpatriotic than other Americans than Democrats (23 percent) are to say this of Republicans.

Other studies show that both parties' partisans dislike and distrust other party elites even more than other party voters.[19] Moreover, all Americans have stereotypic misconceptions of the two parties' composition. Based on a national 2015 survey, Ahler and Sood wrote: "Americans believe that 32 percent of Democrats are gay, lesbian, or bisexual (only 6.3 percent are in reality), and that 38 percent of Republicans earn over $250,000 per year (just 2.2 percent do in reality)."[20]

Republicans and Democrats form different opinions about the world because they draw their political news from very different sources. A 2020 Pew survey found Democrats naming more sources of national news than Republicans: "About nine-in-ten of those whose main source is Fox News (93 percent) identify as Republican, very close to the 95 percent of those who name MSNBC and identify as Democrats."[21] However, a majority of Democrats named six other sources—ABC, CBS,

NBC, CNN, NPR, and the *New York Times*. None of these was named by a majority of Republicans. The two sets of partisans also watch different entertainment programs. In 2019 a marketing research firm stated: "*Brooklyn Nine-Nine*, with its diverse cast, is the top Democratic comedy, and *Last Man Standing*, starring a father with conservative views taking jabs at liberals, is the top comedy for Republicans."[22]

THE RISE OF TRIBAL POLITICS

In the past, American citizens proudly associated themselves with one or the other of the nation's major parties. Republicans boasted of their "Grand Old Party," and Democrats praised Franklin Delano Roosevelt for leading the country out of the Great Depression. Given that Republicans were often employers and Democrats their employees, Republican pride was biased toward wealth. Republicans bonded in boardrooms and golf courses. Excepting some university faculties, upper-class Democrats enjoyed few opportunities to bond over their common party identification.

What happened around 2000 that caused some Republican and Democratic partisans to behave like political tribes and make "we-them" distinctions of the opposition? People smarter than I am have tried to account for the rise in tribal politics. Briefly, they cite five major factors:

1. Decades of migration within the United States that have "sorted" people into homogeneous communities: In his 2008 book *The Big Sort*, Bill Bishop found that over time, prosperous and economically secure Americans who moved "reordered their lives around their values, their tastes, and their beliefs . . . clustering in communities of like-mindedness, and not just geographically."[23] Churches, voluntary associations, and political parties all became more homogeneous.

2. A decline in membership in the kinds of civic associations that promote a sense of community: In his 2000 book *Bowling Alone*, Robert Putnam documents the decline of social clubs and fraternal organizations that cross-cut social divisions, bolster democratic institutions, and

foster feelings of community.[24] Two decades later, in *The Upswing*, he returned to the topic and summarized the situation: "Organizational records suggest that for the first two thirds of the twentieth century Americans' involvement in civic associations of all sorts rose steadily, stalled only temporarily by the Great Depression."[25] Citizens today have fewer civic connections.

3. The growth of cable television and an increase in viewers' choices: which news, or no news? Before 1980, only three television networks—ABC, CBS, and NBC—broadcast political news across America. Using public airways, networks were subject to censorship. Gatekeepers tended to choose the same events to report, and all three networks interrupted regularly programmed entertainment to cover major presidential addresses. All viewers, regardless of religion, race, region, or party, were exposed to essentially the same information. By 2000, more than half of all households had cable television, which did not use public airwaves and offered uncensored entertainment and different political news. Some cable channels selected and reported stories slanted to viewers' biases. Cable also offered the chance to avoid such news entirely and watch entertainment exclusively. As Samuel Kernell and Laurie Rice found, audiences for presidential addresses not only shrank but became more homogeneous as presidents were "preaching to a choir" of their partisans.[26]

4. The end of the "Fairness Doctrine" in broadcasting and the rise of talk radio and then Fox News: In 1949, the Federal Communications Commission required television and radio broadcasts to adhere to its "Fairness Doctrine." Broadcasters had to discuss controversial topics honestly and equitably and had to provide contrasting views in a balanced way. That rule ended in 1987 under the Reagan administration. "Almost overnight, the media landscape was transformed," wrote the newspaper reporters Kevin Kruse and Julian Zelizer.[27] By 1995, the number of all-talk radio stations grew from two in 1960 to 1,130 in 1995, and "conservatives accounted for roughly 70 percent of all talk-radio listeners."[28] Fox News was launched in 1996 in response to a perceived market for conservative views. MSNBC was also founded in 1996 but did not become an outlet for liberal views until late in the 2000s. Politics of social identity and consequent political polarization, said Kruse and Zelizer, "can be traced, in large part, to the end of the Fairness Doctrine."

5.   The rise of social media as a facilitator of in-group political con-
formity: In the early 1980s, academics routinely communicated over the
internet. During the 1990s, large segments of the public were emailing
relatives and friends about social and political life. By the 2000s, dedicated interactive technologies—called social media—facilitated social
and political communications among millions of people with similar
backgrounds or interests. Facebook (founded in 2004), Twitter (2006),
and other internet sites allowed like-minded strangers to commiserate
over politics. Research determined that interacting over social media
often "results in competing worldviews while providing little opportunity for finding common ground."[29]

   Given that (1) people will not move back to places they left, (2) civic
associations are unlikely to flourish again, (3) cable television will not
disappear, (4) the Fairness Doctrine will not be reinstated, and (5) social
media are here to stay, the causes of tribal behavior seem destined to continue. Those factors affect both parties. The lead article in a psychology
journal held that the liberal biases of social scientists caused them to
"find" more tribal behavior among Republicans than among Democrats,[30] and another article in the same journal agreed that Democrats
were tribal too. However, after reviewing numerous studies, the second
article found "a broader definition of the tribe among liberals than conservatives, as well as less importance ascribed to group-based moral
principles, more favorable attitudes toward cooperation and compromise, and less unfavorable evaluations of their ideological opponents."[31]
Nevertheless, both Republican and Democratic partisans exhibit tribal
behavior and will for the foreseeable future.

TRIBAL SOLIDARITY

Before this sociological interpretation of party identification, scholars
explained voters' preferences in terms of politics. In 1957, Anthony
Downs's highly influential book *An Economic Theory of Democracy*

advanced the "axiom" that "each citizen casts his vote for the party he believes will provide him more benefits than any other."[32] Their supposed benefits came in the form of economic policies (tax rates, subsidies, regulation, welfare), social policies (education, race relations, immigration), and foreign policies (anticommunism, free trade).[33] The rational course of action for voters was to identify with the party that served their policy interests.

In historical and cross-national perspective, this rational-choice model of party identification in America clashed with European party models. In their heyday, European "mass" parties had formal members drawn from sectors of society and appealed to their voters' sense of social and political solidarity.[34] In a sense, the electorate was separated into sociopolitical "silos" or "pillars," in a process called "pillarization": "the cultural, political, and cultural organization of society into separate strata" in the party system.[35] In contrast, American parties then were described in the contemporary postwar literature as socially rootless.

In a series of publications in the 1950s and 1960s, Otto Kirchheimer characterized American parties as "catch-all" parties that sought to bridge the "socio-economic and cultural cleavages among the electorate in order to attract a broader 'audience.'"[36] Theoretically, both parties in a two-party system should propose policies that appeal to voters in the middle—the so-called median voter—and thus both parties will inevitably converge in their offerings. Like the twins "Tweedledee" and "Tweedledum" in *Alice in Wonderland*, they would become practically indistinguishable. In fact, Alabama's governor George Wallace called them that in 1968, declaring that there wasn't "a dime's worth of difference" between the Democratic and Republican presidential candidates that year.

If American parties followed the "catch-all" model in the 1950s and 1960s, they have not for the last few decades sought to become a "big tent" for all sorts of voters. Analysts today speak instead of political polarization, of Democrats and especially Republicans being sorted into socially distinct groups. Mason writes:

In particular, the Republican Party is now largely made up of White, Christian, self-identified conservatives, while the Democratic Party is generally characterized by non-White, non-Christian, self-identified liberals. . . .

In Democratic congressional districts, citizens were more likely to buy food at stores like Whole Foods, Dunkin Donuts, and Trader Joe's. In Republican congressional districts, hungry shoppers headed to Arby's, Cracker Barrel, and Kroger. Clothing shoppers went to American Apparel and L.L. Bean in Democratic districts and to Dillard's and Old Navy in Republican districts.[37]

Republican and Democratic partisans today operate in social silos that resemble the party pillarization that occurred in Europe, except that our parties are not connected to ancillary organizations, partly because voluntary associations have declined in America since the 1960s. Today, Republicans and Democrats link together without much social contact by their social identity, and so do Democrats. Without organizing for the purpose, Republican partisans act in lockstep with other Republicans, as Democrats act in lockstep with other Democrats. Consider that over a series of Gallup polls in 2020, 91 percent of Republicans—separately interviewed—approved of President Trump's job performance, versus only 6 percent of Democrats.[38] Before 2000, identifiers of the sitting president's party averaged approval rates ranging from as low as 20 percent to a maximum of 70 percent.[39] That nearly all Republicans approved of Trump's performance while nearly all Democrats disapproved indicates that both behaved like loyal tribal members, not independently rational voters.

EXISTENTIAL ISSUES

In international politics, an "existential threat" is defined as something "likely to cause damage to such a degree that it terminates one's existence."[40] For example, in 2015 the chairman of the Joint Chiefs of Staff testified that "Russia posed the greatest existential threat to the United States."[41] That perception dominated the Joint Chiefs' thinking about military policy. In domestic politics, certain social groups may perceive that other groups pose an existential threat, perhaps not to their survival but to life as they know it. To southern whites in 1860, life as they knew it depended on slavery, so Abraham Lincoln's election threatened their continued existence. To them, the threat to slavery overruled all other considerations, caused southern states to secede from the Union, and produced the Civil War.

Today, white Christians (Protestants and Catholics) perceive an existential threat from the inexorable growth of nonwhites and non-Christians in the electorate. Numbers alone show that white Christians are a minority in a country that many remember as predominantly white and Christian. According to the Public Religion Research Institute (PRRI): "The last year that WASPs (white Anglo-Saxon Protestants) comprised a majority was 1993. In 2018: if you combined all white, non-Hispanic Christians—Protestant, Catholic, Orthodox, and other non-denominational groups—they comprised only 42 percent of the country, down from 54 percent just a decade ago in 2008."[42]

Figure 15.4 plots the dramatic decrease in the proportion of white Christians and the concomitant increase in respondents who are non-white or non-Christians, including atheists, agnostics, and those saying they are "nothing in particular."[43] National surveys only estimate religious composition. The 39 percent white Christians in figure 15.4 is close to the PRRI estimate of 42 percent.

In August 2021, the U.S. Census Bureau reported that the nation's total white population in 2020 had *shrunk* for the first time in history. From 2010 to 2020, the non-Hispanic white population declined 2.6 percent, reducing the whites' share of the total U.S. population to 57 percent.[44] A 2021 national survey found slightly over 60 percent of all Americans (both Republicans and Democrats) thought the declining proportion of whites was neither good nor bad. However, the news confirmed the fears of many Republican voters. Analyzing the survey by party, only 24 percent of all Democrats saw the news negatively, versus 38 percent of conservative Republicans.[45]

For some time, whites have been wary of losing social control. Non-whites already dominated competitive sports, were ascendant in

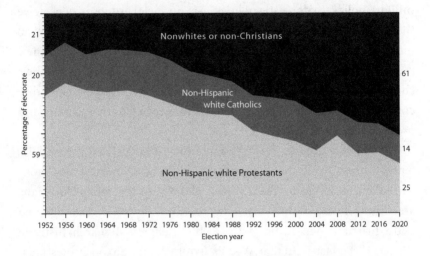

FIGURE 15.4. Decline in white Christians as a proportion of the American electorate, 1952–2020.

Source: Data from 1952–2016 ANES surveys and Democracy Fund Voter Study, group data release no. 1, published January 2020.

entertainment, and had wrested political offices away from whites at the local, state, and national levels. Electing a Black man president of the United States in 2008, reelecting him in 2012, and electing a mixed-race woman vice president in 2020 was particularly galling to some whites. Ashley Jardina in *White Identity Politics* quoted comments by the radio talk host Rush Limbaugh the day after the 2012 election: "I went to bed last night thinking we're outnumbered. I went to bed last night thinking all this discussion we'd had about this election being the election that will tell us whether or not we've lost the country. I went to bed last night thinking we've lost the country. I don't know how else you look at this."[46]

Jardina's book carefully distinguished between racism and the white in-group's desire "to protect their group's collective interests and to maintain its status."[47] Moreover, when asked, "How important is being white to your identity?" about 30 percent of white respondents in a 2016 national sample replied, "Not important at all."[48] Nevertheless, about half conceded that it was "Important" to "Very important." When the former Southern Baptist preacher Robert Jones administered his fifteen-question racism index in a 2018 national survey, he found that white Christians "overall are more likely than white religiously unaffiliated Americans to register higher scores on the Racism Index, and the differences between white Christian subgroups (white evangelical Protestants, white mainline Protestants, and white Catholics) are largely differences of degree rather than kind."[49]

Racism is one cultural trait that, surveys show, distinguishes many white Christians from white non-Christians. Sexism is another trait that characterizes a substantial subset of white Christians who believe that the "Government of Man" is inferior to the "Kingdom of God."[50] The evangelical theology of "complementarism" asserts that, while men and women were "equal before God," God has assigned the genders different roles. Men were to lead women.[51] Many evangelicals fume at social changes that infringe on men's traditional role as the head of the household, that allow women to have abortions, and that permit same-sex marriage. To them, Democrats back government policies that violate God's laws.

Instead of accommodating to the nation's demographic and cultural changes, Republican leaders saw political advantage in opposing them. The same political party whose planks once urged political equality for former slaves, civil rights for Blacks, and equal rights for women now backed "states' rights" to prevent further advances by women and racial minorities. When Ronald Reagan, in accepting the 1980 Republican nomination, welcomed people into a "national crusade to Make America Great Again," many white Christians got the message. Donald Trump certainly grasped the hidden meaning of the phrase "Make America Great Again" when in 2012 he filed paperwork to copyright the slogan years before using it in his presidential campaign.[52] White Christians understood Reagan in 1980 and Trump in 2016: MAGA meant returning to a time when white Christians dominated America's culture and politics.[53] Donald Trump's campaign was more socially reactionary (restoring the past) than politically conservative (planning for an orderly future).

Robert Jones at the Public Religion Research Institute writes:

By activating the white supremacy sequence within white Christian DNA, which was primed for receptivity by the perceived external threat of racial and cultural change in the country, Trump was able to convert white evangelicals in the course of a single political campaign from so-called values voters to "nostalgia voters." Trump's powerful appeal to white evangelicals was not that he spoke to the culture wars around abortion or same-sex marriage, or his populist appeals to economic anxieties, but rather that he evoked powerful fears about the loss of white Christian dominance amid a rapidly changing environment.[54]

Goldwater in 1964, Reagan in 1980, and Trump in 2016 chose to parlay the nation's demographic and cultural changes into an existential issue for white Christians. By promising to restore life as it had been, Republicans would draw votes from white Christians hoping to protect their way of life. In her article "Casting the Other as an Existential Threat," May Darwich writes: "By portraying a sectarian Other as the source of an existential threat to a particular society, elites move the issue from normal politics to the 'exceptional.'"[55] Tribal solidarity becomes paramount: vote only for your own.

Party politics became structured around an existential issue, as in 1860. Once again the issue involved white southerners, but a century later they found refuge in a different party. The ironies mount. After the Civil War, Republicans sometimes campaigned by "waving the bloody shirt"—a reference to Union soldiers who died in battle. According to the Republican historian Lewis L. Gould, the bloody shirt "became a coded slogan for Republican emphasis on the passions of the war over more reasoned and presumably important issues."[56] During the party's ethnocentrism era, the slogan "Make America Great Again" reminded white Christians of what they thought they had lost to nonwhites and non-Christians, focusing their attention on voting for Republicans and against Democrats.

Existential threats to political tribes provide a sociological explanation of changes in the Republican Party since the 1960s. Donald Trump's recent role in accelerating party change has invited psychological explanations. In *Authoritarian Nightmare*, John Dean, former White House counsel for President Nixon, and Bob Altemeyer, professor emeritus of psychology at the University of Manitoba, wrote about the psychological connection between the Republican political tribe and Donald Trump.[57] Analyzing responses to questions concerning social dominance and authoritarianism for a national survey in 2019, Dean and Altemeyer found that most of Trump's supporters

> have one of the two authoritarian personalities that have been scientifically established, plus a unique group that combines these two. They are:
> *Social Dominators*. People who believe in inequality between groups. Predictably, they usually believe their groups should be more prestigious and powerful than others. . . .
> *Authoritarian Followers*. These people are submissive, fearful, and longing for a mighty leader who will protect them from life's threats. . . .
> "*Double Highs*." Some people score highly in both being a Social Dominator and being an Authoritarian Follower.[58]

Of 990 respondents divided into those who approved and disapproved of Trump, those who approved rated substantially higher on authoritarian and social dominance scales.[59] Trump offered a way to deal with the existential threat: do not give in to social change, confront it, and stop it using any available means. These findings also relate to the personality cult surrounding Donald Trump.

SUMMARY

Tribal behavior occurs among Democrats as well as Republicans. Elsewhere I have compared partisan identifiers with sports fans at some length.[60] Individuals in both groups bond over the successes and failures of their political or athletic teams. Although die-hard sports fans often visibly grieve over their team's defeat, a loss is not seen as an existential threat. If some partisans view an election defeat that way, their tribal behavior may escalate into cult behavior. Directed by their losing but still acknowledged leader, they may take unprecedented, undemocratic action to overturn the defeat. This danger lurks in the politics of ethnocentrism, which pits social groups against one another.

The Republican Party entered its ethnocentrism era in 1964 but engaged in normal politics against Democratic opponents throughout the rest of the twentieth century. Then a set of factors—internal migration, civic disorganization, changes in technology and communications policies—caused many voters to morph their identification with a political party into a social identity. Being a Republican (or a Democrat) no longer meant favoring different sets of government policies but being included in a desirable social and political club, a tribe with clear "we" versus "them" distinctions, a tribe that demanded strict loyalty in opinions and, above all, in voting. Party politics in the twenty-first century were very different from party politics in the twentieth.

Donald Trump did not inaugurate the Republican Party's ethnocentrism era, but he exploited it. When Trump announced on June 16, 2015, that he was seeking the Republican presidential nomination, he appealed openly and plainly to his targeted electorate:

> It is way past time to build a massive wall to secure our southern border . . .
>
> When Mexico sends its people, they're not sending their best. They're not sending you [gesturing to audience]. They are not sending you [pointing to audience].
>
> They're sending people that have lots of problems, and they're bringing those problems with us. They're bringing drugs, they're bringing crime, they're rapists, and some, I assume are good people. . . .
>
> It's coming from more than Mexico. It's coming from all over South and Latin America, and it's coming probably, probably from the Middle East. . . . We don't know what's happening. And it's got to stop, and it's got to stop fast.[61]

After Trump's election, politics became further complicated in the second decade of the twenty-first century by the rise of a personality cult around the former president of the United States.

16

THE PERSONALITY CULT

Whereas a political tribe is steered by group intelligence and ignorance, a personality cult obeys the whims of a single person. Chapter 1, "Political Parties," stated that "cult" does not ordinarily fit into a discussion of American political parties. Nor does "personalist parties," a term often applied to Latin American political parties.[1] The term "personalism"—the unique, motivating appeal of an individual, independent of party—is often cited as the basis of a dictator's power.[2] Such a dictator rules by loyalty to his person. Abraham Lincoln, Teddy Roosevelt, Franklin Delano Roosevelt, and Ronald Reagan were enormously popular; their popularity won them elections and public support. Unlike Donald Trump, however, they were not widely idolized by their followers. To an NBC News/*Wall Street Journal* poll question asked repeatedly of Republicans during Trump's presidency, "Do you consider yourself to be more of a supporter of Donald Trump or more of a supporter of the Republican Party?," 52 percent chose Trump, and only 39 percent chose the party.[3]

The term "cult" involves more than just personalism. According to the American Psychological Association, a personality cult is based on "exaggerated devotion to a charismatic political, religious, or other leader, often fomented by authoritarian figures or regimes as a means of maintaining their power."[4] The clearest, most bizarre, and most tragic example of a cult in American history was the Reverend James Warren Jones's People's Temple Christian Church Full Gospel. Jones founded his temple in Indiana, moved it to San Francisco, and then in 1977 relocated to a "socialist paradise" in Guyana, South America, which he named Jonestown. In 1978, U.S. Representative Leo Ryan flew to Jonestown to investigate stories of human abuse—mind control, beatings, imprisonment. While attempting to return with some temple members who asked Ryan to take them back to the United States with him, Ryan and his party were killed by Jones's gunmen. Afterward, Jones convinced his followers to drink a fruit punch laced with cyanide. Over nine hundred people died, including three hundred children. Jones killed himself.[5]

Nothing as grotesque has occurred in the history of American political parties, but some observers charge that Lyndon LaRouche, who ran eight times for president, also surrounded himself with a supportive cult. In the 1970s, LaRouche had thirty-seven offices in North America and twenty-six abroad, and in the 1980s he created an armed compound in Virginia.[6] He usually sought nomination as a Democrat and received thousands of votes, once running from jail after his conviction for defaulting on loans from supporters. In 2008, LaRouche ran against Obama for the Democratic nomination, later supported Trump, and died in 2019 at ninety-six. His obituary in the *New York Times* identified him as a "cult figure." In June 2021, a website maintained by LaRouche's followers claimed that he "was framed" and jailed by the same "global elites" that had "waged the coup against Donald Trump, a coup which denied him his duly-elected second term."[7]

On June 7, 2018, a year before LaRouche's 2019 death, the *New York Times* identified another "cult figure" in an editorial titled "The Cult of Trump":

> This week's primary elections underscored the striking degree to which President Trump has transformed the Republican Party from a political organization into a cult of personality. By contrast, Democrats show signs of taking a more pluralistic approach, fielding candidates who are

willing and even eager to break with their national leaders—the House minority leader, Ms. Pelosi, in particular.

But Mr. Trump's grip on the Republican psyche is unusually powerful by historical standards, because it is about so much more than electoral dynamics. Through his demagogic command of the party's base, he has emerged as the shameless, trash-talking, lib-owning fulcrum around which the entire enterprise revolves.[8]

Soon after that editorial, Steven Hassan, a defector from Sun Myung Moon's Unification Church cult who became a mental health professional, published the three-hundred-page *The Cult of Trump*. Hassan identified others who concluded that Trump's supporters constituted a cult: "Former Tennessee Republican senator Bob Corker was quoted in the *Washington Post* as saying, 'It's becoming a cultish thing, isn't it?' In 2019, Maryland Democratic representative Jamie Raskin said, 'The Republican party is almost like a religious cult surrounding an organized crime family. That's the mentality.' Former White House staffer and Apprentice contestant Omarosa Manigault Newman ends her book, *Unhinged*, with these memorable words: 'I've escaped from the cult of Trump world. I'm free.'"[9] While in the past the concept of "personalism" was applied only to foreign political parties, today the cult concept fits into discussing a major American political party.

TRUMP THE CANDIDATE

The political website *Ballotpedia* summarized Donald Trump's background and political experience at the start of his presidential campaign:

A New York–based real estate developer, author, chairman of The Trump Organization, and former executive producer of "The Apprentice"—a reality television show in which he also starred—Trump had never before sought or held elected public office prior to his 2016 run, though he flirted with political bids off and on between the late 1980s and 2015. He became more active in national politics in 2011 when he began publicly questioning whether Barack Obama was a natural citizen. That same year, Trump indicated some interest in seeking the Republican nomination for president but ultimately declined to run.

Trump's candidacy for the Republican nomination in 2016 was initially seen as something of a long shot, but the New York businessman's outsider status, mastery of the media, and no-holds-barred campaign style propelled him to the front of the field.[10]

A wealthy person and flamboyant personality, Donald Trump had attracted attention, publicity, and controversy in New York since the 1980s. He drew criticism for razing an Art Deco building to make way for Trump Tower and gained praise for rebuilding the Wollman ice-skating rink in Central Park. In 1987, Gary Trudeau, the Pulitzer Prize–winning editorial cartoonist, anticipated that the showy billionaire might run for president and began to ridicule him in his syndicated and popular comic strip Doonesbury as an orange-haired womanizer of low intelligence and lower morals.[11]

Political observers widely joked about Trump's June 16, 2015, announcement to seek the 2016 Republican nomination for president. Yet that fall, he was one of seventeen Republican aspirants who drew national attention. The ten hopefuls who scored highest in opinion polls were invited to the first of twelve scheduled debates. Donald Trump—seen by millions for years as the host of The Apprentice reality television program—averaged 20 percent in those early polls, almost twice as high as the next person, Scott Walker.[12] Although his poll results ensured that he received ample television coverage, Trump initially drew weak reviews, and he lost the Iowa caucuses on February 1 to Senator Ted Cruz. However, Trump won the February 20 primary in South Carolina and did well enough elsewhere to lead the six Republicans still competing for the prize. By May 4, the other five had dropped out, and Trump was assured of the party's nomination at the July 2016 Republican convention.

This brief recap of Trump's quest for the Republican nomination reminds us that most Americans were amused by his announcement to run, that political analysts expected him to fail, and that he struggled to win primaries to gain the nomination. During the primary campaigns, many prominent Republicans denounced Trump, only to court him after he won the presidency. Consider this 2019 report:

> In 2015, Senator Lindsey Graham, Republican of South Carolina, labeled Mr. Trump a "race-baiting, xenophobic, religious bigot" and called him the "ISIL man of the year," referring to the Islamic State. That was in addition to describing him as a "kook," "crazy" and a man who was "unfit for office." [He later became Trump's confidant.] . . .
>
> Senator Ted Cruz, the second-to-last man left standing in the ugly 2016 Republican primary race, called Mr. Trump a "pathological liar" who was "utterly amoral," a "serial philanderer" and a "narcissist at a level I don't think this country's ever seen." [Later, Cruz defended Trump.] . . .
>
> Mick Mulvaney, the former Republican congressman who now serves as the president's acting chief of staff, in 2016 called him a "terrible human being" who had made "disgusting and indefensible" comments about women. . . .
>
> "Rick Perry called him a 'cancer' and then became a cabinet secretary."[13]

A former adviser to Republican Paul Ryan, the former House Speaker, said: "Everything is tribal at this point. . . . If you're with him, you're with him, in spite of or because of the way that he is."[14]

Trump's electoral team had a rocky beginning. Roger Stone, who had advised Richard Nixon and other Republican presidential candidates, was Trump's adviser until they fell out in 2015. Corey Lewandowski became his first campaign manager in 2015, was fired in June 2016, and was replaced by Paul Manafort, who resigned in August. Kellyanne Conway became campaign manager, and Stephen Bannon of *Breitbart News* was named campaign chief executive. Trump himself had already laid out the campaign template the previous summer in announcing his candidacy. He would campaign against immigration, against global trade agreements, and for "America First" and would "Make America Great Again." In *The Politics of Losing*, Rory McVeigh and Kevin Estep present evidence showing that "Donald Trump found his core support among those who felt they were on the losing end of a newly global economy."[15] Trump also denounced so-called leaders in Washington and later promised to "drain the swamp." Castigating government elites as the "enemy" gave his campaign a "populist" slant and appealed to workers who lost manufacturing jobs when companies opened plants abroad.

Donald Trump was a long shot to win his party's nomination, but he won it nevertheless. He was given no chance to win the 2016 general election against former secretary of state Hillary Clinton, but he won the office nevertheless. Although Clinton won almost three million more popular votes than Donald Trump, he won a majority of the electoral votes and thus became president. Clinton carried twenty states (plus Washington, DC) with a population of 67 million. Trump won thirty states with 62 million people. Trump won ten of the eleven states in the old Confederacy by an average of 16 points, losing only Virginia. Exit polls showed Trump winning 81 percent of white evangelical Christians, 67 percent of whites lacking a college degree (which overlaps with the preceding category), and 62 percent of voters in "small cities or rural areas."[16]

Scholars have scratched their heads bloody to explain Trump's electoral appeal. One experienced team examined responses to national surveys and social and economic data from the nation's counties and congressional districts. They concluded:

> Above all, our evidence makes clear that economic aspects of Trump's message—often explicitly linked to more or less plausible policy proposals—were central. His deviations from Republican orthodoxy on trade and immigration were crucial in the primaries and powerful in the general election as well. His nods to criticisms of the wealthy and support for left-leaning economic policies (on infrastructure, jobs, Social Security and Medicare) undoubtedly helped defuse the usual advantage they bring to Democrats in general elections.[17]

These researchers disputed those who argued that "social anxieties overwhelmingly predominated" in the general election but granted that social factors were important in Republican primary elections, which gave Trump the party's presidential nomination.[18] In fact, several researchers found "virtually no correlation between the vote for Trump in the primary and caucus elections and the vote for Trump in the general election."[19] That is, worries about America's changing social composition mattered more to Republican primary voters than to all voters in the national electorate.

The Russian professor Elizaveta Gaufman offered a secular explanation for Trump's social appeal, especially his appeal to his primary voters. She argued that Donald Trump unwittingly but successfully tapped into a "carnival culture" prevalent in Russia. The antielite nature of a common carnival "allows for 'low culture' to come to the high world (of politics), wherein all people are also allowed to curse and swear without social sanction." Although himself a wealthy businessman and media celebrity, Trump's blunt, crude talk separated him from the elites he attacked. According to Gaufman, he drew support from threatened groups by his "anti-establishment battle-cry . . . as a means of rallying voters against his opponent, who was portrayed as mainstream and experienced—part of the 'Washington DC swamp.'" Trump's unprecedented daily stream of messages on social media both confounded his electoral team and won "likes" from partisans in his political tribe. Gaufman explained: "Freedom is the core value of carnival and 'telling it like it is' without a semblance of politesse and etiquette created an illusion of a supposedly real-world town square clashing with the world dominated and mapped out by elites."[20] Even bragging about his sexual escapades played into the carnival culture.

The Calvinist historian Kristen Kobes Du Mez offered a religious account of his victory to explain why 81 percent of white Evangelical Christians crammed into his tent. In *Jesus and John Wayne*, Du Mez wrote that Evangelicals' support for Trump reflected their "embrace of militant masculinity, an ideology that enshrines patriarchal authority and condones the callous display of power, at home and abroad." "Donald Trump was the culmination of their half-century-long pursuit of a militant Christian masculinity. He was the reincarnation of John Wayne, sitting tall in the saddle, a man who wasn't afraid to resort to violence to bring order, who protected those deemed worthy of protection, who wouldn't let political correctness get in the way of saying what had to be said or the norms of democratic society keep him from doing what needed to be done." "Sure, Trump was a notorious womanizer, married three times. So was John Wayne. . . . Trump was 'the John Wayne stand-in' his evangelical supporters were looking for."[21]

Evangelicals in "God's Own Party," as the Republican Party was described almost a decade earlier, opened their political arms to Donald Trump.[22] Their religious faith engendered a cult-like attraction to their candidate. As president, Donald Trump would Make America Great Again. He would deal with the threat that nonwhites and non-Christians posed to white Christian dominance.

A 2017 Gallup poll found that 85 percent of Trump's supporters viewed him as a "strong leader," and 83 percent thought he "can bring about the changes this country needs"—versus about 40 percent of independents and 12 percent of Democrats.[23] Historians agree that supporters of Joseph Stalin, Benito Mussolini, Adolf Hitler, and Mao Zedong also regarded them as strong leaders. The British political scientist Archie Brown's book *The Myth of the Strong Leader: Political Leadership in the Modern Age* studied political leadership across the world. In the foreword to the 2018 edition, Brown wrote, "A strong leader is not the same as a wise leader," and he found "ample evidence that the likelihood of calamitously bad decision-making is substantially greater under unconstrained, or only weakly constrained, individual rule."[24]

TRUMP THE PRESIDENT

While campaigning for and winning the presidency, Donald Trump created a personal following, his own political tribe. No doubt their attachment to him increased after his victory, but not until 2018 did observers refer to his hold over them as cult-like. On February 5, 2018, the website

Axios released one of the first publications titled "The Cult of Trump." It began:

> *Rarely has a president* changed his party as fast and profoundly as Donald J. Trump. Love him or hate him, you can no longer argue his ability to bend an entire party to his will.
>
> *In the two and a half years* since he announced his candidacy, he has moved the party away from decades of orthodoxy on trade, Russia, deficits and more—and has helped make the law-and-order party skeptical of FBI leadership.[25]

The next day, the *National Interest* published an article, "Conservatives and the Cult of Trump," citing a member of the Republican National Committee who admitted that Trump surpassed his previous favorite, Ronald Reagan. The article quoted this from a conservative columnist: "President Trump has officially transformed himself from merely a great American president into a historic world leader keeping lit the torch of freedom for all people around the world."[26]

Was Donald Trump, not regarded as a political thinker, truly a conservative? He certainly promised to return to the past, when immigration was constrained and whites dominated politics. However, conservatives do not simply seek to restore the past. Conservative thought generally respects learning from the past for application in the present and future. Those who strive to recover an idealized past, says the political theorist Mark Lilla, are reactionaries. They "are not conservatives."[27]

Donald Trump was properly a reactionary, "one who believes in returning to governmental and economic conditions of an earlier time."[28] He based his election campaign not on abstract values in political philosophy but on certain voters' recollections of social history. By evoking voters' nostalgic and imperfect memories of the past, Trump shrewdly appealed to the emotions of two social groups—whites and Evangelical Christians—that had once dominated American politics. Although he portrayed himself a true American patriot, the book *Un-American: The Fake Patriotism of Donald J. Trump*, written by an established conservative scholar and former researcher for the Republican National Committee, detailed Trump's repeated disregard for American principles of equality and democratic government.[29]

As the campaign for the 2018 congressional elections unfolded, more observers compared Trump's authority within the party to that of a cult leader. On June 12, 2019, *Bloomberg News* reported that South Carolina Republicans had voted against a veteran lawmaker said to be disloyal to the president and for his opponent, who proclaimed: "We are the party of President Donald J. Trump." The same story cited a Republican speaking of Trump's hold in Congress: " 'We're in a strange place. I mean it's almost becoming a cultish thing,' Senator Bob Corker, a retiring Tennessee Republican, told reporters Wednesday, a day after lambasting other GOP lawmakers on the floor of the Senate for being too afraid of Trump to rein in his authority to impose tariffs."[30]

The former cult member Steven Hassan, who has taught at Harvard Medical School, wrote a book explaining the nature of a cult, saying that cult leaders employ "a complex array of influence techniques, applied incrementally to control almost every aspect of a person—the way they act (behavior), what they read, watch, or listen to (information), the way they think (thoughts), and how they feel (emotions). Trump has gotten millions of people to believe, support, and even adore him by using techniques in each of these areas."[31]

Cult leaders typically exercise their charismatic influence on followers through personal interactions. Jim Jones gathered a thousand followers around him in Jonestown, Guyana, where they could not escape. Lyndon LaRouche turned an estate in Virginia into an enclosed armed camp. David Koresh, head of the Branch Davidians sect, maintained a compound in Waco, Texas. Federal agents raided the compound in 1993, causing a fire resulting in the deaths of seventy-nine cult members and Koresh's death by gunshot.

President Trump's followers had no direct access to him, nor did he to them. How could he have commanded their loyalty? Hassan says:

I cannot overstate the impact of the digital world on the whole area of undue influence and mind control. People no longer need to be physically isolated to be indoctrinated by destructive cults. Digital technology has provided access and a powerful set of tools for destructive groups and individuals to indoctrinate, control, and monitor believers day and night. When cult members go home for family visits, they are often receiving multiple texts every hour to keep them connected and faithful.[32]

Before and after his election to the presidency, Donald Trump tweeted his thoughts to growing numbers of avid followers. His Twitter social media account had nearly 89 million followers in early 2021. Although Twitter banned Trump from tweeting following the January 6, 2021, Capitol insurrection, a "Trump Twitter Archive" retains more than 56,000 posted to his account since 2009.[33] Before being banned from Facebook after the insurrection, he had about 150 million followers and subscribers.[34] Social media provided a means to influence followers without interacting with them in person.

Relatively few Germans actually met Adolf Hitler. Nevertheless, the Holocaust Museum said: "Election campaign materials from the 1920s and early 1930s, compelling visual materials, and controlled public appearances coalesced to create a 'cult of the Führer' (leader) around Hitler. His fame grew via speeches at rallies, parades, and on the radio."[35]

Hitler's Nazi Party participated in four free parliamentary elections from 1928 to 1932, winning first place in the last three. Named chancellor and head of government in January 1933, Hitler terrorized opponents in the March 1933 elections, won again by a large margin, and assumed dictatorial powers.

Mentioning Hitler returns us to the research cited in chapter 15 on the authoritarian nature of Trump's relationship with his followers. Dean and Altemeyer wrote:

Nothing demonstrates right-wing authoritarians' submission to their leaders as clearly as Trump's supporters' acceptance of his pronouncements and guidance regarding COVID-19. Polls show they believed Trump's dismissal of the threat during January and February and up to March 11, 2020. Accordingly, they would have been more likely to ignore the advice coming from medical experts to socially distance themselves from others. Considerable numbers of them likely became infected and proceeded to infect others, including their loved ones. They did not blame him for leading them, as far as they knew, into the Valley of Death.[36]

TRUMP THE LOSING CANDIDATE

Political parties provide a peaceful way to transfer government power in a democracy. The political scientist Ralph M. Goldman argued that "a stable political party system is the most effective institutional alternative to warfare."[37] Stable party systems require defeated candidates to leave office without a fight—even after close or disputed elections. That norm was observed by American presidential candidates throughout the nineteenth and twentieth centuries and for a time into the twenty-first. Consider these four examples of problematic presidential elections since World War II: two were decided by less than 1 percent of the popular vote, and two saw the popular vote winner lose to the electoral vote winner:

1960   The Democrat Kennedy won by only 0.2 percent of the popular vote over Republican Nixon.
1968   The Republican Nixon won by only 0.7 percent of the vote over Democrat Humphrey.
2000   The Republican Bush lost to Democrat Gore by 0.5 percent but won the electoral vote.
2016   The Republican Trump lost to Democrat Clinton by 2.1 percent but won the electoral vote.

In all four cases, all the losing candidates—including Trump's 2016 opponent, who polled more popular votes—accepted the outcomes.

On September 23, 2020, more than a month before the November 3 presidential election, President Trump refused to guarantee that he would accept the results and leave office if defeated.[38] That was not an offhand remark. He repeatedly failed to commit to honor the people's verdict in October. Political observers wrote articles and even books speculating on the consequences of such unprecedented action.[39] Trump established the precedent.

On November 3, 2020, the Republican president Donald Trump lost decisively to the Democratic challenger Joe Biden by clear majorities in both the popular vote (51 to 47 percent) and the electoral vote (57 to 43 percent). However, close contests in some states took time to determine the outcome. By Saturday after the Tuesday election, the Associated Press and news networks called the election for Biden. The president still did not concede, saying that the election was "far from over."[40] To stay in power, he quickly began to dispute the results. Most Republican officials charged with counting the votes stayed true to the law and verified his defeat, including his unexpected loss in Arizona. But on November 20, the chairwoman of the Arizona Republican Party texted one of the Republican supervisors of Maricopa County, which contains 60 percent of Arizona's voters, protesting the verification: "Seems like you're playing for the wrong team and people will remember. WRONG team."[41]

Millions of Trump's voters bought his claim that their team had really won. Founded in 2013, Just Security, "an online forum for the rigorous analysis of national and international security," scoured social media sites and archives to compile a timeline of relevant actions by President Trump and his supporters nearly every day after the election.[42] Here are a few excerpts from the scores of Just Security postings:

- November 4: "In the early morning hours following Election Day, Trump falsely declares premature victory to his supporters at the White House. He makes several unsubstantiated claims about supposed voter fraud, calling it 'a major fraud on our nation.' He then calls for vote counting to stop."
- November 5: "At 9:12 a.m. ET, Trump tweets, 'STOP THE COUNT!'"
- November 6: "More than 200 protesters, including militia movement members, gather to protest in Detroit, Michigan. A group of Trump

supporters target a local news station for a protest in Youngstown, Ohio. More protests take place in Arizona, Pennsylvania, and Michigan."

- November 10: "Oath Keepers leader Stewart Rhodes tells Alex Jones [Infowars] that he had men stationed outside Washington, DC prepared to engage in violence on Trump's command."

- November 12: "According to notes shared by an Oath Keepers member inside a chat room for dues-paying group supporters, Rhodes says that members of his group will be stationed near Washington, DC until Trump is installed as president."

- November 14: "Trump supporters and far-right extremists gather by the thousands in DC to protest the results of the 2020 election. Trump pays a visit to the Million MAGA March with a presidential motorcade drive-by. That night, members of the Proud Boys and Trump supporters engage in violence in downtown DC, feuding with civil rights counter-protestors."

- November 21: "Trump acknowledges Stop the Steal protesters in Georgia on Twitter in a reaction to a Breitbart News article. 'The proof pouring in is undeniable. Many more votes than needed. This was a LANDSLIDE!' Trump writes."

- December 5: "Armed protesters surround Michigan Secretary of State Joselyn Benson's home, chanting 'Stop the Steal' and spouting conspiracy theories about the election popularized by Trump and his allies. Activist Genevieve Peters live-streams the event, including the caption, 'Michiganders head to Secretary of States Jocelyn Benson's HOUSE in dead of night to let her know: WE AIN'T TAKING THIS CORRUPT ELECTION!! FORENSIC AUDIT PERIOD!'"

- December 19: "Trump tweets out a call for his supporters to protest in DC on the day when Electoral College votes are set to be certified by Congress. 'Statistically impossible to have lost the 2020 Election,' Trump says, adding, 'Big protest in DC on January 6th. Be there, will be wild!'"

- December 25: "Ali Alexander posts a since-deleted video to YouTube on Christmas Day, urging people to come to DC on Jan. 6, the day

that Congress will finalize Biden's election as president. With a triumphant soundtrack, the video features Trump at a rally declaring,
'We will never give in. We will never give up, and we will never back
down. We will never ever surrender.'"

- December 31: "Oath Keepers share details for Jan. 6 protests on its
  website and announce that the group will be present in an article
  titled, 'JANUARY SIXTH, SEE YOU IN DC!'"

- January 1, 2021: "Trump promotes 'Stop The Steal' on Twitter,
  encouraging his supporters to attend the 'BIG Protest Rally in Washington DC.'"

- January 2: "White House Chief of Staff Mark Meadows tweets, 'We're
  now at well over 100 House members and a dozen Senators ready to
  stand up for election integrity and object to certification. It's time
  to fight back.'"

Also on January 2, President Trump called the secretary of state in
Georgia, Republican George Raffensperger, asking him to change the
vote totals and deny Joe Biden his narrow victory in that state. Someone
recorded and released the call. Here are excerpts from the extended con-
versation, Trump speaking:

Hello, Brad and Ryan and everybody. . . . I think it's pretty clear that
we won. We won very substantially, Georgia . . . there were many infrac-
tions, and the bottom line is many, many times the 11,779 margin that
they said we lost by . . . we're many, many times above the 11,779, and
many of those numbers are certified or they will be certified. . . . So
look. All I want to do is this. I just want to find 11,780 votes, which is
one more than we have because we won the state. . . . And the truth, the
real truth is I won by 400,000 votes, at least. That's the real truth.

After the president made his plea, Secretary of State Raffensperger
replied: "Mr. President, you have people that submit information, and
we have our people that submit information. And then it comes before
the court, and the court then has to make a determination. We have to
stand by our numbers. We believe our numbers are right."[43]

President Trump also tried to reverse the election results through the courts via lawsuits. Over two months following the election, his supporters filed "at least 86 contesting election processes, vote counting, and the vote certification process in multiple states, including Arizona, Georgia, Michigan, Nevada, Pennsylvania, and Wisconsin."[44] Virtually all lawsuits were dismissed by judges, some of whom were Trump appointees. Some filings were found to be "frivolous" or "without merit." The Pennsylvania Supreme Court later vacated one minor ruling in Trump's favor.

While President Trump was unsuccessful in altering the Georgia vote count, his supporters pressed on with their rebellious plans. Here are the final excerpts from the Just Security timeline:

- January 3: "Jennifer Lynn Lawrence, also from Women for America First, tweets to her followers urging them to attend protests on Jan. 6. 'The globalists will not win!' she writes. 'We the People are showing up to defend our way of life & our President who has put America First!'"

- January 4: "On TheDonald.win, a popular pro-Trump forum board, more than 50 percent of top posts that day contain calls for violence in the top five responses, according to Advance Democracy. Users on the forum openly fantasize about storming congressional offices. One user replies to a post on the forum with the comment, 'Stop the steal and execute the "stealers,"' according to The Daily Beast. Similar violent rhetoric is present on the platform Parler."

- January 5: "Trump supporters descend on DC, hosting a roughly eight-hour event at Freedom Plaza. That evening, Trump tweets and posts to Facebook, 'I hope the Democrats, and even more importantly, the weak and ineffective RINO section of the Republican Party, are looking at the thousands of people pouring into DC They won't stand for a landslide election victory to be stolen.' His message is addressed to Republican Senators Mitch McConnell, John Cornyn, and John Thune."

- January 6: "At 8:17 a.m., Trump tweets encouragement to Pence, urging him to overturn the election."

Around noon on January 6, 2021, President Trump addressed thousands of supporters he had gathered on the Ellipse south of the White House. Here are excerpts from the transcript of his speech published by the Associated Press:

All of us here today do not want to see our election victory stolen by emboldened radical-left Democrats, which is what they're doing. And stolen by the fake news media. That's what they've done and what they're doing. We will never give up, we will never concede. . . .

Our country has had enough. We will not take it anymore and that's what this is all about. And to use a favorite term that all of you people really came up with: We will stop the steal. Today I will lay out just some of the evidence proving that we won this election and we won it by a landslide. This was not a close election. . . .

We have come to demand that Congress do the right thing and only count the electors who have been lawfully slated, lawfully slated.

We will not let them silence your voices. We're not going to let it happen, I'm not going to let it happen. (*Audience chants: "Fight for Trump."*) . . .

Take third-world countries. Their elections are more honest than what we've been going through in this country. It's a disgrace. It's a disgrace. . . .

We will not let them silence your voices. We're not going to let it happen, I'm not going to let it happen. (*Audience chants: "Fight for Trump."*)

Now, it is up to Congress to confront this egregious assault on our democracy. And after this, we're going to walk down, and I'll be there with you, we're going to walk down, we're going to walk down. . . .

I know that everyone here will soon be marching over to the Capitol building to peacefully and patriotically make your voices heard.[45]

In truth, the president did not march with the protesters, and they did not peacefully make their voices heard.

Instead, an angry mob, armed with various weapons, violently assaulted the Capitol, forcing entrance into the chambers where members of the U.S. Senate and House of Representatives had gathered to verify the states' electoral vote counts and verify the election of Joe Biden as president. Five people died during the insurrection. The mob succeeded in interrupting the vote count and drove members of Congress to seek refuge until order was restored. Late in the day, Congress resumed its constitutional duty, finished the count, and confirmed Joe Biden's election.

On January 13, 2021, just a week after the insurrection, the House of Representatives impeached President Donald Trump for the second time, this time on the charge "incitement of insurrection." Previously on December 18, 2019, the House had impeached him for "abuse of power" and "obstruction of justice." Whereas no House Republicans voted for impeachment in 2019, ten Republicans joined all Democrats on the 2021 charge of insurrection. On February 9, the Republican Senate began its second trial of the House's impeachment. The Senate acquitted him again on February 13, but seven Republicans joined all Democrats in voting for conviction in 2021.

SUMMARY

On December 19, Trump tweeted: "Big protest in DC on January 6th. Be there, will be wild!" He reminded his followers on January 1 to "Stop The Steal," encouraging them to attend the "BIG Protest Rally in Washington DC." Why did thousands of people from across the United States heed Trump's tweet to uproot their lives, during a pandemic, in the middle of the winter, and storm the nation's Capitol? Why did a thousand people in Jonestown, Guyana, drink a poisoned punch at the command of Reverend James Jones?

In both cases, people demonstrated "exaggerated devotion to a charismatic political, religious, or other leader," which the American Psychological Association defines as characteristic of a personality cult. Reverend Jones was white, but his congregation was multiracial. He scared them with death threats from the Ku Klux Klan and of a U.S.

governmental plan to imprison and gas African Americans. Adopting an idea of the Black Panther leader Huey Newton, Reverend Jones prepared his followers to commit "revolutionary suicide"—if necessary—as an act of defiance.[46] Over nine hundred did as he instructed on November 18, 1978, and died along with their leader. Donald Trump encouraged his followers to help overturn the outcome of a presidential election. Thousands of his devotees defied over two hundred years of democratic tradition and stormed the nation's Capitol in an insurrection on January 6, 2021. While hundreds faced criminal charges and scores were sentenced, thousands remained loyal to Donald Trump.

Two chapters in part 5 conclude this book. Chapter 17, "The Party in Peril," examines how far Trump's personal grip on his voters extends to Republicans holding governmental office and leadership positions in his party. Chapter 18, "A Republican Epiphany," hopes for a restored Republican Party.

V

REPUBLICAN RESTORATION

17

THE PARTY IN PERIL

P art 5 closes with two chapters: this one on the party's status in 2021 and the last on its possible future.

On January 13, 2021, the House of Representatives impeached President Donald Trump for "incitement of insurrection." On January 20, Joe Biden was inaugurated as president of the United States without, according to custom, the presence of the outgoing president, who returned to his Florida home before the ceremony. Trump did not comment on the inauguration via his favorite social media platforms, because he could not. Facebook had denied him access indefinitely on January 7, and Twitter banned him permanently on January 8.[1] The former president was effectively cut off from his favorite means of communicating with his devoted supporters.

TRUMP'S REPUBLICAN CRITICS

Even before Trump's impeachment on January 13, some Republicans questioned his leadership. On January 11, South Dakota senator John Thune stated: "We've got to chart a new course. I think our identity for the past several years now has been built around an individual. And we've got to get back to where it is built on a set of ideas and principles and policies, and I'm sure those conversations will be held." That same day, the GOP strategist Scott Reed said, "I think the Trump brand is close to destroyed," and another strategist, Rick Tyler, elaborated: "Unless the party fully rejects Trump, it will quickly become irrelevant. The type of candidates a Trumpcentric Republican Party will nominate will be easily beaten in most general elections, relegating themselves to being a perpetual minority and regional party."[2]

In 2019, the House of Representatives had impeached President Trump for abuse of power and obstruction of Congress, but the Senate failed to convict him. After the House impeached him a second time for inciting an insurrection, how would the Republican leadership in Congress react to the former president?

Although the Senate Republican leader, Mitch McConnell, had voted against Trump's impeachment, he unexpectedly and forcefully criticized President Trump afterward on the Senate floor, saying in part:

> American citizens attacked their own government. They used terrorism to try to stop a specific piece of democratic business they did not like.
>
> Fellow Americans beat and bloodied our own police. They stormed the Senate floor. They tried to hunt down the Speaker of the House. They built a gallows and chanted about murdering the vice president.
>
> They did this because they had been fed wild falsehoods by the most powerful man on Earth—because he was angry he'd lost an election.
>
> Former President Trump's actions preceding the riot were a disgraceful dereliction of duty.

Many who watched or read McConnell's devastating speech expected him to oppose Donald Trump's attempts to control the party. Also on January 13, the Republican representative and minority leader, Kevin McCarthy, who did not vote to impeach Trump, nevertheless delivered this speech on the House floor: "The President bears responsibility for Wednesday's attack on Congress by mob rioters. He should have immediately denounced the mob when he saw what was unfolding. These facts require immediate action by President Trump, accept his share of respon-sibility, quell the brewing unrest and ensure that President elect Biden is able to successfully begin his term."

Many who watched or read McCarthy's critical speech also expected him to oppose attempts by Donald Trump to control the party, especially since McCarthy supported his colleague Liz Cheney, chair of the Republican Conference, who voted to impeach Trump on January 13. Cheney, the third-highest-ranking Republican in the House, released this statement on her vote: "The President of the United States sum-moned this mob, assembled the mob, and lit the flame of this attack. Everything that followed was his doing. None of this would have hap-pened without the President. The President could have immediately and forcefully intervened to stop the violence. He did not. There has never been a greater betrayal by a President of the United States of his office and his oath to the Constitution."[3]

Given Cheney's damning comments about President Trump, some Republicans in the House sought to oust her as chair of the Republican Conference. They forced Kevin McCarthy to schedule a vote on her retention by secret ballot in a closed meeting on February 2. According to media accounts, Kevin McCarthy defended his deputy against oth-ers who accused her of "aiding the enemy" by criticizing Trump. Cheney won the secret vote by a large margin (reported as 145 to 61), which seemed to signal that Trump's grip on congressional Republicans had loosened.[4]

TRUMP'S REPUBLICAN DEFENDERS

On January 13, Republican Minority Leader Kevin McCarthy criti-cized President Trump by name on the House floor. On February 2, he opposed Liz Cheney's removal from her leadership post for denouncing the president on the House floor. Nevertheless, between those two dates, McCarthy on January 28 traveled to Florida to meet with the president. Although McCarthy had said that President Trump "bears responsibility" for the January 6 attack on the Capitol, McCarthy afterward released a statement saying, "Today, President Trump committed to helping elect Republicans in the House and Senate in 2022."[5] Clearly, the former president still had influence within the Republican Party.

The February 25–28 Conservative Political Action Conference (CPAC) in Florida soon demonstrated the extent of his influence. CPAC invited Donald Trump to speak in the prime spot at the end of the conference. During his ninety-minute speech, Trump promised not to start a new party but claimed that the 2020 election "was rigged, and the Supreme Court and other courts didn't want to do anything about it," to which the crowd repeatedly cheered: "You won. You won. You won. You won."[6] Present at CPAC, Senator Ted Cruz noted, "Donald J. Trump ain't goin' anywhere."[7]

Rank-and-file CPAC attendees expressed to reporters their personal devotion to Donald Trump. One worker at a booth selling Trump merchandise complained about the party: "We're so disgusted by Republicans that, honestly, if Trump's not running, we don't care who wins." Another lifelong Republican claimed that the Lord told her in 2015, "I want you to pray for Donald Trump," and she was "very upset" when "seven Republicans turned on him" to vote for conviction in the Senate. A third person thought that Vice President Pence "let down" his president by presiding over the Electoral College votes.[8]

CPAC is independent of the Republican Party organization, which up to then had not taken a position on the former president. A month later in early April, the National Republican Committee invited him to headline a retreat for party donors in Florida, four miles from Mar-a-Lago. One GOP donor commented: "The venue for the quarterly meeting along with Trump's keynote speech at CPAC shows that the party is still very much in Trump's grip" and that it "doesn't seem to have the ability to hit escape velocity from its former standard-bearer." A former RNC staffer and now Trump critic said that the party had the chance to move on after January 6, "but they didn't choose to do that. This is who the party is."[9]

The last week in April, House Republicans met for their annual retreat, again in Florida. This time, Majority Leader McCarthy and Conference Chair Liz Cheney were on different paths. In keeping with McCarthy's

statement after meeting with Trump on January 28, McCarthy emphasized party unity, working with the former president on the 2022 elections. Cheney urged distancing the party from Trump, arguing that it
was "damaging to perpetuate the notion that in 2020 the election was
stolen."[10] Trump's defenders returned to arguing she should be dethroned
from her House leadership position.

On May 4, Republican Minority Leader Kevin McCarthy, previously
Cheney's defender, told Fox News: "I have heard from members concerned about her ability to carry out the job as conference chair, to
carry out the message."[11] On May 12, House Republicans met for about
fifteen minutes, rejected a request for a recorded vote, and by voice vote
quickly removed Liz Cheney from her leadership position. On May 14,
House Republicans elected the Trump-endorsed representative Elsie Stefanik chair of the Republican Conference. Stefanik stated her view:
"Voters determine the leader of the Republican Party, and Donald Trump
is the leader they look to."[12]

It took almost four months for McCarthy to forget his denunciation
of President Trump for causing the January 6 assault on the Capitol and
to accept Trump's leadership of the Republican Party. In less than two
months, Mitch McConnell, Senate Republican leader, forgot his more
damning denunciation and forgave the former president. When asked
on February 24 whether he would support Donald Trump for election
in 2024, McConnell replied: "the nominee of the party? Absolutely."[13]

PERPLEXED REPUBLICANS

Perplexed Republicans were at a loss to understand what had happened
to their party. Mark Meckler, a former Tea Party leader and conservative activist, confessed his puzzlement: "I'm unaware of a GOP agenda.
I would love to see one. . . . Nobody knows what they're about. They do
this at their own peril."[14]

High-ranking Republican government and party officials began to
speak out. In the last chapter of his 2021 memoir, John Boehner,
speaker of the House from 2011 to 2015, stated: "My Republican

Party—my party of smaller, fairer, more accountable government and not conspiracy theories—had to take back control from the faction that had grown to include everyone from garden-variety whack jobs to insurrectionists. If the conservative movement in the United States was going to survive, there couldn't be room for them. Time will tell how successful that mission will be, but I hope to be able to do my part, even in retirement."[15]

Republican Paul Ryan had replaced Boehner as House speaker in 2015 and served during Trump's election and administration until 2019. Speaking at the Ronald Reagan Presidential Library on May 27, 2021, Ryan avoided mentioning President Trump by name but told the crowd, "If the conservative cause depends on the populist appeal of one personality . . . then we're not going anywhere. Voters looking for Republican leaders want to see independence in metal. They will not be impressed by the sight of yes-men and flatterers flocking to Mar-a-Lago. We win majorities by directing our loyalty and respect to voters and by staying faithful to the conservative principles that unite us."[16]

Speaking at the Ronald Reagan Library on June 24, Republican vice president Mike Pence defended his role in counting the electoral votes that certified Joe Biden's election as president, saying, "I will always be proud to have played a small part on that tragic day when we reconvened the Congress and fulfilled our duty under the Constitution and the laws of the United States."[17]

Other self-identified Republicans or political conservatives publicly disassociated themselves with Donald Trump's administration, including

- Joe Scarborough (host of *Morning Joe*)
- George Will (conservative columnist)
- Max Boot (conservative columnist)
- Richard Painter (Bush ethics lawyer)
- Steve Schmidt (Republican Party strategist and top George W. Bush aide)
- Jennifer Rubin (author of the "Right Turn" blog for *The Washington Post*)

- Bill Kristol (neoconservative political analyst)
- Colin Powell (former U.S. secretary of state)
- Joe Walsh (former representative and radio host)[18]

To some, the problem was more than just Donald Trump; the party itself had a problem by prioritizing winning votes over respecting principles. It was behaving more like a *team* than a *party*. In 2016, before Trump won the party's nomination, some prominent Republicans formed an informal "Never Trump Movement" to stop him from succeeding. Observers across the country thought him unfit for the presidency given his (lack of) experience, temperament, values, and morals. Even the nation's daily newspapers, owned by traditionally conservative publishers, endorsed Hillary Clinton 243 to 20 over Donald Trump.[19] Disregarding Trump's fitness to be president of the United States and de facto leader of the Republican Party, some once-active Trump critics became fervent supporters, for example, Senator Lindsey Graham and Wisconsin governor Scott Walker. Other Republicans fell into line after witnessing Trump's strength among Republican voters.

THE PARTY SURRENDERS TO THE TEAM

Stuart Stevens worked on several high-profile Republican campaigns and was senior strategist to Mitt Romney's 2012 presidential campaign. He left the party after Trump's election and in 2020 published *It Was All a Lie: How the Republican Party Became Donald Trump*, which blamed the party for Trump's presidency:

> There is nothing strange or unexpected about Donald Trump. He is the logical conclusion of what the Republican Party became over the last fifty or so years, a natural product of the seeds of race, self-deception, and anger that became the essence of the Republican Party. Trump isn't an aberration of the Republican Party; he is the Republican Party in a purified form. . . .

In the end, the Republican Party rallied behind Donald Trump because if that was the deal needed to regain power, what was the problem? Because it had always been about power.

The rest? The principles? The values? It was all a lie.[20]

Academics also wrote critically of the current state of the Republican Party. The distinguished historian Lewis Gould authored a series of books on the party's history.[21] His final book, published in 2014, before Trump's presidency, began:

> Republicans took justified pride in their record in the nineteenth century of freeing the slaves and enacting the Reconstruction amendments to the Constitution. Democrats had taken an unduly long time to discard their racist past. In the 1960s and 1970s, however, the parties passed each other in opposite directions. The party of Kennedy and Lyndon Johnson became as identified with the aspirations of African Americans as previous members of their party had been with keeping alive segregation and discrimination. Republicans, for their part, found reasons to champion the cause of white southerners and like-minded northerners in the service of victory at the polls and the opportunity to hold power.[22]

Gould wrote before Donald Trump's 2016 quest for the party's nomination and his campaign for winning the election. Both actions capitalized on Republicans' acceptance of Goldwater's attempt to capture votes from white southerners, which repudiated the party's historical stance on civil rights. In a 2021 personal communication, Professor Gould wrote, "I now believe that the Republican Party I wrote about has ceased to exist."[23]

As Republicans entered its ethnocentrism era, the "Party of Lincoln" became the party of expediency. Stevens wrote in the last chapter of *The Big Lie*: "A political party without a higher purpose is nothing more than a cartel, a syndicate. No one asks what is the greater good OPEC is trying to achieve. Its purpose is to sell oil at the highest prices possible. So it is with today's Republican Party. It is a cartel that exists to elect

Republicans. There is no organized, coherent purpose other than the acquisition and maintenance of power."[24]

Political parties acquire and maintain power in democratic systems by winning elections. In both major parties, their electoral teams are entrusted to campaign for votes within two sets of parameters: party principles and electoral rules. Some party principles are malleable. Electoral teams can skirt or amend them for electoral advantage without altering the party's character. Consider the Republicans' position on the "protective tariff." As discussed in chapter 7, the 1888 Republican platform stated: "We are uncompromisingly in favor of the American system of protection." A century later, the 1980 Republican platform switched position, stating, "The Republican Party believes that protectionist tariffs and quotas are detrimental to our economic well-being." The public in general and Republicans in particular quietly accepted this change in party principles.

Over the years, the Republican Party has changed its policies numerous times. Figure 13.1 in chapter 13 depicted a dozen changes in the party's platforms just since 1924. But the changes that happened in 1964 were different. Having lost the 1960 election and seeking to garner votes from southern whites, who had voted solidly against Republican candidates since the Civil War, the Republican Party backed a strategy that contradicted the party's two founding principles: (1) embracing national authority and (2) ensuring citizens' political rights. In 1952, by contrast, the party had reacted very differently to a series of electoral losses.

In 1952, Republicans ended a string of five consecutive losses in presidential elections (1932 to 1948) by nominating a sure "winner" (General Dwight David Eisenhower), who was less conservative than their ideal candidate. Republicans then chose to be on a winning *team* rather than being in a principled, but losing, *party*. In 1964, Republicans finally selected a staunchly conservative candidate, Barry Goldwater, despite his support of states' rights against national authority, one of the party's founding principles. The convention delegates were undeterred that pundits projected Goldwater to lose to President Lyndon Johnson. They seem to prefer being in a principled losing *party* than on an unprincipled winning *team*.

Goldwater's dedicated followers and Goldwater himself believed that they would win the election *because* of their principled, uncompromising, conservative stance. Frank Annunziata's 1980 article—written close to that period—summarized their reasoning: "Conservative Republicans attributed the party's narrow defeat in 1960 to the party's derivative and imitative liberalism. Millions of conservatives, they claimed, refused to vote because no real choice existed. . . . 'We who are conservatives,' Goldwater commented, 'will stoutly maintain that 1960 was a repeat performance of 1944 and 1948, when we offered the voters insufficient choices.' "[25] Goldwater famously promised to offer voters "a choice, not an echo."[26]

Few knew at the time that Republicans were also changing the politics for winning in future elections. The former Republican strategist Stevens described Barry Goldwater's opposition to the 1964 Civil Rights Act as "the defining moment for the modern Republican Party." The party entered its ethnocentrism era committed to courting southern white voters under the guise of states' rights. As nonwhites increased their share of the electorate, Republicans' appealed more to northern whites. After the party abandoned support for women's rights in 1980, Republicans drew increasing support from Evangelical Christians. As white Christians' share of the electorate declined, so did Republicans' share of the popular vote. Eventually, Republicans chose "to fight the demographic trend of declining white voters by making it more difficult for nonwhite voters, particularly black voters, to participate in the election."[27]

Results of presidential elections since 1952 reveal a sharp change in voting patterns for both parties, but the change is especially stark for the Republican Party. In ten elections, from 1952 to 1988, Republican candidates captured a majority of the popular vote six times—not simply a plurality of the popular vote but a *majority* of it. Whereas in six elections from 1996 to 2020, only once did Republicans win even a plurality of the popular vote. Twice (2000 and 2016) Republican candidates lost the vote but won the presidency by winning the Electoral College. Thus, the party became increasingly dependent on electoral votes from less populated southern, central, and plains states, where white Christians predominated. The percentage of the two-party vote for presidential candidates is given in figure 17.1, along with the leading percentage for third-party candidates.

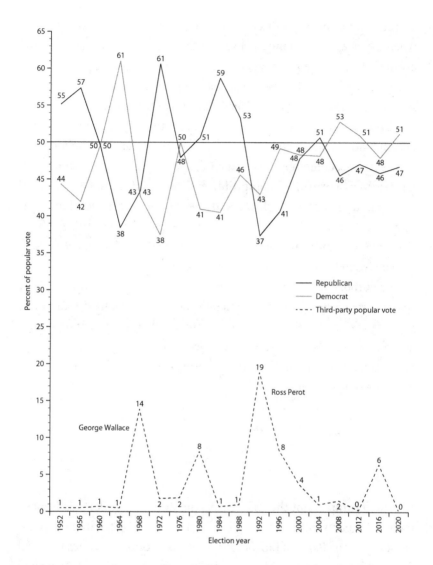

FIGURE 17.1. Parties' percent of popular vote, 1952–2020.

Note: Democrats won a plurality of the popular vote in five of six elections (1996–2020) and a majority three times. Since 1992, Republicans won a plurality (and majority) of the popular vote only in 2004.

The Republican Party discredited its reputation in the 1960s. That was when it turned from being the Party of Lincoln, using the national government to advance political equality and provide public goods, to the Party of Goldwater, leveraging states' rights to impede social equality. Already in 2012, two distinguished scholars at the conservative American Enterprise Institute acknowledged that the Republican Party had become "an insurgent outlier" in our two-party system. It was "ideologically extreme; contemptuous of the inherited social and economic policy regime; scornful of compromise; unpersuaded by conventional understanding of facts, evidence, and science; and dismissive of the legitimacy of its political opposition. When one party moves this far from the center of American politics, it is extremely difficult to enact policies responsive to the country's most pressing challenges."[28]

The authors issued that judgment in a book published in 2012. They renewed it in a revised 2016 edition published before Donald Trump was elected president. They are unlikely to change their judgment now, after Trump became the first president to reject electoral defeat yet enjoy support from a majority of Republican members of Congress and Republican state officeholders across the country.

SUMMARY

Donald Trump is not the sole reason the Republican Party is in peril today. The party entered its perilous state in 1964 by trading its moral authority as the Party of Lincoln for votes from southern whites who had fought for generations against Lincoln's party. In 1877, Republicans had negotiated a similar trade, when Rutherford Hayes ended Reconstruction in the South to win the disputed 1876 election. Hayes's act reneged on Republicans' commitment to political equality for the former slaves, but it was not a complete betrayal. Nonetheless, the party signaled to what lengths it might go to hold on to the presidency, to retain power.

Whereas Hayes made a self-serving bargain to retain the presidency in 1877, Republicans in 1964 traded away the party's founding principles for Goldwater's "Southern Strategy." Seeking to win national elections by converting the previously Democratic "solid South" into their own bastion, Republicans reversed both their commitment to national authority over state authority and their embracement of political equality. The Republican Party in its ethnocentrism era became a fundamentally different party from the Grand Old Party during its nationalism epoch. The change repelled many lifelong Republican officials, activists, and dedicated conservatives.

Before the 1932 election, a majority of American voters favored Republican candidates in national elections. Afterward, more voters identified themselves as Democrats than as Republicans. After World War II, Republicans overcame their numerical disadvantage in the electorate by nominating popular figures, such as General Dwight Eisenhower and the actor Ronald Reagan, or by benefiting from unpopular Democratic nominees, such as Hubert Humphrey and Hillary Clinton.

Although Goldwater's Southern Strategy failed miserably for him in 1964, it worked well enough to narrowly elect Richard Nixon in 1968, to produce Nixon's smashing reelection in 1972, and to generate huge victories by Reagan in 1980 and 1984. By the 1990s, however, demographic changes began to undermine the party's dependence on white Christian voters, as nonwhites and non-Christians grew in the electorate. Nevertheless, the white Christian tank retained enough gas for Donald Trump to extract an electoral vote victory in 2016. The fuel level dropped in 2020, and he failed to secure reelection.

Some prominent Republicans left the party in protest over Donald Trump's nomination in 2016. More left after his election and still more because of his actions as president of the United States—especially his failure to concede defeat in the 2020 election. Additional Republican leaders disassociated themselves from the party after Trump incited supporters to storm the Capitol on January 6, 2021, to prevent certifying Joe Biden's election. This is the status of the Republican Party in 2021:

- It remains the minority party in its share of party identifiers in the electorate.

- Its core constituency, white voters, has continued to decline as a share of the electorate.
- It suffered having some Republicans in Congress vote to impeach or convict their own president for "inciting an insurrection."
- Its former president experienced new lows in approval, falling to 39 percent in a June 2020 Gallup poll, with 57 percent disapproving his performance.
- Its congressional leadership still professes allegiance to the former president.
- Its Republican identifiers profess more loyalty to Donald Trump personally than to their party.

Being led by a twice-impeached, unpopular former president and being criticized by prominent party leaders who fear for the party's future, the Republican Party is a party in peril. Despite—or perhaps because of—its perilous state, the party poses a danger to American democracy.

18

A REPUBLICAN EPIPHANY

GOP stands for "Grand Old Party" and is synonymous with "Republican Party." In fact, the website of the Republican National Committee is www.gop.com. Writers usually fix the first usage of "Grand Old Party" in the 1870s, but an 1868 item in the *Chicago Tribune* praised "the grand old Republican party" for carrying on the war, putting down the rebellion, making soldiers of colored men, freeing them, and granting their citizenship.[1] Lincoln lived in Illinois, so the *Chicago Tribune* often ran articles about the GOP's accomplishments, like this one in 1879:

> Col Ricaby came up and thanked the Convention for the complement paid him, coming as it did from the Chicago representatives of the *grand old party* which erased the blighting stain of slavery from the national escutcheon, and the *grand old party* which would never cease its aggressive action until every American citizen,—white, red, black, or yellow,—no matter what his creed or nationality, should be permitted to walk forth as a man and exercise his right of conscience in his political views independently of rifle-clubs, mobs, or ex-rebels. (Great applause.)[2]

Many other contemporary items in the *Chicago Tribune* reflected the GOP's themes of national authority and political equality during the party's nationalism epoch.

Today, those words do not fit the Republican Party, a party in peril yet a party we need. Peggy Noonan, President Reagan's speechwriter, in a 2021 *Wall Street Journal* column conceded that "the party is split, if not shattered," but said, "America Needs the GOP, and It Needs Help." She continued: "It is worth saving, even from itself. At its best it has functioned as a friend and protector of liberty, property, speech and religious rights, an encourager of a just and expansive civic life, a defender of the law, without which we are nothing, and the order it brings, so that regular people can feel as protected on the streets as kings."[3] Noonan argued against trying to start a new party, saying, "Two parties are better for the country, and better for Democrats. A strong Republican party keeps them on their toes. As Oscar Hammerstein once said, 'liberals need conservatives to hold them back and conservatives need liberals to pull them forward.'"

Unlike Hammerstein, a musical impresario who won multiple Tony and Academy awards, I am a nationally unknown academic. Nevertheless, I am devoted to studying political parties, find merit in Hammerstein's aphorism, and agree with Peggy Noonan. While other European democracies function well with multiple political parties, our democratic form of government and constitutional framework require having two major parties responsibly engaged across the country in competitive elections.[4] Geoffrey Kabaservice wrote, "One of the likeliest ways America might in fact be destroyed would be if one of its two major parties were rendered dysfunctional."[5]

THE PARTY ORGANIZATION TRIES

Kabaservice also thought that while the Republican Party had "cut itself off from its own history, and indeed has become antagonistic to most of its own heritage," millions of moderate Republicans and millions of other voters "would vote for moderate Republican candidates if they could find them."[6] Even in the 2000s, former national chairs of the Republican National Committee under George W. Bush worried about the party's future in a changing electorate. Kenneth Mehlman (2005–2007) warned: "America is every day less of a white country. We rely too hard on white guys for votes," and Edward Gillespie (2007–2009) said, "Our majority already rests too heavily on white voters, given that current demographic voting percentages will not allow us to hold our majority in the future."[7]

Republican leaders thought similarly in 2013 and took action, seeking to strengthen the party by ending its ethnocentric slant. Reince Priebus, chairman of the Republican National Committee, confronted the facts: In 2008, 53 percent of the voters elected Democratic candidate Barack Obama president; in 2012, Obama was reelected with a smaller absolute majority of the popular vote but 62 percent of the electoral vote. Responding to these Republican losses, the RNC launched what leaders called their Growth and Opportunity Project:[8]

> Following the 2012 Election, the American people sent a clear message that *it was time for the Republican Party to grow.* In response, Chairman Priebus issued an assessment of the party by the Growth and Opportunity Project task force. Reaching out to hundreds of party leaders and grassroots activists across the country, the task force issued a list of recommendations to the RNC to help pave a path to victory. This project is an ongoing commitment to get input from people all across the country on ways to grow our party.[9]

Chairman Priebus charged the GOP group with "making recommendations and assisting in putting together a plan to grow the Party and improve Republican campaigns. We were asked to dig deep to provide an honest review of the 2012 election cycle and a path forward for the Republican Party to ensure success in winning more elections."[10]

The project's authors met with thousands of people "both outside Washington and inside the Beltway"; spoke with "voters, technical experts, private sector officials, Party members, and elected office holders"; conducted polls; and consulted pollsters before issuing its hundred-page report.[11] It began by noting: "Republicans have lost the popular vote in five of the last six presidential elections."[12] A section titled

"America Looks Different" urged the party to recognize "the nation's demographic changes":

> In 1980, exit polls tell us that the electorate was 88 percent white. In 2012, it was 72 percent white. Hispanics made up 7 percent of the electorate in 2000, 8 percent in 2004, 9 percent in 2008 and 10 percent in 2012. According to the Pew Hispanic Center, in 2050, whites will be 47 percent of the country while Hispanics will grow to 29 percent and Asians to 9 percent.
>
> If we want ethnic minority voters to support Republicans, we have to engage them and show our sincerity.[13]

A section titled "Demographic Partners" began:

> The Republican Party must focus its efforts to earn new supporters and voters in the following demographic communities: Hispanic, Asian and Pacific Islanders, African Americans, Indian Americans, Native Americans, women, and youth. . . .
>
> *Unless the RNC gets serious about tackling this problem, we will lose future elections; the data demonstrates this.* In both 2008 and 2012, President Obama won a combined 80 percent of the votes of all minority voters, including not only African Americans but also Hispanics, Asians, and others. The minority groups that President Obama carried with 80 percent of the vote in 2012 are on track to become a majority of the nation's population by 2050. Today these minority groups make up 37 percent of the population, and they cast a record 28 percent of the votes in the 2012 presidential election, according to the election exit polls, an increase of 2 percentage points from 2008. We have to work harder at engaging demographic partners and allies.
>
> By 2050, the Hispanic share of the U.S. population could be as high as 29 percent, up from 17 percent now. The African American proportion of the population is projected to rise slightly to 14.7 percent, while the Asian share is projected to increase to approximately 9 percent from its current 5.1 percent. Non-Hispanic whites, 63 percent of the current

population, will decrease to half or slightly less than half of the population by 2050.[14]

The added emphasis in the second paragraph shows that the RNC understood the party was headed toward permanent minority status. Unfortunately, the Republican National Committee, the top party organ, had no control over who would seek the party's nomination and where its nominee would drive the party.

On June 16, 2015, Donald Trump announced his candidacy for the Republican presidential nomination, during which he said: "When Mexico sends its people, they're not sending their best. They're sending people that have lots of problems, and they're bringing those problems with us. They're bringing drugs. They're bringing crime. They're rapists. And some, I assume, are good people."[15] If candidate Trump knew about the RNC's advice to "show our sincerity" to "ethnic minority voters," he did not take it. Instead, he explicitly flaunted its recommendations and appealed directly to the dwindling white portion of the American electorate. Nonetheless, Reince Priebus, who sponsored the study, backed Trump's ethnocentric campaign strategy. Trump won the 2016 presidential election, and Priebus became his first chief of staff. The long and expensive RNC report was later purged from the national committee's website.[16]

HUNTING FOR VOTERS IN 1964

In 1964, Barry Goldwater proposed "to go hunting where the ducks were." According to Joseph Aistrup's *The Southern Strategy Revisited*, Goldwater aimed for the "strongly ideological, racially motivated white conservatives." Aistrup described his Southern Strategy as "merely an attempt to attract states rights voters to the Republican party."[17] Viewed from that perspective, Goldwater simply sought a victory for the Republican electoral *team*—not to reverse the basic principles of the Republican Party. However, Aistrup also wrote, "Republican heavyweights such as former RNC chair Meade Alcorn and New York Senator Jacob Javits felt the party should not abandon its historic commitment to civil rights to win the votes of Southern segregationists, and Republican Senator John Sherman Cooper believed it would deny constitutional and human rights of our citizens."[18] In retrospect, Goldwater failed in achieving his electoral objective but succeeded in jettisoning his party's principles.

The 2013 RNC report urged "efforts to earn new supporters and voters"—that is, hunting for new ducks. Instead, Donald Trump chose to double down on ethnocentrism. Candidate Trump foresaw that he just might win by exploiting his showmanship and marketing himself to the dwindling but still numerous white Christians in the electorate as their Great White Hope. Against the odds, he won in 2016, drawing enough votes from supporters in less populous states for an electoral vote majority. In 2020, Goldwater's 1964 Faustian bargain expired. Demographic changes had already returned the former capital of the Confederacy, Virginia, to the Democratic column in 2008. In 2020, another Confederate state, Georgia, voted Democratic, as did previously reliably Republican Arizona, Goldwater's home state.

By concluding that "it was time for the Republican Party to grow," the 2013 RNC report relied on established theory about how two-party politics operated in America. In most U.S. elections, candidates need only a simple plurality of votes to win. In some countries, such as France, candidates must win a majority for election to office. Our plurality rule, dubbed "first-past-the-post," tends to produce two-party competition. Any third party that falls short of winning pluralities gains nothing for its effort, thus discouraging the creation of third parties. That leaves the two largest parties competing for votes from a common electorate. Theoretically, each party would propose policies designed to attract more voters than the other party. As stated in chapter 2, their platforms typically promise direct benefits in the form of Public Goods or indirect benefits packaged as Freedom, Order, or Equality.

Arguably, our party system operated that way up to the middle of the twentieth century. Republicans and Democrats campaigned by telling voters how their economic, social, and foreign policies would benefit the country generally and them personally. Both parties, according to theory, sought votes from the middle of the electorate, and thus the parties converged in their policies. They competed mainly over Public Goods: who would get what from government and at what costs. Typically, Democrats offered people more benefits but higher taxes. Republicans countered by proposing lower taxes but fewer benefits. With the parties thus engaged in bargaining with the electorate, compromises on all sides were possible. This thumbnail account oversimplifies the situation but echoes Peggy Noonan's description.

In 1964, Republican leaders changed the competitive dynamics by campaigning against granting rights to a racial minority. Their actions resurrected the existential issue that provoked the Civil War. Then in 1980, Republican activists created a new existential issue by opposing equal rights for women, causing some to fear that they would never be viewed as equal to men. Some white Christians countered that granting equal rights for women would erode their culture. Unlike disagreements over Public Goods, disagreement on existential issues discourages electoral bargaining, which party theory would argue precludes rational behavior.

The first three columns in figure 18.1 plot the 2012 poll data that confronted the 2013 RNC report authors. They already knew that Democrats had enjoyed an edge in party identification since the 1930s. Seeing that

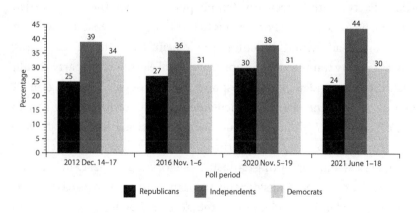

FIGURE 18.1. Gallup poll report of party identification, 2012–2021.

Source: Gallup, https://news.gallup.com/poll/15370/party-affiliation.aspx.

Democrats in 2012 led by almost 10 percentage points, they rationally concluded it was "time for the Republican Party to grow."

However, figure 18.1 also revealed that by November 2016 the Democratic advantage had declined from nine to four points. By November 2020, the parties were neck and neck. Perhaps their 2013 analysis and remedy were incorrect. Perhaps Trump was right in doubling down on an ethnocentric strategy. He lost in 2020, but perhaps he could win again in 2024. Legions of Republicans still pledged him their support. On June 26, 2021, in Wellington, Ohio, thousands of Trump's faithful flocked to his first rally since leaving office. They cheered when he lashed out at the ten Republican House members who had voted to impeach him and chastised Vice President Mike Pence for failing to stop the electoral vote count.[19] No one could tell whether Trump would run again in 2024 or what influence he would have in determining the Republican nominee.

HUNTING FOR VOTERS AFTER 2016

Notwithstanding the electoral success of former president Trump in 2016, party theory still supports the 2013 RNC prescription for the Republican Party's path to recovery. Simply put, even then the party needed to look beyond its base. For reasons to be discussed in what follows, that was easy to advise but difficult to implement. Nevertheless, assuming that the party wants to win future presidential elections, the party should rethink how independents respond to its policies. Look again at figure 18.1 for the share of independents, who constitute from 38 to 45 percent of the electorate. True, independents are less likely to vote in presidential elections than those who identify as Republicans or Democrats, but, excepting landslide victories, independents always decide the outcome. Consider the partisan sources of votes cast for the major presidential candidates in the 2016 and 2020, as displayed in figure 18.2.[20]

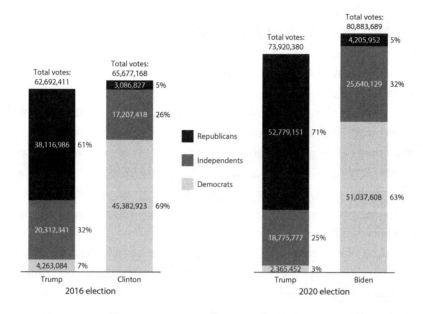

FIGURE 18.2. Partisan sources of presidential votes, 2016 and 2020.

Figure 18.2 reveals that if the 2016 and 2020 presidential elections were decided *only* by Republicans and Democrats voting for their parties' candidates, *both* winning candidates would have lost. In 2016, over 7 million more Democrats voted for Clinton than Republicans voted for Trump. Yet Clinton lost. In 2020, 1.6 million more Republicans voted for Trump than Democrats voted for Biden. Yet Trump lost.

Donald Trump won in 2016 by getting an estimated 3,104,923 more votes from independents than Clinton. Joe Biden won in 2020 by getting an estimated 6,864,353 more votes from independent voters than Trump. Clearly, independents decided the outcome of both presidential elections. From a theoretically rational prospective, the Republican Party should do more to court independent voters in the electorate. Unfortunately for the party and the country, rational Republicans are hampered in appealing broadly to independent voters in the electorate given the narrow concerns of the party's "selectorate."

THE ELECTORATE VERSUS THE SELECTORATE

Political scientists distinguish between the *electorate*, the enfranchised citizens who choose which candidates are elected to government office, and the *selectorate*, the party activists who select the candidates presented for the electorate's decision. While nations differ somewhat in how they define eligible voters, countries differ far more in how they select party candidates for election. In the United States, both parties follow candidate selection laws that give local party activists great power. Winning votes in the electorate is very different from getting chosen by the selectorate. One cross-national study put it this way: "In U.S. primary elections, voters may select congressional nominees without reference to what any higher party organization might prefer. This is candidate selection at its most purely inclusive and decentralized."[21]

The Republican National Committee has no control over the Republican selectorate nationwide. State laws define how both parties select their candidates, which they usually do though primary election. Across the country, Republicans vote in primary elections to nominate Republican candidates for general elections to the U.S. House or Senate and to select Republican convention delegates to nominate the party's presidential candidate. As of 2021, Donald Trump appears to exercise considerable control over how his tribe/cult votes in Republican primaries. If he continues to promote ethnocentric policies, the Republican selectorate is unlikely to increase the party's share of the electorate.

As party polarization increased during the twenty-first century, academics began to examine conditions for rational behavior in the context of tribe/cult politics. Patir, Dreyfuss, and Shayo described such politics as "the existence of a set of voters whose overriding concern is 'who is with us and who is against us' and who support candidates representing their ethnic, religious, or national group whatever the policy they promote."[22] Consistent with research on tribes, they note that "individuals do not identify with a group simply because they belong to it. People are more likely to identify with their group if it provides them with a sense of pride or 'status.' "[23] Typically, they said, tribal politics is rooted in "the middle and lower ranks of the socioeconomic distribution," and "non-tribal regimes are characterized by centrist policies, catering to the median voter in society as a whole, whereas tribal regimes are typically characterized by more extreme policies."

If a party's policies appeal mainly to its partisans, it is not catering to the "median voter"—that is, the one in the middle, the average voter. Wherever the median voter stands on an issue, the position is likely to be among independents, not partisans. Rational political parties in a two-party system try to propose policies that fit its basic principles (satisfying its partisans) while also appealing to independent voters. That the Republican Party has captured a plurality of the popular vote for president only once (2004) in eight elections since 1992 suggests that it has campaigned to the Republican selectorate and not to the American electorate. That contradicts the origin and history of the Grand Old Party.

DEMEANING GOVERNMENT

This book's subtitle refers to Republicans in 1860 as the "Governing Party," and Abraham Lincoln famously promised "government of the people, by the people, for the people" in his 1863 Gettysburg Address. Over the next century, the GOP largely practiced popular government as Lincoln proposed. However, the book's subtitle contends that by 2020 Republicans had evolved into an antigovernment party. Readers might wonder whether antigovernment tribe or cult more accurately described its organizational form in 2020. Neither: Republicans existed as a party alongside their partisan tribe and Trump cult. The GOP still fits the definition of a political party as stated in chapter 1. It is an organization whose goal is *to place its avowed representatives in government positions.* The GOP nominates candidates for elections to local, state, and national offices across the country. It remains a political party, but one with very different principles.

Founded in 1854 to oppose the spread of slavery, the 1860 Republican Party won every northern state except New Jersey, fought to maintain the Union, ended slavery, freed the slaves, and made them citizens. While fighting the Civil War, Republicans funded the creation of land-grant colleges and the construction of a transcontinental railroad. Subsequent Republican administrations established the Interstate Commerce Commission to regulate railroads, enacted the Sherman Anti-Trust Act to preserve economic competition, the Pure Food and Drug Act to prohibit the sale of adulterated food and drugs, and undertook building a canal across the Isthmus of Panama. Republicans created the National Forest Service and the first national parks. Republicans introduced legislation leading to a national income tax, regulation of child labor, and the establishment of an eight-hour day for workers. The Republican Party was a governing party throughout its nationalism epoch. If I'd lived then, I'd choose to be a Republican rather than aligning with Democrats and their racist southern wing.

Today, Republicans fly the libertarian banner of freedom from government. As stated in chapter 1, "to govern" means "to control." All government requires surrendering some freedoms; only anarchy elevates freedom above government. Democratic government entrusts voters to decide how much Freedom they are willing to trade for Order, Equality, and Public Goods. During their nationalism epoch, Republicans won elections on party platforms that promoted all three values at the cost of certain freedoms. As "the Party of Lincoln," Republicans then were governing "for the people."

In accepting the 1964 Republican presidential nomination, Barry Goldwater extolled the virtue of "freedom under a government limited by laws of nature and of nature's God." He saw strict limits on what governments could do. In Goldwater's book *The Conscience of a Conservative*, he even viewed employee retirement insurance as infringing on freedom. He wrote, "The government takes 6% of most payrolls in Social Security Taxes and thus compels millions of individuals to postpone until later years their enjoyment of wealth they might otherwise enjoy today."[24] President Ronald Reagan's 1981 inaugural address echoed Goldwater's view. Reagan said, "Government is not the solution to our problem, government is the problem."[25] In his news conference on August 12,

1986, Reagan quipped: "The nine most terrifying words in the English language are: 'I'm from the Government, and I'm here to help.'"[26]

While claiming to be antigovernment, the Republican Party's 2016 platform also says it is *a party of law and order*. It favors imposing harsh sentences for drug offenses, executing prisoners for capital crimes, and building walls to keep out immigrants. It also supports laws that force women to give birth to unwanted children, that keep schools from teaching about racial discrimination, and that prevent businesses and schools from requiring face masks to prevent spreading the COVID-19 virus. In a contradictory or hypocritical way, the antigovernment party relies a lot on government when politically expedient. Consider mandatory vaccination laws. They originated in the early nineteenth century and were upheld by the Supreme Court in 1905. Republicans in power then accepted mandated vaccinations against smallpox; Republicans in power in 2021 opposed requiring vaccinations to stop a resurgence of the COVID-19 pandemic.[27]

Rational parties in a two-party system compete for voters by promising government benefits. Typically, parties propose and dicker over providing and funding Public Goods. Republicans did this successfully during their nationalism epoch up to the 1920s but stopped during their neoliberalism epoch of antistatism and free-market capitalism. They surrendered the tax-and-spend strategy to Democrats, who won voter support over the decades for such government programs as Social Security, Medicare, minimum wages, health care expansion, and Head Start. Social Security became so popular that politicians called it the "third rail" of American politics: "touch it, and you will die." Medicare was similarly embraced; one conservative warned her bemused Republican congressman, "Keep your government hands off my Medicare."[28]

Some Republicans see the party replacing the Democratic Party as the voting home for blue-collar workers. Missouri senator Josh Hawley declared on Twitter, "We are a working class party now. That's the future."[29] In the past, "blue collar" referred to many millions of voters with good-paying jobs. Today, it refers to far fewer voters with poorly paying jobs. Republican presidential candidates, Donald Trump in particular, won support from this dwindling group by feeding them cultural benefits—by attacking minorities and immigrants. Republican candidates who decried losing manufacturing jobs in America neglected to mention that Republicans' core principles of free trade and economic freedom led to making goods abroad and buying foreign products. Also, few Republicans favored spending money on government programs to help the poor and unemployed, relying instead on laws that propped up Republican cultural values. Carlos Curbelo, a former Republican congressman from Florida, said, "Eventually, if you don't take action to improve people's quality of life, they will abandon you."[30] A researcher at a conservative think tank said that using the state "to directly affect the economic well-being of Americans" was very difficult for Republicans.[31]

CONCLUSION

Chapters 6 through 13 in part 2 reviewed hundreds of planks in the quadrennial platforms of the Republican Party since its founding. Those chapters detailed how the "Party of Lincoln"—a governing party—evolved into an antigovernment party. Once a champion of national authority and political equality, the Republican Party in 1964 deliberately reversed its positions, advocating states' rights and defending racial inequities. In effect, the party traded its founding principles for votes from southern whites. By 1980, it sank further into social inequality, trading women's rights for votes from Evangelical Christians.

The 1964 story involved more than just winning votes. Republicans knowingly selected a candidate, Barry Goldwater, who *believed* in states' rights and thought that national government should *not* enforce racial equality. The Grand Old Party lost its way on principles in 1964 and has continued going in a different direction since. The book by Amy Fried and Douglas Harris describes at length how the Republican Party "from Goldwater to Trump" has been *At War with Government*.[32]

Because chapters 6 through 13 only dealt with party planks concerning government policy, it did not report this passage that appeared in the Republican Party's 2016 platform and was readopted in 2020: "The next president must restore the public's trust in law enforcement and civil order by first adhering to the rule of law himself. Additionally, the next president must not sow seeds of division and distrust between the police and the people they have sworn to serve and protect. The Republican Party, a party of law and order, must make clear in words and action that every human life matters."

Running on that platform, Trump was elected president in 2016. When he ran again in 2020 but lost, he did not adhere to the rule of law and accept his loss. Instead, he sowed "seeds of division and distrust" among the people—against the promise in the 2020 Republican Party platform.

To make their party Grand again, Republicans must experience a collective epiphany, a revelation, a widespread admission that they are no longer the historic "party of Lincoln" but a reactionary rear-guard against social change. Former Republican speaker John Boehner once saw his party standing for "smaller, fairer, more accountable government." By 2021, he awakened to realize that it was controlled by a "faction that had grown to include everyone from garden-variety whack jobs to insurrectionists."[33] Other Republicans need to wake up and take action to restore the GOP as a truly democratic party in a two-party system.

That can be done, but only Republicans can do it. As described in chapter 14, the Democratic Party accomplished something comparable in 1948, when its convention adopted its first civil rights plank over the objections of its powerful southern wing. The 1948 Democratic civil rights plank was proposed by a young Hubert Humphrey, whose biographer wrote: "Democratic Senate minority leader Scott Lucas of Illinois, who called Humphrey a 'pipsqueak,' warned him that his action would 'split the party wide open' and 'kill any chance of Democratic victory in November,' and Rhode Island senator J. Howard McGrath threatened, 'This will be the end of you.'"[34]

The plank *did* split the party, southern delegations *did* walk out of the convention, and the party *did* lose the votes of white southerners. In the

1948 election, President Truman lost four southern states, but he still won—and Democrats had ended their tacit support of racism. The party "did the right thing" again in 1964, when President Lyndon Johnson backed the Civil Rights Act, fully expecting it to cost the party in the South, which it did, with Republicans stepping in to win southern votes. By embracing ethnocentrism, Republicans won a string of presidential elections. It profited electorally as it discarded its principles.

The party scholar John Kenneth White likened the GOP's electoral situation as an "imprisonment" that the party can escape only by undergoing a "metamorphosis."[35] Major costs would be incurred in remaking the party. In October 2021, two former Republican officeholders published an op-ed piece in the *New York Times* proposing that they along with other Republicans opposed to Trump "form an alliance with Democrats" to defeat Trump-backed Republican candidates.[36] Although these prominent Republican leaders publicly backed an electoral strategy to discredit Trump indirectly, who will challenge him directly in the party organization?

Who will emerge as the Republican heroes to restore the Grand Old Party as the governing "Party of Lincoln" that led social change in America? Who will return the GOP to being a democratic party, one that accepts electoral outcomes and participates responsibly in legislative politics? Who will remake the party to be truly conservative and not just reactionary? Who will help the GOP regain its modern role in our two-party system to stand for fairer, smaller, more accountable government against a Democratic Party left free to spend without respectable opposition? Who will lead Republicans out of its ethnocentrism era and into one of genuine conservatism? Who will head the Republican epiphany?

EPILOGUE

The Next Republican Era

What might result from a Republican epiphany? In the first paragraph of my introduction to this book, I wrote, "More than fifty years of research and writing on democracy and party politics have convinced me that no nation can practice democratic government in the absence of a responsible, competitive party system. Given its constitutional structure, the United States cannot endure as a democracy without two major parties—two parties that compete for popular votes, accept election outcomes, and govern responsibly."

The United States needs a vigorous Republican Party to challenge an energetic Democratic Party over how government should promote the Public Good—defined in chapter 2 as actions that benefit the public. The parties' electoral competition should extend across the nation into every state and into all areas within each state. Both parties should be inclusive in attracting partisans, and they should adopt policies that appeal to independent voters. Above all, democracy requires government to encourage all citizens to vote and both parties to abide by electoral decisions, resulting in the peaceful transfer of power.

Today, neither party competes adequately across and within the nation. Democrats appeal more to metropolitan residents in populous states, while Republicans count more on residents living outside urban areas in states with fewer people. Since the 1960s, the parties have diverged even more in their partisan composition. In an earlier book, *A Tale of Two Parties*, I documented differences in the social bases of Democratic and Republican partisans since 1952.[1] Simply put, the Republican Party has not attracted substantial numbers of minority social groups to identify as Republicans. Since 1952, Republican partisans have been overwhelmingly white and Christian. Seven decades ago, white Christians constituted a majority of the electorate. Today, they are in the minority.

More disturbing for democracy is that most Republican partisans and party leaders refuse to accept that its presidential candidate lost the 2020 election. Donald Trump's unprecedented denial of the outcome led to his supporters' January 6, 2021, "Stop the Steal" assault on the U.S. Capitol during Congress' official count of electoral votes. A national survey in May 2021, six months after the 2020 election, found that "56% of Republicans believe the election was rigged or the result of illegal voting, and 53% think Donald Trump is the actual President, not Joe Biden."[2] While some Republican governmental leaders, most notably Wyoming representative Liz Cheney, denounced Donald Trump's failure to concede losing, most Republican members of Congress failed to do so.

Democracy cannot succeed anywhere if candidates do not accept election results. If the Republican Party intends to function as a responsible, democratic party in the future, it must remake itself into one. It should become socially inclusive instead of ethnocentric. Like the former "Party of Lincoln," it should return to being authentically conservative instead of archaically reactionary. Instead of trying to resurrect a former society, it should work to improve the current one by using powers of government institutions for the Public Good.

" 'Conservatism' is a word whose usefulness is matched only by its capacity to confuse, distort, and irritate."[3] That is how Clinton Rossiter, the distinguished historian and political scientist, began his lengthy entry in the *International Encyclopedia of the Social Sciences*. Despite the term's many uses, Rossiter asserted that "an ordered, constitutional society" was the core value that "in the most meaningful sense" defined conservative parties.[4] He also distinguished conservatism from being reactionary, describing "reaction as the position of men who sigh for the past more intensively than they celebrate the present and who feel that a retreat back to it is worth trying."[5] Conservative principles motivated antislavery citizens to govern together as Republicans. They sought constitutional means to combat a present threat and to ensure future social and economic progress.

The Republican Party was formed in 1854 to impose order on the various states concerning the spread of slavery. After the Civil War, the party imposed constitutional government across the United States, developed the nation's economy, and advanced its society. The GOP was a conservative party that employed government power to promote and preserve political and social institutions. It served the national community by generating Public Goods. Throughout the nineteenth century, the Republican Party flourished during what was defined in chapter 4 as its *nationalism* era.

By the end of the first quarter of the twentieth century, however, Republicans began to elevate the value of individual freedom over governmental order. From the late 1920s to the early 1960s, party principles evolved from a conservatism that promoted nationalism and Public Goods to a classical liberal conservatism steeped in economic freedom. The Republican Party entered its *neoliberalism* era during these decades, as Democrats almost completely shut Republicans out of the presidency. Under President Dwight Eisenhower's administration, however, key governmental programs—for example, the interstate highway system—resembled those of the party's nationalism period.

Beginning with Barry Goldwater's presidential campaign in 1964, the Republican Party turned 180 degrees away from national authority (the key principle of the Republican Party's nationalism era) and toward states' rights (the key principle of the Democratic Party after the Civil War). That reversal led to the Republican Party's entrance into its era of *ethnocentrism*. Moreover, Goldwater inverted the priorities of "order" and "freedom" on the conservative scale of values. Government's role in maintaining order became subservient to preserving freedom. Understanding this development requires some historical background.

The original dilemma of government concerned the tradeoff between two abstract values.[6] "Order" through government had always been the goal of political conservatives, who valued strong government. "Freedom" from government restrictions was the objective of their political opponents—deemed "liberals" at the time. Then in the latter half of the nineteenth century, "Equality"—distinct from Freedom—emerged as a cherished political value. Today, Equality's advocates are widely recognized as liberals, while Freedom's advocates have been mistakenly labeled as conservatives.

In truth, government action is required to achieve both Order and Equality in a society. Neither value can be secured without government intervention. Freedom, in contrast, comes merely from blocking government. Libertarians differ from anarchists mainly in the extent they demand Freedom from government. Both groups are philosophical opposites of conservatives. Today's media describe the many Republicans in the House Freedom Caucus as "extreme" conservatives. More accurately, Freedom Caucus members are libertarian, not conservative at all.

The inherent conflict between the values of Order and Freedom poses a conundrum for the Republican Party, composed of avowed conservatives and avowed libertarians. Goldwater himself struggled with the value contradiction. In one place he proposed balancing the values: "The Conservative looks upon politics as the art of achieving the maximum amount of freedom for individuals that is consistent with the maintenance of the social order." On the next page he seems to have made his value choice, saying, "the Conservative's first concern will always be: *Are we maximizing freedom?*"[7] Perhaps his 1960 book, titled *The Conscience of a Conservative*, should have been titled "The Conscience of a Libertarian."[8]

The Republican Party today espouses incompatible principles and undemocratic politics. Libertarians in the Freedom Caucus constitute an organized faction that opposes policies proposed by the majority of Republican conservatives. Many Republicans up for election fail to acknowledge that Democrat Joe Biden was duly elected president, fearing retaliation from his defeated opponent, Donald Trump. The former president, widely recognized as the party leader, has already attacked Republican Senate Leader Mitch McConnell, who blamed Trump for the

January 6 assault on Congress. The party is split ideologically and politically.

For decades, the Democratic Party was also split ideologically and politically between its northern and southern wings. In southern states, the party was dominated by racism, and southern Democrats in the U.S. House and Senate often voted with conservative Republicans. In 1948, the Democratic Party experienced its own epiphany and adopted its first civil rights plank. The party remade itself by following a more coherent philosophy oriented to equality.

How should the GOP remake itself? That is for Republicans to decide. I am not a Republican, but I offer these suggestions:

- Disavow Donald Trump's claim that he won the election and avow the integrity of our highly decentralized system of counting and reporting election returns. Reaffirm the Republican Party's long held democratic credentials.

- Consider returning to a version of the GOP's *nationalism* era—of using government to advance the Public Good instead of trusting private enterprises to serve public rather than private interests. Recall that Republican president Teddy Roosevelt was acclaimed as a "trust-buster."

- Celebrate the exceptional history of the United States of America—a country founded by immigrants. Welcome immigrants, recruit them into the party, and recognize that they are the key to population growth in America.

- Decide whether the GOP is a conservative party that governs an orderly society or a libertarian party that frees individuals to do as they please. Should government limit the availability of firearms used in homicides and mass shootings, or should anyone be able to buy and carry a deadly weapon of choice?

APPENDIX A

VALIDATING THE CODING

I dentifying, classifying, and coding planks in party platforms raises questions about the validity of the research. A measurement procedure has concurrent validity if it matches results produced by an alternative procedure. Unfortunately, there is no established method for coding American party planks over time, but there is an alternative data set. Over eighty years ago, a PhD student at Northwestern University catalogued platform planks adopted by all U.S. political parties at national conventions from 1840 to 1936.[1] Richard G. Browne earned his degree for that effort and had a long and distinguished career as a teacher and academic administrator, but he apparently never published anything afterward on party platforms. Only one of the many sources consulted in writing this book cited Dr. Browne's painstaking research.[2]

Browne doggedly identified 1,666 individual platform planks for thirty-four different American parties from 1840 to 1936. He listed all of the planks in a forty-five-page appendix.[3] I used only the 373 Republican planks he identified in the party's twenty-one presidential elections from 1856 to 1936. Perhaps the best way to indicate what Browne gave as a platform plank is through examples. Table A.1 lists, verbatim from Browne's thesis, the first five of twenty Democratic planks and of eight Republican planks in 1856 and the first five of twenty Democratic and twenty-two Republican planks in 1936.

TABLE A.1 Browne's first five Democratic and Republican planks:
1856 and 1936

Democratic 1856	Republican 1856
Strict construction of the Constitution	Maintain the Union
Oppose internal improvements	No slavery in territories
Oppose assumption of state debts	Oppose polygamy
Equal protection of all persons, industries	Favor punishment for Kansas outrages
Economy	Favor admitting Kansas as a free state

Democratic 1936	Republican 1936
Protect citizens from kidnapping and banditry	Maintain constitutional government
Protect savings	Preserve free enterprise
Favor old-age pensions and unemployment	Restore employment
Protect consumers against exploitation	Provide federal aid to states and localities who will administer relief
Provide cheap power	Old-age pensions and unemployment insurance

Browne's unadorned allusion to "Economy" in the 1856 Democratic platform simply reflected the party's promise to "practice the most rigid economy in conducting our public affairs," not to "improve" the economy. Presumably, Browne counted "economy" as a plank because it occurred in a numbered sentence. Acknowledging some latitude in interpreting the meaning of a plank, one must concede that nearly all of Browne's twenty planks in table A.1 are readily interpretable and meaningful.

Using printed texts of party platforms and doing his research by hand, Browne identified 373 planks in the twenty-one Republican platforms he studied. Using online texts and aided by computers, I found 540 planks in the same platforms. I classified all Browne's Republican planks according to the 114 detailed codes in my coding scheme, reported in table 5.1.

TABLE A.2 Major code headings for classifying party planks

Code Type	General Category	General Category Description
1 - -	Freedom	Policies limiting government
2 - -	Order	Policies restricting citizens' freedom
3 - -	Equality	Policies benefiting disadvantaged people
4 - -	Public Goods	Policies benefiting the public
5 - -	Government	Actions pertaining to the government
6 - -	Military	Actions benefiting the military
7 - -	Foreign Policy	Relations with foreign states
8 - -	Symbolic	Expressions of support, regret

The major headings of that coding scheme are restated here for convenience as table A.2.

Table A.3 illustrates how some of Browne's specific planks were classified under those eight broad types of codes. The examples come from early and later sets of Browne's Republican planks.

Browne's planks can be compared with mine by considering examples of our codings for Republican planks from 1856 to 1936. Under code 110 States' Rights—Browne listed three planks, I found four; code 210 National Rights—Browne had eight planks to my thirteen; code 508 Territories—Browne had fourteen planks to my fifteen. While the planks that Browne found did not match exactly with those that I found, they corresponded fairly well. Over fifty-eight such comparisons, our frequencies of usage correlated 0.77. Correlations close to 0.80 are widely acceptable as indicating reliable measurement.

COMPARING BROWNE WITH GERRING

Browne's platform also data compare favorably with Gerring's findings for his Republican "epochs." (Gerring comingled the early Whigs, who

TABLE A.3 Examples of Republican planks classified
under major code headings

1 - - Freedom		5 - - Government	
1864	Favor encouraging immigration	1872	Abolish franking privileges
1936	Preserve free enterprise	1876	Oppose patronage
2 - - Order		6 - - Military	
1880	Restrict Chinese immigration	1888	Strengthen navy/merchant marine
1912	Regulate monopolies	1928	Build navy to full strength
3 - - Equality		7 - - Foreign Policy	
1856	No slavery in territories	1896	Build Nicaraguan Canal
1920	Adopt federal antilynching law	1920	Oppose League of Nations
4 - - Public Goods		8 - - Symbolic	
1856	Federal aid to railroads/ highways	1868	Sympathy for all oppressed peoples
1900	Extend rural mail delivery	1892	Support Chicago's World's Fair

faded in 1856, with its successor Republican Party.) Gerring held that
Republicans experienced only two epochs:

Epoch	Central Dichotomy
Nationalism (1828–1924)	order versus anarchy
Neoliberalism (1928–1992)	the individual versus the state

Figures A.1 and A.2 exclude Whigs' platforms and include only Browne's
data on Republican Party planks from 1856 to 1936. Figure A.1 portrays
all eight types of planks in the twenty-one Republican platforms. Figure A.2 displays percentages for only the four main types. The period
covers nearly all of Gerring's nationalism epoch but only a small portion of his neoliberalism epoch.

In both Republican epochs, most platform planks related to Public
Goods. Consistent with Gerring's characterization, Order planks far

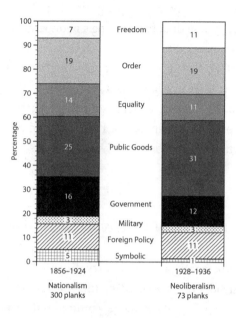

FIGURE A.1 All eight types of planks during Republican eras.

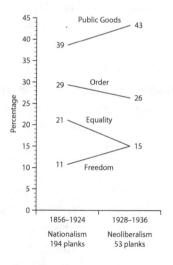

FIGURE A.2 Four main types of planks during Republican eras.

outdistanced Freedom planks during the Republican's nationalism epoch. Browne's sparse data for Gerring's neoliberalism epoch showed a rise in Freedom planks with decreases in Order and Equality planks— consistent with Gerring's portrayal of favoring the individual over the state. Browne's readily available data on platform planks to 1936 produced results close enough to Gerring's much larger study of party platforms and presidential speeches. It encouraged collecting my own data on all Republican platform planks since 1856.

MORE ON BROWNE'S STUDY

Curiously, Browne barely analyzed party differences in the planks that he so laboriously identified. Regarding the political differences between Democrats and Republicans, Browne ventured only general statements in chapter 1 of his dissertation. Toward the end of his thesis, he wrote:

> In all but one or two modern campaigns the parties have clashed over the tariff, and, while the difference may have been one of degree rather than of principle, such difference exists. There have also been other clashes. They are sometimes intensified, as in 1896, 1912, and in 1932, but they sometimes subside, as in 1928.
>
> In general these differences between the parties have been pointed out: (1) the Democratic party is more progressive, and (2) it has showed this particularly in its earlier endorsement of labor legislation, which endorsement has won for it, at least most of the time since 1908, the support of the leaders of organized labor.[4]

In his chapter on the development of party platforms, Browne established that platforms had gotten progressively longer in words and contained more planks. He accounted for the increases in words and planks by increases in the scope of national politics. Browne explained that the post–Civil War platforms of both parties "dealt with problems which arose out of the war." He wrote:

The first reference in any major party platform to one of the chief problems of the twentieth century, the relationship of the government to business, appeared in the Democratic platform of 1884 and in the Republican platform of the same year. The Democratic plank aimed at the control of monopoly in general and the Republican plank dealt with the regulation of the railroads. In 1892 the Democratic platform contained two planks proposing labor legislation, and in 1896 the Republicans followed suit. By 1920 the Democratic platform contained five planks relating to government control over business, and four planks dealing with labor. The Republican platform for the same year contained 10 planks on these two subjects.[5]

The relationship between length of platform and number of planks is stronger for Democrats than Republicans, but both showed more planks after 1900. Regulation of business and labor along with federal aid to agriculture were new topics in party platforms. The turn of the century also introduced foreign policy into the platforms through U.S. territorial expansion and the construction of what became the Panama Canal. World War I brought new fiscal concerns. In summary, Browne wrote: "The increased number of planks has been due chiefly to, (1) the growth in importance of the government's relationship to business, agriculture, and labor, (2) the control assumed by the United States over noncontiguous territory, and, (3) the impact of the World War."[6]

Although Browne offered important observations on the political content of the Democratic and Republican parties' planks, most of his thesis addressed other aspects of national party platforms. One chapter detailed the process of drafting platforms. Another assessed the significance of platforms before 1908, and one assessed their significance after 1908. Browne concluded his thesis on the national party platform as a political instrument by saying that he examined "(1) its function, (2) its development, (3) the manner of its formulation, and (4) its significance."[7] He did not claim credit for detailing what the parties' platform planks actually stated.[8]

APPENDIX B

ACCOUNTING FOR ALL 2,722 REPUBLICAN PLATFORM PLANKS

Chapters 6 to 12 in part 3 considered Republican platform planks adopted since 1856 on key topics, but the chapters did not cover all 2,722 planks found in the platforms. Readers should know what was omitted. Two main criteria determined inclusion: (1) the importance of the topic politically and (2) the number of planks devoted to the topic. The topic's importance was more important than the number of planks. For example, nearly every Republican platform after the Civil War contained a plank on "providing for veterans," and nearly every Republican plank promised to support the "civil service." Nevertheless, these planks were excluded from consideration; they were not important from the standpoint of partisan politics. Although spending on the space program was politically important, the topic was excluded because few such planks appeared. Figure B.1 begins the overview of coverage by displaying the distribution of the 968 planks covered in the figures and text of part 3.

The 968 planks specifically tallied in those chapters account for 36 percent of the 2,722 planks cataloged for the forty-one Republican Party platforms. Many of the missing 64 percent are scattered in small numbers over all 114 coding categories.

Most of the planks considered in part 3 pertained to the four core governmental values of Freedom, Order, Equality, and Public Goods. Some topics in the Public Goods category did not fit comfortably in the

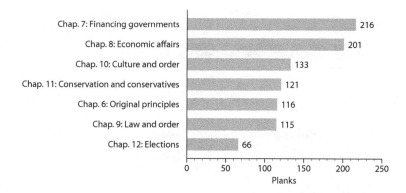

FIGURE B.1 Topics of the 968 party planks discussed in chapters 6–12.

previous chapters but drew a large number of planks since the 1930s. Four topics—Energy, Health and Welfare, Agriculture, and Foreign Policy—generated many planks and deserve reporting.

Energy planks fell under Public Goods, coded +410 for positive government action concerning energy production or consumption and code −410 for government reliance on private companies. Figure B.2 summarizes the results for 101 energy planks.

The first Republican plank on energy came in 1924. The party promised to "use publicity to contain coal prices and supply." In 1932 it asked to "coordinate conservation of oil" and in 1964 went on record to "favor atomic power and coal." Almost all of the sixteen planks in this period proposed positive government action. By 1976, the party's approach to energy had changed to encouraging deregulation and promoting private enterprise, as shown by these planks from the 1976 platform:

- "Eliminate price controls on oil and newly-discovered natural gas"
- "Oppose divestiture of oil companies"
- "Remove regulation on coal mining"

Republican planks were coded separately concerning Health and Welfare, both under Public Goods. Health code +406 applied to positive government actions; code −406 to actions against governmental actions.

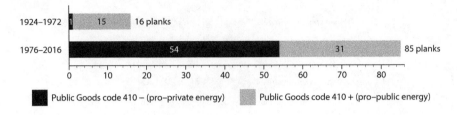

FIGURE B.2 Energy in 101 planks, 1924–1972 vs. 1976–2016.

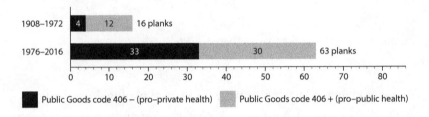

FIGURE B.3 Health in seventy-nine planks, 1908–1972 vs. 1976–2016.

The first of seventy-nine Health planks came in 1908, promising to "secure greater efficiency in National Public Health Agencies." The data are in figure B.3.

Up to 1972, most Republican planks on health favored government action. After 1972, a slight majority was negative. Throughout both periods, most negative planks opposed government health insurance and favored private programs. Here are some examples:

1952   "Opposed to Federal compulsory health insurance"
1960   "Provide for the option of purchasing private health
          insurance"
1968   "Broaden private health insurance programs"
1972   "Oppose nationalized compulsory health insurance"
1976   "Oppose compulsory national health insurance"
1980   "Further health coverage through tax incentives"
          "Oppose socialized medicine"
          "Reject compulsory health insurance"

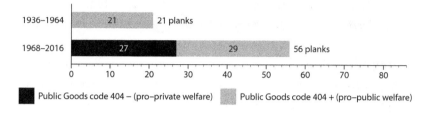

FIGURE B.4 Welfare in seventy-seven planks, 1936–1964 vs. 1968–2016.

Public Welfare was addressed in 77 Republican planks. Code +404 referenced positive governmental actions on Welfare; code −404 indicated other preferences. See figure B.4 for the coding results.

The party's Welfare planks followed a similar pattern as its planks on Health: very positive in earlier periods and mostly negative afterward. Republicans did not adopt a platform plank on welfare until 1936, during the Great Depression. From 1936 to 1960, all its planks were positive; after 1964, they turned negative. Here are the first post-1964 planks:

1968   "Modify rigid welfare requirements that stifle work"
1972   "Oppose government-guaranteed income"
1976   "End welfare fraud"
       "Strengthen work requirements"

Agriculture has faded from the Republican Party's attention over time. In the nineteenth and early twentieth centuries, farming and business associated with farming employed much of America, and party platforms addressed agricultural issues. The 1984 election year divides the total number of Republican planks into two nearly equal groups. Since 1856, agriculture (code 409 under Public Goods) drew a total of seventy-four planks, but 81 percent of those came before 1984. The 2016 Republican platform spoke about the importance of agricultural exports and praised farmers as the backbone of America, but it contained no planks concerning farming.

The 402 Foreign Policy planks represented 15 percent of the total planks. They scattered widely over twelve coding categories. A nation's foreign policy varies with the times, which upsets longitudinal comparisons. Germany was our enemy twice in two twentieth-century wars and is now an important close ally. A few global areas warrant mentioning. Republican platforms contained no planks on the Soviet Union or Russia (code 706) until one in 1952; afterward, Soviet Union/ Russia drew another thirty-five planks. Republicans adopted their first plank on the Middle East (code 708) in 1944 (Palestine), followed by another forty-two planks on the Middle East, most relating to Israel. Figure B.5 displays the distribution of planks by decreasing frequency.

In a geographic sense, the largest number of Foreign Policy planks (fifty) pertained to the Americas, including Canada and Latin American countries (code 704). Two codes applied to International Organizations, code +700 for positive planks and code –700 to negative planks. As befits the party's differing positions over time concerning the League of Nations, the United Nations, and the World Court, twenty planks were positive, and nineteen were negative.

Military planks, like Foreign Policy, are adopted or not according to the international situation. A total of 114 planks fell under the Military. Code 600 applied to thirty-four planks that favored more spending, and code 601 to the single plank favoring less spending, which came after President G. H. W. Bush won the 1990–1991 Gulf War. The 1992 Republican platform called for "a controlled defense drawdown, not a freefall." Otherwise the party consistently supported military spending. In addition, Republican platforms had six planks on Nuclear Weapons (code

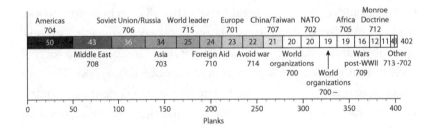

FIGURE B.5 All 402 foreign policy planks.

Note: Negative codes –700 for world organizations and –702 for NATO signaled opposition.

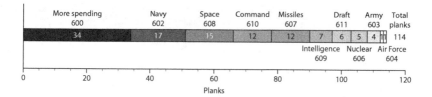

FIGURE B.6 All 114 military planks.

FIGURE B.7 All 244 governmental planks.

606), twelve on Missiles (code 607), and seven on Intelligence (code 609). Republicans favored a strong military capability. Figure B.6 reports Military planks by frequency of use.

The Governmental category had 244 planks. Most of them were noncontroversial, except for the Elections and Statehood planks discussed in chapter 12. Figure B.7 accounts for all others.

Finally, Republican Party platforms had only eighteen planks in the Symbolic category, and nearly all came early in the party's history.

ACKNOWLEDGMENTS

This book analyzes 2,722 planks I found in the forty-one Republican Party platforms from 1856 to 2016 and also refers to corresponding Democratic Party platform texts. (In 2020, both parties readopted their 2016 platforms.) All platform texts were obtained from the website of the American Presidency Project at the University of California, Santa Barbara, to which I am indebted.

A scholar whom I never met but whose paths crossed mine inspired me to build a database of Republican Party platform planks. In 1936, Richard G. Browne earned his PhD from Northwestern University for his dissertation "National Party Platforms and Their Significance." He cataloged 1,666 platform planks for virtually *all* American political parties to 1936. In 1957, I got my bachelor's degree in social science from Illinois State Normal University, where Browne had served as department head. In 1961, I joined the faculty at Northwestern, the same department that granted Browne's degree. Indulge me for describing Browne's life, for he had an important role in structuring my education and that of others in the state of Illinois.

Richard Browne was assistant professor of social science at Illinois State Normal University when he did his graduate work at Northwestern. In 1942, he coauthored a popular sociological textbook, *America in Transition*, with John A. Kinneman, his ISNU colleague. In 1946, Browne became head of ISNU's Department of Social Sciences and in 1951 was appointed executive officer and education coordinator to the Illinois Teachers College Board, where he served up to 1961. Occupied with administrative work, however, he published little of a scholarly nature. Searches of *The Social Science Citation Index* returned no entry for "Richard G. Browne," and Google Scholar returned no references to any of his publications relating to political parties.

ISNU was still a "Normal" school, a teacher's college, when I enrolled there in 1953 and read assignments from Browne's coauthored text *America in Transition*. Browne had already left the department, but Kinneman, his coauthor, was department chair, and he arranged for my graduate study at Indiana University. One final connection: the preface to Browne's thesis credits "Miss Dorrit Keirn who counted the length of the major party platforms and typed the entire manuscript." Miss Keirn was a social studies teacher at Wilmington High School, from which I graduated in 1953. So Browne's paths and mine crossed over many decades, and I am pleased to draw on his significant doctoral research.

Another scholar whom I never met, John Gerring at the University of Texas, wrote a book that provided the foundation for my study. In *Party Ideologies in America, 1826–1996*, Gerring used party platforms and presidential speeches to identify how the Democratic and Republican parties were guided by different basic principles in distinct "epochs" over time. For the Democrats, Gerring identified three epochs: Jeffersonianism (1828–1892), populism (1896–1948), and universalism (1952–1992). For the Whigs/Republicans, Gerring identified only two: nationalism (1828–1924) and neoliberalism (1928–1992). Unlike Gerring, I concentrated on the Republican Party, and my independent analysis supported his in broad outlines except that I identified a third Republican "epoch," which started in 1964 and that I called "ethnocentrism."

Although I had met Rutgers University professor Gerald Pomper and knew of his celebrated publications on how well parties delivered on the pledges made in their platforms, I did not fully appreciate his pioneering research until working on this book. I drew heavily on Pomper's original framework and then benefited from his constructive advice in revising my text. We are contemporaries, but I came very late to the work he began decades earlier. Books by Lewis Gould, the foremost historian of the Republican Party, were important to my research, as were his encouraging thoughts he emailed to me early in my writing. The British political scientist Archie Brown helpfully directed me to research about "strong leaders" in politics.

My Twin Cities neighbor John Flynn, professor emeritus of history and geography at Saint Catherine University, carefully read the first draft of my manuscript, caught far more errors than I thought it contained, constructively questioned some historical interpretations, and improved my writing in many places. I owe him a lot. Syracuse University historian David Bennett, to whom I was directed by Democratic Party historian Arnold Offner at Lafayette College, read a later draft and provided additional information and helpful advice that shaped the final version.

My wife, Ann Janda, served for many years as Northwestern's official representative to the Inter-University Consortium for Political and Social Research, winning its Distinguished Service Award in 1999. A published author and editor herself, Ann checked and smoothed my early writing, as she has done for most of my books, invariably improving them. Jerry Goldman, my longtime Northwestern colleague, steered me in fruitful directions, as he did in coauthoring our American government textbook decades ago.

Stephen Wesley, editor of American politics at Columbia University Press, showed interest from the start in my book proposal and then guided me through the publication process. Few authors are fortunate to have such knowledgeable and supportive assistance.

NOTES

PREFACE

1. In alphabetical order, the other authors were Cornelius P. Cotter, Roger H. Davidson, Charles R. Dechert, Alfred de Grazia, Edward de Grazia, Lewis Anthony Dexter, Heinz Eulau, Kenneth G. Olson, James A. Robinson, and Aaron Wildavsky.
2. Kenneth Janda, *Data Processing: Applications to Political Research* (Evanston, IL: Northwestern University Press, 1965).
3. Alfred de Grazia, ed., *Congress: The First Branch of Government* (Washington, DC: American Enterprise Institute for Public Policy Research, 1966).
4. Kenneth Janda, "Computer Applications in Political Science," *AFIPS Fall Joint Computing Conference*, vol. 31 of AFIPS Conference Proceedings (Washington, DC: AFIPS/ ACM/Thomson, 1967) 339–45.
5. Robert Chartrand, Kenneth Janda, and Michael Hugo, eds., *Information Support, Program Budgeting, and the Congress* (New York: Spartan, 1968).

INTRODUCTION

1. The cross-national relationship between competitive party systems and democratic government is studied in Kenneth Janda with Jin-Young Kwak, *Party Systems and Country Governance* (Boulder, CO: Paradigm, 2011).
2. Forms of democratic government are described in Kenneth Janda, Jeffrey Berry, Jerry Goldman, Deborah Schildkraut, and Paul Manna, *The Challenge of Democracy: American Government in Global Politics*, 15th ed. (Boston: Cengage, 2021).
3. Thomas E. Mann and Norman J. Ornstein, *The Broken Branch: How Congress Is Failing America and How to Get It Back on Track*, Institutions of American Democracy (New York: Oxford University Press, 2006).

4. Thomas E. Mann and Norman J. Ornstein, *It's Even Worse Than It Looks: How the American Constitutional System Collided with the New Politics of Extremism*, rev. ed. (New York: Basic Books, 2016); E. J. Dionne Jr., Norman J. Ornstein, and Thomas E. Mann, *One Nation After Trump: A Guide for the Perplexed, the Disillusioned, the Desperate, and the Not-Yet Deported* (New York: St. Martin's, 2017).

5. Geoffrey Kabaservice, *Rule and Ruin: The Downfall of Moderation and the Destruction of the Republican Party, from Eisenhower to the Tea Party* (New York: Oxford University Press, 2013).

6. Amy Fried and Douglas B. Harris, *At War with Government: How Conservatives Weaponized Distrust from Goldwater to Trump* (New York: Columbia University Press, 2021).

7. Barry M. Goldwater, *The Conscience of a Conservative* (Princeton, NJ: Princeton University Press, 1960), 15, 66.

1. POLITICAL PARTIES

1. This section draws heavily from Kenneth Janda, *Political Parties: A Cross-National Survey* (New York: Free Press, 1980), 5.

2. There is more to this story. In 2010, five congressional candidates did list themselves on election ballots under the Tea Party label, but none was endorsed by significant Tea Party groups, and all lost.

3. Leon Epstein, "Political Parties in Western Democratic Systems," in *Essays in Political Science*, ed. Edward H. Burehrig (Bloomington: Indiana University Press, 1966), 104.

4. Sigmund Neumann, ed., *Modern Political Parties: Approaches to Comparative Politics* (Chicago: University of Chicago Press, 1956), 395.

5. Joseph A. Schlesinger noted that some scholars "want to define party to include all the numerous political organizations that call themselves by the name." He continued, "However useful a theory of party based on such a broad definition would be, the theory I propose to elaborate is less ambitious" and applies only to "parties that contest in free elections, and primarily those parties that are able to win elections over time." Joseph A. Schlesinger, *Political Parties and the Winning of Office* (Ann Arbor: University of Michigan Press, 1991), 6.

6. E. E. Schattschneider wrote nearly eighty years ago, "Political parties created democracy, and modern democracy is unthinkable save in terms of the parties." E. E. Schattschneider, *Party Government* (New York: Rinehart, 1942), 1.

7. John Aldrich, *Why Parties?* (Chicago: University of Chicago Press, 1995), 23. See also his *Why Parties? A Second Look* (Chicago: University of Chicago Press, 2011), 21.

8. Edmund Burke, *Thoughts on the Cause of the Present Discontents* (1770).

9. "The History of the Parliamentary Franchise," House of Commons Library, Research Paper 13.14, March 2013, 19.

10. Anthony Downs, *An Economic Theory of Democracy* (New York: HarperCollins, 1957), 25.

11. Qtd. in Siobhan Hughes, "McConnell Eyes a Role in Primaries," *Wall Street Journal*, February 16, 2021.

12. Other scholars wrote about political parties and tribes. The connection is explicit in Lilliana Mason and Julie Wronski, "One Tribe to Bind Them All: How Our Social Group Attachments Strengthen Partisanship," *Advances in Political Psychology*, 39 suppl. 1 (2018): 257–77. Mason expands on the psychological, sociological, and political linkage in Lilliana Mason, *Uncivil Agreement: How Politics Became Our Identity* (Chicago: University of Chicago Press, 2018), but avoids using the term "tribe." However, a review of her book found "convincing evidence that the two party tribes in the United States are much less concerned with the substance of policy issues than of triumphant victory or, alternatively, staving off the humiliation of defeat." See Richard K. Ghere, "Review: *Uncivil Agreement: How Politics Became Our Identity*," *Public Integrity* 21 (2019): 214.

13. James N. Druckman et al., "The Role of Race, Religion, and Partisanship in Misperceptions About COVID-19," *Group Processes & Intergroup Relations* 24 (2021): 638–57.

14. Pew Survey, "Republicans, Democrats Move Even Further Apart in Coronavirus Concerns," June 25, 2020, https://www.pewresearch.org/politics/2020/06/25/republicans -democrats-move-even-further-apart-in-coronavirus-concerns/.

15. Jesse Van Berkel, "Rift Grows as Walz Weighs Mask Rule," *Minneapolis StarTribune*, July 13, 2020.

16. Cary Funk and John Gramlich, "10 facts About Americans and Coronavirus Vaccines," *Pew Research Center*, September 20, 2021.

17. Edward Shils, "Charisma," in *The International Encyclopedia of the Social Sciences*, vol. 2, ed. David L. Sills (New York: Macmillan/Free Press, 1968), 387.

18. U.S. Holocaust Memorial Museum, "The Cult of the Führer," https://www.ushmm.org /propaganda/themes/making-a-leader/.

19. Tatiana Kostadinova and Barry Levitt, "Toward a Theory of Personalist Parties: Concept Formation and Theory Building," *Politics and Policy* 42 (2014): 490–512.

20. Steven Hassan, *The Cult of Trump: A Leading Cult Expert Explains How the President Uses Mind Control* (New York: Simon & Schuster, 2019).

21. *The American Heritage Dictionary of the English Language*, 3rd ed. (Boston: Houghton Mifflin, 1992).

22. Richard G. Browne, "National Party Platforms and Their Significance," PhD diss., Northwestern University, 1936, 8; Gerald M. Pomper with Susan S. Lederman, *Elections in America: Control and Influence in Democratic Politics*, 2nd ed. (New York: Longman, 1980), 128; and Edward F. Cooke , "Origin and Development of Party Platforms," *Social Studies* 51 (1960): 175.

23. In 1831, the National Republican Party, later called the Whigs, adopted a "list of resolutions" that some have called a platform, but Porter and Johnson say that the "real business of platform making did not begin until 1840." Kirk H. Porter and Donald Bruce Johnson, *National Party Platforms 1840–1964* (Urbana: University of Illinois Press, 1966), 1.

24. Republican Party, "2016 Republican Party Platform," July 18, 2016, https://www
.presidency.ucsb.edu/documents/2016-republican-party-platform. Except as otherwise noted, all quotations from party platforms come from the American Presidency Project website, https://www.presidency.ucsb.edu/people/other/republican
-party-platforms.

2. GOVERNMENT BENEFITS

1. For a wide-ranging review of "conservatism" in philosophy, see Andy Hamilton,
"Conservatism," in *The Stanford Encyclopedia of Philosophy*, spring 2020 ed., ed.
Edward N. Zalta, https://plato.stanford.edu/archives/spr2020/entries/conservatism/.

2. Wikipedia, "Anarchy," https://en.wikipedia.org/wiki/Anarchy#Overview.

3. Liberalism constitutes a nebulous doctrine for theorists. Louis Hartz, in his classic
The Liberal Tradition in America (New York: Harcourt, Brace & World, 1955), says it
is an "even vaguer term" than feudalism (3–4). David G. Smith calls it "too ecumeni-
cal and too pluralistic to be called, properly, an ideology" in *The International Encyclopedia of the Social Sciences* (New York: Macmillan/Free Press, 1968), 9:276. More
recently, Robert Eccleshall admitted that "in everyday usage," liberalism "often stands
for little more than a collection of values and principles which no decent person would
reject" but then proceeds to find substance in an "incoherent doctrine." Robert Eccleshall, *Political Ideologies: An Introduction*, 3rd ed. (London: Routledge, 2003), 18.

4. Quoted in Pauline Maier, *Ratification: The People Debate the Constitution, 1787–1788*
(New York: Simon & Schuster, 2010), 460.

5. Strictly speaking, a public good has two characteristics: "nonrivalry in consumption
and nonexcludability." Nonrivalry means that one person's consumption does not
reduce that of another, and nonexcludability means that people cannot be prevented
from consuming it. John B. Taylor, *Economics*, 4th ed. (Boston: Houghton Mifflin,
2004), 375. Gareth D. Myles, *Public Economics*, 2001 ed. (Cambridge University Press,
1995), 258, https://people.exeter.ac.uk/gdmyles/papers/pdfs/pubec.pdf.

6. "Total general government spending in Europe is 48 per cent of GDP (60 percent in
Sweden). In the US, total government spending is 35.5 percent of GDP." See Alberto
Alesina, Edward Glaeser, and Bruce Sacerdote, "Why Doesn't the US Have a
European-Style Welfare System?," National Bureau of Economic Research, Working
Paper 8524, October 2001, http://www.nber.org/papers/w8524.

7. Alberto Alesina, Reza Baqir, and William Easterly, "Public Goods and Ethnic Divisions," National Bureau of Economic Research, Working Paper 02138, April 1997.

8. In 1889, Germany adopted an old-age social security system backed by its chancellor, Otto von Bismarck.

9. Karl Marx and Friedrich Engels, *Critique of the Gotha Programme* (New York: International Publishers, 1938), 10. Originally written in 1875 and published in 1891.

10. Kenneth Janda, *A Tale of Two Parties: Living Amongst Democrats and Republicans
Since 1952* (New York: Routledge, 2021).

3. PARTY PLATFORMS AND PRINCIPLES

1. According to the 1937 *Oxford Universal English Dictionary*, "platform," meaning a plan or representation on a plane [flat] surface, was used in sixteenth-century England.

2. William Safire, *Safire's Political Dictionary* (New York: Random House, 1978), 537–38.

3. Perhaps the best known is Kirk H. Porter and Donald Bruce Johnson, *National Party Platforms, 1840–1980* (Urbana: University of Illinois Press, 1982). The 1982 edition appears to have been the last of its numerous editions.

4. American Presidency Project, https://www.presidency.ucsb.edu/documents/app -categories/elections-and-transitions/party-platforms.

5. Edward F. Cooke, "Origin and Development of Party Platforms," *Social Studies* 51 (1960): 175.

6. Kimberly H. Conger, "Party Platforms and Party Coalitions: The Christian Right and State-Level Republicans," *Party Politics* 16 (2010): 652.

7. Terri Susan Fine, "Party Platforms as Tools of Presidential Agenda Setting," *White House Studies* 3 (Spring 2003).

8. L. Sandy Maisel, "The Platform-Writing Process: Candidate-Centered Platforms in 1992," *Political Science Quarterly* 108 (Winter 1993–1994): 671.

9. Gerald Pomper, "'If Elected, I Promise': American Party Platforms," *Midwest Journal of Political Science* 11 (August 1967): 319.

10. James Bryce, *The American Commonwealth* (London: MacMillan, 1888), 2:331.

11. Moisey Ostrogorsky, *Democracy and the Organization of Political Parties* (Garden City, NY: Doubleday Anchor, 1964), 2:138–39.

12. Richard G. Browne, "National Party Platforms and Their Significance," PhD diss., Northwestern University, 1936, 115.

13. Theodore White, *The Making of the President* (New York: Atheneum, 1961), 7.

14. Browne, "National Party Platforms and Their Significance," 7, credited his professor Kenneth Colegrove for the popular phrases "point with pride" and "view with alarm," which authors often substitute for points 1 and 2.

15. Browne, "National Party Platforms and Their Significance," 9–10.

16. Browne, "National Party Platforms and Their Significance," 10–11.

17. Pomper, "'If Elected, I Promise,'" 325–26. This list is identical to that contained later in Gerald M. Pomper with Susan S. Lederman, *Elections in America: Control and Influence in Democratic Politics*, 2nd ed. (New York: Longman, 1980), 133–35.

18. Pomper with Lederman, *Elections in America*.

19. Lee W. Payne, "'If Elected, I [Still] Promise': American Party Platforms—1980–2008," *Journal of Political Science* 41 (2013): 33–60.

20. Judith Bara, "A Question of Trust: Implementing Party Manifestos," *Parliamentary Affairs* 58 (2005): 585–99; Lucy Mansergh and Robert Thomson, "Election Pledges, Party Competition, and Policymaking," *Comparative Politics* 39 (April 2007): 311–29; Payne, "'If Elected, I [Still] Promise.'"

21. T. J. Royed and S. A. Borelli, "Parties and Economic Policy in the USA: Pledges and Performance, 1976–1992," *Party Politics* 5 (1999): 115–27.

22. Kostas Gemenis, "What to Do (and Not to Do) with the Comparative Manifestos Project Data," *Political Studies* 61 (S1, 2013): 3, traces the history of the Manifesto Project: "Ian Budge and his colleagues established the Manifesto Research Group (MRG) in 1979. The MRG embarked on an ambitious task, namely to collect and code the manifestos of all major political parties in nineteen countries. Ten years later, the project was renamed the Comparative Manifestos Project (CMP) and under the direction of Hans-Dieter Klingemann its coverage was extended to include parties in Central and Eastern European countries. In 2009, the project was once more renamed as Manifesto Research on Political Representation (MARPOR) with plans to extend its coverage to political parties in Asia and Latin America under a twelve-year grant from the German Science Foundation (DFG)."

23. Francois Petry and Benoît Collette, "Measuring How Political Parties Keep Their Promises: A Positive Perspective from Political Science," October 2007, 17, later published with the same title in L. M. Imbeau, ed., *Do They Walk Like They Talk?* (Dordrecht: Springer, 2009).

24. Robert Thomson et al., "The Fulfillment of Parties' Election Pledges: A Comparative Study on the Impact of Power Sharing," *American Journal of Political Science* 61 (July 2017): 527, 540.

25. David Thackeray and Richard Toye, "An Age of Promises: British Election Manifestos and Addresses 1900–97," *Twentieth Century British History* 31, no. 1 (March, 2020): 9.

26. Thackeray and Toye, "An Age of Promises," 10, 2.

27. Thackeray and Toye, "An Age of Promises," 11. Word counts for American party platforms come from the American Presidency Project.

28. Allan Brimicombe, "Text Mining the Election Manifestos," *British Society of Criminology Newsletter* 76 (Summer 2015), table 1.

29. Many studies have documented the decentralized nature of American political parties compared with parties in other countries. This literature is reviewed in Robert Harmel, Matthew Biebert, and Kenneth Janda, *American Parties in Context: Comparative and Historical Analysis* (New York: Routledge, 2016).

30. Craig Allen Smith and Kathy B. Smith, "A Rhetorical Perspective on the 1997 British Party Manifestos," *Political Communication* 17 (2000): 460.

31. "Formal responsibility for deciding what goes into Labour's programme lies with the annual Conference. . . . Within the Conservative Party the ultimate authority of the leader is clear." Dennis Kavanagh, "The Politics of Manifestos," *Parliamentary Affairs* 34 (Winter 1981): 15, 19.

32. Browne, "National Party Platforms and Their Significance," 71.

33. Edward F. Cooke, "Drafting the 1952 Platforms," *Western Political Quarterly* 9 (September 1956): 708, 710.

34. Paul T. David, "Party Platforms as National Plans," *Public Administration Review* 31 (May–June 1971): 306.

35. Jeff Fishel, *Presidents and Promises* (Washington, DC: Congressional Quarterly, 1985), 63, 64.

36. Susan Fine, "Interest Groups and the Framing of the 1988 Democratic and Republican Party Platforms," *Polity* 26 (Spring 1994): 517.

37. Fine, "Interest Groups and the Framing," 524.

38. Maisel, "The Platform-Writing Process," 696, 687.

39. Browne, "National Party Platforms and Their Significance," 63.

40. Jennifer Nicoll Victor and Gina Yannitell Reinhardt, "Competing for the Platform: How Organized Interests Affect Party Positioning in the United States," *Party Politics* 24 (2018): 275.

41. Caitlin Oprysko, "Biden, Sanders Unity Task Forces Release Policy Recommendations," *Politico* (July 8, 2020), https://www.politico.com/news/2020/07/08/biden-sanders-unity-task-force-recommendations-353225.

4. BEYOND LIBERAL AND CONSERVATIVE

1. Kostas Gemenis, "What to Do (and Not to Do) with the Comparative Manifestos Project Data," *Political Studies* 61 (S1, 2013): 3, 12.

2. Gemenis, "What to Do (and Not to Do)," 12, 19–20.

3. Verlan Lewis, "The Problem of Donald Trump and the Static Spectrum Fallacy," *Party Politics* 27 (2021): 605–18.

4. This chapter draws heavily from Kenneth Janda, *A Tale of Two Parties: Living Amongst Democrats and Republicans Since 1952* (New York: Routledge, 2021), chap. 10.

5. Philip E. Converse thoroughly explores the importance of coherence to ideology in "The Nature of Belief Systems in Mass Publics," in *Ideology and Discontent*, ed. David E. Apter (New York: Free Press, 1964), 206–61.

6. Kathleen Knight traces the history of the term in "Transformations of the Concept of Ideology in the Twentieth Century," *American Political Science Review* 100 (November 2006): 619–26. Also see Terence Ball and Richard Dagger, "Ideologies, Political," in George Thomas Kurian, *The Encyclopedia of Political Science* (Washington, DC: CQ Press, 2011), 3:759–62.

7. Frances E. Lee, *Beyond Ideology: Politics, Principles, and Partisanship in the U.S. Senate* (Chicago: University of Chicago Press, 2009), 27.

8. Lee, *Beyond Ideology*, 31–32.

9. Verlan Lewis, *Ideas of Power: The Politics of American Party Ideological Development* (Cambridge: Cambridge University Press, 2019), 2.

10. Lewis, *Ideas of Power*, 5–7.

11. Samuel H. Beer, "In Search of a New Public Philosophy," in Samuel H. Beer et al., *The New American Political System* (Washington, DC: American Enterprise Institute for Public Policy Research 1978), 15.

12. The observed shift to attack mode in Republican platform rhetoric in 1984 is consistent with the analysis of Walter J. Stone, Ronald B. Rapoport, and Alan I. Abramowitz, "The Reagan Revolution and Party Polarization in the 1980s," in *The Parties*

Respond: Changes in the American Party System, ed. L. Sandy Maisel (Boulder, CO: Westview, 1990), 67–93.

13. See surveys taken in presidential years since 1972 by the American National Election Studies.

14. CBS News poll, February 22–26, 2006, found using iPoll at the Roper Center website, http://www.ropercenter.uconn.edu/about_roper.html.

15. Lewis, *Ideas of Power*, 8.

16. Lewis, *Ideas of Power*, 29.

17. Lewis, *Ideas of Power*, 126.

18. Lewis, *Ideas of Power*, 36.

19. Walter R. Houghton, *History of American Politics (Non-Partisan) Embracing a History of the Federal Government and of Political Parties in the Colonies and United States from 1607 to 1882* (Chicago: F. T. Neely, 1883).

20. The social psychologist Matt Motyl examined changes in the parties' "moral intuitions" from 1850 to 2008. He found that "the clearest instance of party evolution in their moral intuitions occurred between 1896 and 1932, suggesting a fundamental shift in both parties' views of the federal government's role in promoting individual welfare." See Matt Motyl, "Party Evolutions in Moral Intuitions: A Text-Analysis of US Political Party Platforms from 1856–2008," unpublished paper. Adam Silver studied party polarization in platforms from 1840 to 1896. He found that while the parties generally offered divergent positions on most issues, they were more divergent on economic issues than on any other issue except for slavery. Adam Silver, "Consensus and Conflict: A Content Analysis of American Party Platforms, 1840–1896," *Social Science History* 42 (Fall 2018): 441–67.

21. John Gerring, *Party Ideologies in America, 1826–1996* (Cambridge: Cambridge University Press, 1998), 14, 294.

22. The information was extracted from Gerring, *Party Ideologies in America*, 17, table 2.

23. Gerring, *Party Ideologies in America*, 15.

24. Gerring, *Party Ideologies in America*, 204, 40.

25. Gerring, *Party Ideologies in America*, 15.

26. The prominent historian Heather Cox Richardson claims instead that the party focused on the "central unresolved problem" of tension between "equality of opportunity and protection or property." Heather Cox Richardson, *To Make Men Free: A History of the Republican Party* (New York: Basic Books, 2014), xi. I disagree with Richardson, as did the historian Lee Edwards, who wrote in her review, "The continuing tension in the Republican Party is not between advocates of equality and protectors of property but between proponents of liberty and proponents of order." Lee Edwards, "Book Review: *To Make Men Free* by Heather Cox Richardson," *Wall Street Journal*, September 19, 2014. I agree with Edwards and Gerring that the central dichotomy for the party was Freedom versus Order.

27. Richardson, *To Make Men Free*.

28. Gerring, *Party Ideologies in America*, 142–43.

29. Gerring, *Party Ideologies in America*, 62.

30. John E. Gerring, *The Development of American Party Ideology, 1828–1992* (Berkeley: University of California, 1994), app. D.

31. In a brief epilogue, Gerring lapsed into talking about the parties moving left or right, but he saw no essential changes in the Republican Party's ideology by the 1996 election. Gerring, *Party Ideologies in America*, 283–86.

5. REPUBLICAN PLATFORM PLANKS SINCE 1856

1. American Presidency Project, https://www.presidency.ucsb.edu/documents/app-categories/elections-and-transitions/party-platforms.

2. Richard G. Browne, "National Party Platforms and Their Significance," PhD diss., Northwestern University, 1936, 29.

3. Charles Merriam and Harold Gosnell, *The American Party System* (1929), cited by Browne, "National Party Platforms and Their Significance," 31.

4. The term "plank" was used this way as early as 1844. William Safire, *Safire's Political Dictionary* (New York: Random House, 1978), 537–38.

5. Robert Harmel, "The How's and Why's of Party Manifestos: Some Guidance for a Cross-National Research Agenda," *Party Politics* 24 (November 2018): 229–39.

6. "Plank" is also unmentioned in Kostas Gemenis, "What to Do (and Not to Do) with the Comparative Manifestos Project Data," *Political Studies* 61 (S1, 2013): 3–23.

7. Browne, "National Party Platforms and Their Significance," 57–58.

8. For a historian's judgment, see Lewis L. Gould, *The Republicans: A History of the Grand Old Party* (New York: Oxford University Press, 2003). Josh Kraushaar, "The Crackup of the Republican Party," *National Journal*, January 19, 2021, provides a journalist's judgment. See Stuart Stevens, *It Was All a Lie: How the Republican Party Became Donald Trump* (New York: Knopf, 2020), for an appraisal by a former Republican campaign strategist to George W. Bush.

6. ORIGINAL PRINCIPLES

1. Joseph J. Ellis, *Founding Brothers* (New York: Vintage, 2002), won a Pulitzer Prize.

2. Ellis, *Founding Brothers*, 106.

3. Lewis L. Gould, *Grand Old Party: A History of the Republicans* (New York: Random House, 2003), 14.

4. Because the Constitution said nothing about slavery, slavery's opponents looked to the Declaration of Independence for the principles underlying the Constitution. See Philip F. Detweiler, "Congressional Debate on Slavery and the Declaration of Independence, 1819–1821," *American Historical Review* 63 (April 1958): 598–61.

5. Edmund Burke, *Thoughts on the Cause of the Present Discontents* (1770).

6. Properly speaking, the FBI should be the NBI, National Bureau of Investigation, because it operates independently of state governments.

7. FINANCING GOVERNMENT

1. Michael A. Martorelli, "From Tariffs to Taxes," *Financial History* (Spring 2019): 20, https://www.moaf.org/publications-collections/financial-history-magazine/129/_res /id=Attachments/index=0/From%20Tariffs%20to%20Taxes.pdf.
2. Martorelli, "From Tariffs to Taxes," 21.
3. Lewis L. Gould, *Grand Old Party: A History of the Republicans* (New York: Random House, 2003), 90.
4. Gould, *Grand Old Party*, 91.
5. Gould, *Grand Old Party*, 484.
6. Jeff Mason and Doina Chiacu, "Trump Promises Tariffs on Companies That Leave U.S. to Create Jobs Overseas," Reuters, August 27, 2020.
7. Alexander Agadjanian, "When Do Partisans Stop Following the Leader?," *Political Communication* 38 (2021): 352.
8. Agadjanian, "When Do Partisans Stop Following the Leader?," 436.
9. Bureau of the Budget, *Historical Tables, FY2021* (Washington, DC, 2020), table 1.3.
10. Presidents are elected in November of even-numbered years. When new presidents take office in January of the following year, they face a budget already outlined by the previous administration. They do not create entirely new ones. So presidents are credited for the fiscal year after they take office.
11. The 2020 pandemic cost huge sums not represented in President Trump's budgets. So the FY2020 and FY2021 deficits are vastly underestimated.
12. Ronald Reagan with Richard G. Hubler, *Where's the Rest of Me?* (New York: Duell, Sloan and Pearce, 1965), 233.
13. N. Gregory Mankiw, *Principles of Economics*, 7th ed. (Boston: Cengage Learning, 2014), 170–71.
14. Ronald Brownstein, "Bush Breaks with 140 Years of History in Plan for Wartime Tax Cut," *Los Angeles Times*, January 13, 2003, https://www.latimes.com/archives/la-xpm -2003-jan-13-na-outlook13-story.html.
15. Tribune News Services, "O'Neill Says Cheney Told Him, 'Deficits Don't Matter,'" *Chicago Tribune*, January 12, 2004, https://www.chicagotribune.com/news/ct-xpm -2004-01-12-0401120168-story.html.

8. ECONOMIC AFFAIRS

1. Lewis L. Gould, *Grand Old Party: A History of the Republicans* (New York: Random House, 2003), 29.
2. Gould, *Grand Old Party*, 69.
3. Rex Hammock, "The 150-Year History of the Term 'Small Business,'" December 27, 2019, https://smallbusiness.com/history-etcetera/history-of-the-term-small-business/. Hammock used Google's Ngram Viewer, which scans millions of pages in thousands of documents.

4. Stacy Mitchell, "Monopoly Power and the Decline of Small Business: The Case for Restoring America's Once Robust Antitrust Policies," Institute for Self-Reliance, August 2016, https://ilsr.org/monopoly-power-and-the-decline-of-small-business/.

9. LAW AND ORDER

1. Hannes Wimmer, "The State's Monopoly on Legitimate Violence: Violence in History and in Contemporary World Society as Challenges to the State," 2003, https://homepage.univie.ac.at/johann.wimmer/Wimmer-AkadWiss.pdf.
2. Weber said this in a 1918 lecture, "Politics as a Vocation," delivered in Munich. The lecture was published in 1919, translated, and reprinted in H. H. Gerth and C. Wright Mills, eds., *From Max Weber: Essays in Sociology* (New York: Oxford University Press, 1946), 77–128.
3. Melanne A. Civic and Michael Miklaucic, "Introduction: The State and the Use of Force," in *Monopoly of Force: The Nexus of DDR and SSR*, ed. Melanne A. Civic and Michael Miklaucic (Washington, DC: National Defense University Press, 2011), xvi.
4. "Death Penalty: How Many Countries Still Have It?," BBC News, December 11, 2020, https://www.bbc.com/news/world-45835584.
5. Brennan Weiss and James Pasle, "Only 3 Countries in the World Protect the Right to Bear Arms in their Constitutions: The US, Mexico, and Guatemala," *Business Insider*, October 2017, https://www.businessinsider.com/2nd-amendment-countries-constitutional-right-bear-arms-2017-10.
6. "Second Amendment," Legal Information Institute, https://www.law.cornell.edu/wex/second_amendment.
7. "US Gun Control: What Is the NRA and Why Is It So Powerful?," BBC News, August 6, 2020, https://www.bbc.com/news/world-us-canada-35261394.
8. "Gun Control Act of 1968," Wikipedia, https://en.wikipedia.org/wiki/Gun_Control_Act_of_1968.
9. Robert Shoemaker, "Male Honour and the Decline of Public Violence in Eighteenth-Century London," *Social History* 26 (May 2001): 190–208.
10. Some complicate the nature of "life" by distinguishing a "being" from a "person." See Dianne N. Irving, "When Do Human Beings Begin? 'Scientific' Myths and Scientific Facts," *International Journal of Sociology and Social Policy* 19 (1999): 22–36.

10. CULTURE AND ORDER

1. "Culture," American Sociological Association, https://www.asanet.org/topics/culture.
2. Edward Prince Hutchinson, *Legislative History of Immigration Policy, 1789–1985* (Philadelphia: University of Pennsylvania Press, 1981), 136.
3. Julie Byrne, "Roman Catholics and Immigration in Nineteenth-Century America," National Humanities Center, http://nationalhumanitiescenter.org/tserve/nineteen/nkeyinfo/nromcath.htm.

4. "To be an evangelical, according to the National Association of Evangelicals, is to uphold the Bible as one's ultimate authority, to confess the centrality of Christ's atonement, to believe in a born-again conversion experience, and to actively work to spread this good news and reform society accordingly." Kristin Kobes Du Mez, *Jesus and John Wayne: How White Evangelicals Corrupted a Faith and Fractured a Nation* (New York: Liveright, 2020), 5.

5. Robert Jones, *White Too Long: The Legacy of White Christianity in American Christianity* (New York: Simon & Schuster, 2020), 13.

6. The 77 percent comes from a Pew Survey. Ruth Igielnik, Scott Keeter, and Hannah Hartig, "Behind Biden's 2020 Victory," Pew Research Center, June 30, 2021, https://www.pewresearch.org/politics/2021/06/30/behind-bidens-2020-victory/. Exit polls in 2016 reported 81 percent voting for Trump.

7. Igielnik, Keeter, and Hartig, "Behind Biden's 2020 Victory."

8. Du Mez, *Jesus and John Wayne*, 73.

11. CONSERVATION AND CONSERVATIVES

1. The historian Douglas Brinkley documents the case for Roosevelt as the conservation president in *The Wilderness Warrior: Theodore Roosevelt and the Crusade for America* (New York: HarperCollins, 2009).

2. "Theodore Roosevelt," National Park Service, https://www.nps.gov/thro/learn/historyculture/theodore-roosevelt-and-conservation.htm.

12. ELECTIONS

1. This section is drawn from Kenneth Janda et al., *The Challenge of Democracy* (Boston: Cengage, 2021), chap. 9.

2. See David A. Crockett, "Dodging the Bullet: Election Mechanics and the Problem of the Twenty-Third Amendment," *PS: Political Science and Politics* 36 (July 2003): 423–26.

3. The transcript of Liz Cheney's speech was reported in Philip M. Bailey and Ledyard King, " 'I Know the Topic Is Cancel Culture': What Rep. Liz Cheney Said in Her House Floor Speech About Trump," *USA Today*, May 11, 2021.

4. Jonathan Martin, "Overthrow of a Party Leader Risks Worsening Republican's Headaches," *New York Times*, May 13, 2021.

5. Martin, "Overthrow of a Party Leader."

6. Nathaniel Rakich and Elena Mejía, "Where Republicans Have Made It Harder to Vote (So Far)," *FiveThirtyEight*, May 11, 2021, https://fivethirtyeight.com/features/republicans-have-made-it-harder-to-vote-in-11-states-so-far/#fn-1.

13. EVOLVING TO ETHNOCENTRISM

1. John Gerring, *Party Ideologies in America, 1826–1996* (Cambridge: Cambridge University Press, 1998), 125–126. Later, Gerring says, "What is missed in this conventional narrative, however, is the sense in which Goldwater himself was the intellectual stepchild of Hoover" (155). I sharply disagree.

2. Heather Cox Richardson, *To Make Men Free: A History of the Republican Party* (New York: Basic Books, 2014), 273. She continues: "Observers in November 1964 thought Movement Conservatives were extremists, soon to be relegated to a footnote in history books."

3. Geoffrey Kabaservice, *Rule and Ruin: The Downfall of Moderation and the Destruction of the Republican Party, from Eisenhower to the Tea Party* (New York: Oxford University Press, 2012), 401.

4. David H. Bennett, *The Party of Fear: From Nativist Movements to the New Right in American History*, rev. ed. (Chapel Hill: University of North Carolina Press, 1988, 1995), 379, 389.

5. Gerring, *Party Ideologies in America*, 101.

6. Bennett, *The Party of Fear*, 395.

7. Most Evangelicals are Protestant, but some are Catholic. Evangelical Catholics, like Evangelical Protestants, emphasize the Gospel and Jesus Christ. "What Is an Evangelical Christian?," *Economist*, March 1, 2021, https://www.economist.com/the-economist-explains/2021/03/01/what-is-an-evangelical-christian; Father Jay Scott Newman, Pastor of St. Mary's Catholic Church, Greenville, South Carolina, "Evangelical Catholicism," https://stmarysgvl.org/wp-content/uploads/2016/08/Evangelical-Catholicism-Explained.pdf. Father Newman writes: "By our Baptism we are called to receive the Gospel as a complete, coherent, comprehensive Way of Life; in other words, we are called to be disciples, or students, of the Lord Jesus."

8. Earl Black and Merle Black, *The Rise of Southern Republicans* (Cambridge, MA: Harvard University Press, 2002), 214.

9. Edric Huang, Jenny Dorsey, Claire Mosteller, and Emily Chen, "Understanding Anti-Intellectualism in the U.S., and How It Is Literally Killing Us," *Studio ATAO*, November 13, 2020, https://www.studioatao.org/post/understanding-anti-intellectualism-in-the-u-s.

10. Richard Hofstadter, *Anti-Intellectualism in American Life* (Berkeley: University of California, 1963).

11. Bennett, *The Party of Fear*, 398–99.

12. Moira Fagan and Christine Huang, "Many Globally Are as Concerned About Climate Change as About the Spread of Infectious Diseases," Pew Research Center, October 16, 2020, https://www.pewresearch.org/fact-tank/2020/10/16/many-globally-are-as-concerned-about-climate-change-as-about-the-spread-of-infectious-diseases/.

13. Lisa Friedman, "Republicans Begin to Tackle an Issue They've Long Scorned: Climate Change," *New York Times*, June 24, 2021.

14. Gerring, *Party Ideologies in America*, 142–43.

15. Gerring, *Party Ideologies in America*, 147.
16. Amy Fried and Douglas B. Harris, *At War with Government: How Conservatives Weaponized Distrust from Goldwater to Trump* (New York: Columbia University Press, 2021), 17.
17. Bennett, *The Party of Fear*, xi.
18. Andrew Stuttaford, "Where (Some of) Lincoln's Words Came from," *National Review*, November 19, 2013.
19. Marc Bühlmann and Hanspeter Kriesi, "Models for Democracy," in *Democracy in the Age of Globalization and Mediatization*, ed. Hanspeter Kriesi et al. (New York: Palgrave, 2013), 44–68.

14. ELECTORAL TEAMS

1. Edmund Burke, *Thoughts on the Cause of the Present Discontents* (1770).
2. Anthony Downs, *An Economic Theory of Democracy* (New York: Harper Collins, 1957), 25.
3. Cornelius Cotter and Bernard C. Hennessy, *Politics Without Power: The National Party Committees* (New York: Atherton, 1964).
4. Frank Annunziata, "The Revolt Against the Welfare State: Goldwater Conservatism and the Election of 1964," *Presidential Studies Quarterly* 10 (Spring 1980): 254–65.
5. Lewis L. Gould, *Grand Old Party: A History of the Republicans* (New York: Random House, 2003), 15.
6. Gregory Borchard, *Abraham Lincoln and Horace Greeley* (Carbondale: Southern Illinois University Press, 2011), reviewed by Reed Smith, *Journal of the Abraham Lincoln Association* 33 (Summer 2012): 56–60; Michael S. Green, *Lincoln and the Election of 1860* (Carbondale: Southern Illinois University Press, 2011), reviewed by Mitchell Snay, *Civil War History* 58 (December 2012): 487–89.
7. Gould, *Grand Old Party*, 122.
8. Wesley M. Bagby, "The 'Smoke Filled Room' and the Nomination of Warren G. Harding," *Mississippi Valley Historical Review* 41 (March 1955): 659.
9. Robert J. Brake, "The Porch and the Stump: Campaign Strategies in the 1920 Presidential Election," *Quarterly Journal of Speech* 55 (1969): 257.
10. Brake, "The Porch and the Stump," 257.
11. Lewis L. Gould, *The Republicans: A History of the Grand Old Party* (New York: Oxford University Press, 2014), 214.
12. Si Sheppard, *The Partisan Press: A History of Media Bias in the United States* (Jefferson, NC: McFarland, 2008), 300–4.
13. Gould, *Grand Old Party*, 330.
14. Theodore H. White, *The Making of the President 1960* (New York: Pocket Books, 1962), 86–88.
15. Matthew Robert Bonito, "Sons of Abraham: A History of the Republican Party, Richard Nixon's Southern Strategy, and the Formation of Twenty-First Century Conservatism," MA thesis, Southern Connecticut State University, 2018, 83.

16. Gould, *Grand Old Party*, 346.

17. Gould, *Grand Old Party*, 75.

18. Gould, *Grand Old Party*, 76.

19. Gould, *Grand Old Party*, 224

20. Earl Black and Merle Black, *The Rise of Southern Republicans* (Cambridge, MA: Harvard University Press, 2002), 2.

21. Arnold Offner, *Hubert Humphrey: The Conscience of the Country* (New Haven, CT: Yale University Press, 2018), 6.

22. White, *The Making of the President 1960*, 387.

23. Gould, *The Republicans*, 254.

24. Kevin Phillips, *The Emerging Republican Majority* (New Rochelle, NY: Arlington, 1969), 74.

25. Phillips, *The Emerging Republican Majority*, 22.

26. Nelson Polsby, "An Emerging Republican Majority? Review Essay," *Public Interest* 17 (Fall 1969): 119.

27. Warren Weaver Jr., "The Emerging Republican Majority," *New York Times*, September 21, 1969.

28. Aaron Wildavsky, "The Goldwater Phenomenon: Purists, Politicians, and the Two-Party System," *Review of Politics* 27 (July 1965): 386–413.

29. Wildavsky, "The Goldwater Phenomenon," 395.

30. Jelani Cobb, "How Parties Die," *New Yorker*, March 15, 2021.

31. Stewart Alsop, "Can Goldwater Win in '64?" *Saturday Evening Post*, August 24, 1963.

32. Daniel J. Galvin, "Presidential Partisanship Reconsidered: Eisenhower, Nixon, Ford, and the Rise of Polarized Politics," *Political Research Quarterly* 66 (2013): 46–60. Galvin also described the "Southern Strategy" organizational efforts.

33. Robert S. Erikson, "The Influence of Newspaper Endorsements in Presidential Elections: The Case of 1964," *American Journal of Political Science* 20 (May 1976): 207–8.

34. Nicholas D'Angelo, "In Reckless Pursuit: Barry Goldwater, a Team of Amateurs, and the Rise of Conservatism," Honors thesis, Union College, Schenectady, NY, 2014, 54. See also Charles Mohr, "Goldwater Gets Ideas from Many," *New York Times*, March 31, 1964.

35. Richard H. Rovere, "The Campaign: Goldwater," *New Yorker*, September 25, 1964, https://www.newyorker.com/magazine/1964/10/03/the-campaign-goldwater.

36. Gould, *Grand Old Party*, 349.

37. "Historical Polling for United States Presidential Elections," *Wikipedia*.

38. Robert Axelrod, "Where the Votes Come From: An Analysis of Electoral Coalitions, 1952–1968," *American Political Science Review* 66 (March 1972): 13.

39. Bonito, "Sons of Abraham," 102; David Stout, "Harry Dent, an Architect of Nixon 'Southern Strategy', Dies at 77," *New York Times*, October 2, 2007.

40. Phillips, *The Emerging Republican Majority*, 186.

41. Phillips, *The Emerging Republican Majority*, 479.

42. Phillips, *The Emerging Republican Majority*, 470.

43. Phillips, *The Emerging Republican Majority*, 474.

44. David Domke and Kevin Coe, *The God Strategy: How Religion Became a Political Weapon in America* (New York: Oxford University Press, 2010), 3.

45. Rens Crevits, "'I Will Be the Greatest Jobs President That God Ever Created': The God Strategy and the 2016 Primaries," MA thesis, Universetit Gent, 2016, 10.

46. "'God Bless America' in Presidential Speeches Has a Little-Known, Uncomfortable Beginning," *Huffington Post*, January 28, 2014, https://www.huffpost.com/entry/god-bless-america_n_4676177.

47. Jeffrey D. Howison, *The 1980 Presidential Election: Ronald Reagan and the Shaping of the American Conservative Movement* (New York: Routledge, 2014), 128.

48. Stephen T. Pfeffer, "Hostile Takeover: The New Right Insurgent Movement, Ronald Reagan, and the Republican Party, 1977–1984," PhD diss., Ohio State University, 2012, 127.

49. David H. Bennett, "The Witches' Brew: The Origins of the Trump Base, the Trumplican Party and the Politics of Resentment," unpublished paper, Syracuse University, January 2021; Howison, *The 1980 Presidential Election*, 126.

50. Stuart Stevens, *It Was All a Lie* (New York: Knopf, 2020), 21.

51. Pfeffer, "Hostile Takeover," 251.

52. Wildavsky "The Goldwater Phenomenon," 411.

53. Gould, *The Republicans*, 298.

15. THE POLITICAL TRIBE

1. Some passages in this chapter were drawn from Kenneth Janda, *A Tale of Two Parties: Living Amongst Democrats and Republicans Since 1952* (New York: Routledge, 2021), chap. 2.

2. Henri Tajfel and John Turner, "An Integrative Theory of Intergroup Conflict," in *The Social Psychology of Intergroup Relations*, ed. W. G. Austin and S. Worchel (Monterey, CA: Brooks/Cole, 1979), 33–47.

3. Here, "social crowds" means desirable friends and not physical crowds. The relationship between social identity theory and crowd psychology is explored in John Drury and Steve Reicher, "The Intergroup Dynamics of Collective Empowerment: Substantiating the Social Identity Model of Crowd Behaviour," *Group Processes & Intergroup Relations* 2 (1999): 402. The social identity model argues that, in the mass, personal identity becomes less salient and that people act in terms of that social identity which is associated with the relevant social category. Control over behavior is not lost but rather governed by the understandings and values that define social identity.

4. Donald Green, Bradley Palmquist, and Eric Schickler, *Partisan Hearts and Minds: Political Parties and the Social Identities of Voters* (New Haven, CT: Yale University Press, 2002); Lilliana Mason, *Uncivil Agreement: How Politics Became Our Identity* (Chicago: University of Chicago Press, 2018).

5. Assaf Patir, Bnaya Dreyfuss, and Moses Shayo, "On the Workings of Tribal Politics," January 26, 2021, 3, https://scholar.harvard.edu/files/dreyfuss/files/tribal_politics_v13.pdf.

6. Mary Bernstein, "Identity Politics," *Annual Review of Sociology* 31 (2005): 47–74.

7. Carlos Lozada, "Show Me Your Identification," *Outlook, Washington Post Book Review*, October 18, 2018, https://www.washingtonpost.com/news/book-party/wp /2018/10/18/feature/.

8. Lilliana Mason, "'I Disrespectfully Agree': The Differential Effects of Partisan Sorting on Social and Issue Polarization," *American Journal of Political Science* 59 (January 2015): 130; and Lilliana Mason and Julie Wronski, "One Tribe to Bind Them All: How Our Social Group Attachments Strengthen Partisanship," *Advances in Political Psychology* 39 suppl. 1 (2018): 259.

9. Leonie Huddy, Lilliana Mason, and Lene Aaroe, "Expressive Partisanship: Campaign Involvement, Political Emotion, and Partisan Identity," *American Political Science Review* 109 (February 2015).

10. That ANES question about party identification was followed by an additional pair. Those who answered "Republican" or "Democrat" were asked: "Would you call yourself a strong (REP/DEM) or a not very strong (REP/DEM)?" Those who answered "independent" were asked: "Do you think of yourself as closer to the Republican or Democratic party?" The authors fashioned this set of three questions into a seven-point scale of "party identification." Responses to the first question ("do you think of yourself as") are clearly relying on *self*-categorization as a group member; this relates directly to social identity theory. The second pair of questions—asking respondents if they were strong/weak DEM/REP or if independents were "closer" to either of the parties—suggested the strength of psychological attachment, a somewhat different concept.

11. Data for 1952 to 2016 in figure 15.1 come from the American National Election Studies (https://www.electionstudies.org), supported by the National Science Foundation under grant numbers SES 1444721, 2014–2017, the University of Michigan, and Stanford University. Data for 2020 come from January–April Surveys by Democracy Fund and UCLA Nationscape.

12. Angus Campbell, Warren E. Miller, Philip E. Converse, and Donald E. Stokes, *The American Voter* (Chicago: University of Chicago Press, 1960).

13. Data for figure 15.2 came from 1952–2016 ANES surveys and exit polls for 2020. The 2020 ANES survey showed the vote as 56 to 41 percent for Biden, when the actual split was 51 to 47. The ANES data found 96 percent of Democrats voting for Biden and only 90 percent of Republicans voting for Trump. I suspect that the survey overestimated Democrats' loyalty and underestimated Republicans' loyalty.

14. "2020 General Election Editorial Endorsements by Major Newspapers," American Presidency Project, https://www.presidency.ucsb.edu/statistics/data/2020-general -election-editorial-endorsements-major-newspapers.

15. "List of Republicans who opposed the Donald Trump 2020 presidential campaign," *Wikipedia*, https://en.wikipedia.org/wiki/List_of_Republicans_who_opposed_the _Donald_Trump_2020_presidential_campaign.

16. The ANES feeling thermometer's scale is described at https://electionstudies.org/wp -content/uploads/2018/03/2007ANES_Gallup_QuestionComparisons.pdf.

17. The surveys were for congressional and presidential elections to 2000 but only for presidential elections afterward.

18. "Partisan Antipathy: More Intense, More Personal," Pew Research Center, October 10, 2019, https://www.pewresearch.org/politics/2019/10/10/partisan-antipathy-more -intense-more-personal/.

19. James N. Druckman and Matthew S. Levendusky, "What Do We Measure When We Measure Affective Polarization?," *Public Opinion Quarterly* 83 (Spring 2019): 114–22.

20. Douglas J. Ahler and Gaurav Sood, "The Parties in Our Heads: Misperceptions About Party Composition and Their Consequences," *Journal of Politics* 80 (April 27, 2018): 965.

21. Elizabeth Grieco, "Americans' Main Sources for Political News Vary by Party and Age," Pew Research Center, April 1, 2020.

22. "Favorite Programs of Republicans & Democrats," E-POLL Market Research, February 4, 2019, https://blog.epollresearch.com/2019/02/04/favorite-programs-of -republicans-democrats/.

23. Bill Bishop with Robert G. Cushing, *The Big Sort: Why the Clustering of Like-Minded Americans Is Tearing Us Apart* (Boston, MA: Houghton Mifflin, 2008), 12.

24. Robert D. Putnam, *Bowling Alone: The Collapse and Revival of American Community* (New York: Simon & Schuster, 2000).

25. Robert D. Putnam with Shaylyn Romney Garrett, *The Upswing: How American Came Together a Century Ago and How We Can Do It Again* (New York: Simon & Schuster, 2020), 127.

26. Samuel Kernell and Laurie L. Rice, "Cable and the Partisan Polarization of the President's Audience," *Presidential Studies Quarterly* 41 (December 2011): 693.

27. Kevin M. Kruse and Julian Zelizer, "How Policy Decisions Spawned Today's Hyperpolarized Media," *Washington Post*, January 17, 2019, https://www.washington post.com/outlook/2019/01/17/how-policy-decisions-spawned-todays-hyperpolarized -media/.

28. Kruse and Zelizer, "How Policy Decisions Spawned Today's Hyperpolarized Media."

29. James Hawdon, Shyam Ranganathan, Scotland Leman, Shane Bookhultz, and Tanushree Mitra, "Social Media Use, Political Polarization, and Social Capital: Is Social Media Tearing the U.S. Apart?," International Conference on Human-Computer Interaction HCII 2020, July 2020, 243–60.

30. Cory J. Clark and Bo M. Winegard, "Tribalism in War and Peace: The Nature and Evolution of Ideological Epistemology and Its Significance for Modern Social Science," *Psychological Inquiry* 31 (2020): 1–22.

31. Kimberly A. Quinn, Andrea K. Bellovary, and Christopher E. Cole, "The Tribe Has Spoken: Evidence for the Impact of Tribal Differences in Social Science Is Equivocal," *Psychological Inquiry* 31 (2020): 39.

32. Anthony Downs, *An Economic Theory of Democracy* (New York: HarperCollins, 1957), 36.

33. For a short review of political explanations of voter choice, see Georg Wenzelburger and Reimut Zohlhöfer, "Bringing Agency Back Into the Study of Partisan Politics: A

Note on Recent Developments in the Literature on Party Politics," *Party Politics*, March 2020.

34. Piero Ignazi, *Party and Democracy: The Uneven Road to Party Legitimacy* (Oxford: Oxford University Press, 2017), 224–25.

35. Koen Stapelbroek, "Pillarization," in *The Encyclopedia of Political Science*, ed. George Thomas Kurian (Washington, DC: CQ Press, 2011), 4:1209.

36. Kirchheimer's work is discussed at length by Andre Krouwel, "Party Models," in *Handbook of Party Politics*, ed. Richard S. Katz and William Crotty (London: Sage, 2006), 258.

37. Lilliana Mason, "Losing Common Ground: Social Sorting and Polarization," *Forum* 16, no. 1 (2018): 48.

38. Gary C. Jacobson, "Driven to Extremes: Donald Trump's Extraordinary Impact on the 2020 Elections," *Presidential Studies Quarterly*, May 2021, 3.

39. Putnam with Garrett, *The Upswing*, 91.

40. Nathan J. Powell, "The Myth of the Russian Existential Threat," MA thesis, Maxwell Air Force Base, AL, January 2016/April 2016, https://apps.dtic.mil/sti/pdfs/AD1031566 .pdf.

41. Powell, "The Myth of the Russian Existential Threat."

42. Robert Jones, *White Too Long: The Legacy of White Christianity in American Christianity* (New York: Simon & Schuster, 2020), 11–12.

43. Ryan Burge estimates that those without religion divide as follows: 6 percent atheist, 6 percent agnostic, and 20 percent professing "nothing in particular." See esp. his *The Nones: Where They Came from, Who They Are, and Where They Are Going* (Minneapolis, MN: Fortress, 2021), chap. 4.

44. Paul Overberg and John McCormick, "Census Data Show America's White Population Shrank for the First Time," *Wall Street Journal*, August 12, 2021.

45. Jens Manuel Krogstad, Amina Dunn, and Jeffrey S. Passel, "Most Americans Say the Declining Share of White People in the U.S. Is Neither Good nor Bad for Society," Pew Research Center, August 23, 2021.

46. Ashley Jardina, *White Identity Politics* (Cambridge: Cambridge University Press, 2018), 219.

47. Jardina, *White Identity Politics*, 7.

48. Jardina, *White Identity Politics*, 63.

49. Jones, *White Too Long*, 169.

50. Kingdom Citizens, "The Kingdom of God Versus the Government of Man," 2012, http://www.kingdomcitizens.org/the-kingdom-of-god-versus-the-government-of -man.html.

51. Kristin Kobes Du Mez, *Jesus and John Wayne: How White Evangelicals Corrupted a Faith and Fractured a Nation* (New York: Liveright, 2020), 167.

52. Sam Dangremond, "Who Was the First Politician to Use 'Make America Great Again' Anyway?," *Town and Country*, November 14, 2018, https://www.townandcountrymag .com/society/politics/a25053571/donald-trump-make-america-great-again-slogan -origin/.

53. Alex DiBranco and Chip Berlet, "The Ideological Roots of the Republican Party Shift to the Right in Election 2016," paper presented at the 2016 American Sociological Association annual meeting in Seattle, Washington. On the copyright, see David Martosko, "EXCLUSIVE: Trump Trademarked Slogan 'Make America Great Again,'" *Daily Mail*, May 12, 2015.

54. Jones, *White Too Long*, 15.

55. May Darwich, "Casting the Other as an Existential Threat: The Securitisation of Sectarianism in the International Relations of the Syria Crisis," *Global Discourse* 6 (2017): 4.

56. Lewis L. Gould, *Grand Old Party: A History of the Republicans* (New York: Random House, 2003), 56.

57. John W. Dean and Robert A. Altemeyer, *Authoritarian Nightmare: Trump and His Followers* (Brooklyn, NY: Melville House, 2020).

58. Dean and Altemeyer, *Authoritarian Nightmare*, 108–9.

59. Dean and Altemeyer, *Authoritarian Nightmare*, 217.

60. Janda, *A Tale of Two Parties*, chap. 2.

61. "Donald Trump, Announcement of Candidacy, Trump Tower, New York, NY, June 16, 2015," C-SPAN, http://www.p2016.org/trump/trumpo61615sp.html.

16. THE PERSONALITY CULT

1. Tatiana Kostadinova and Barry Levitt, "Toward a Theory of Personalist Parties: Concept Formation and Theory Building," *Politics & Policy* 42 (2014): 490–512.

2. Barbara Geddes, Joseph Wright, and Erica Frantz, *How Dictatorships Work* (Cambridge, MA: Harvard University Press, 2019).

3. Gary C. Jacobson, "Donald Trump's Big Lie and the Future of the Republican Party," *Presidential Studies Quarterly* 51 (June 2021): 279.

4. "Cult of Personality," *Dictionary of the American Psychological Association*, https://dictionary.apa.org/cult-of-personality.

5. Steven Hassan, *The Cult of Trump* (New York: Free Press, 2019), 218–19.

6. Richard Severo, "Lyndon LaRouche, Cult Figure Who Ran for President 8 Times, Dies at 96," *New York Times*, February 13, 2019.

7. LaRouchePAC, https://www.larouchepac.com/about_larouchepac.

8. Editorial Board, "The Cult of Trump," *New York Times*, June 7, 2018.

9. Hassan, *The Cult of Trump*, xvii.

10. "Donald Trump Presidential Campaign, 2016," *Ballotpedia*, https://ballotpedia.org/Donald_Trump_presidential_campaign,_2016.

11. Michael Cavna, "How 'Doonesbury' Predicted Donald Trump's Presidential Run 29 Years Ago," *Washington Post*, June 23, 2016, https://www.washingtonpost.com/news/comic-riffs/wp/2016/06/23/how-doonesbury-predicted-donald-trumps-presidential-run-29-years-ago/.

12. Charles Aull, "Fox News Republican Debate," *Ballotpedia*, August 6, 2015, https://ballotpedia.org/Fox_News_Republican_debate_(August_6,_2015).

13. Annie Karni, "No One Attacked Trump More in 2016 Than Republicans. It Didn't Work," *New York Times*, August 13, 2019.

14. Karni, "No One Attacked Trump More in 2016 Than Republicans."

15. Rory McVeigh and Kevin Estep, *The Politics of Losing: Trump, the KKK, and the Mainstreaming of Resentment* (New York: Columbia University Press, 2019), 76.

16. Jon Huang, Samuel Jacoby, Michael Strickland, and K. K. Rebecca Lai, "Election 2016: Exit Polls," *New York Times*, November 8, 2016.

17. Thomas Ferguson, Benjamin Page, Jacob Rothschild, Arturo Chang, and Jie Chen, "The Economic and Social Roots of Populist Rebellion: Support for Donald Trump in 2016," New Institute for Economic Thinking Working Paper 83, October 2018, 49.

18. Ferguson et al., "The Economic and Social Roots of Populist Rebellion," 3.

19. McVeigh and Estep, *The Politics of Losing*, 121.

20. Elizaveta Gaufman, "The Trump Carnival: Popular Appeal in the Age of Misinformation," *International Relations* (2018): 8.

21. Kristin Kobes Du Mez, *Jesus and John Wayne: How White Evangelicals Corrupted a Faith and Fractured a Nation* (New York: Liveright, 2020), 3, 271, 258.

22. Daniel K. Williams, *God's Own Party: The Making of the Christian Right* (New York: Oxford University Press, 2010).

23. Megan Brenan, "Trump Still Scores Highest as Strong Leader, but Less So Now," *Gallup News*, August 16, 2017, https://news.gallup.com/poll/216260/trump-scores -highest-strong-leader-less.aspx.

24. Archie Brown, *The Myth of the Strong Leader: Political Leadership in the Modern Age* (London: Vintage, 2018), xxiv.

25. Jonathan Swan, "The Cult of Trump, *Axios*, February 5, 2018, https://www.axios.com /cult-trump-base-maga-republicans-gop-b96102cb-7cb9-46f2-9763-b014e68a261a .html; emphasis in original.

26. Jonathan Chait, "Conservatives and the Cult of Trump," *National Interest*, February 6, 2018, https://nymag.com/intelligencer/2018/02/conservatives-and-the-cult-of-trump .html.

27. John Banville, "*The Shipwrecked Mind: On Political Reaction* by Mark Lilla: Review— How Reactionaries Have Ruined Our World," *Guardian*, December 14, 2016, https:// www.theguardian.com/books/2016/dec/14/the-shipwrecked-mind-on-political -reaction-by-mark-lilla-review.

28. William Safire, *Safire's Political Dictionary* (Oxford: Oxford University Press, 2008), 605.

29. John J. Pitney Jr., *Un-American: The Fake Patriotism of Donald J. Trump* (Lanham, MD: Rowman & Littlefield, 2020).

30. Sahil Kapur, "Trump's 'Cult-Like' Grip on GOP Keeps Most Party Members in Line," *Bloomberg News*, June 13, 2018.

31. Hassan, *The Cult of Trump*, 13–15.

32. Hassan, *The Cult of Trump*, 197.

33. David Yanofsky, "Where to Read Donald Trump's Tweets Now That Twitter Has Closed His Account," *Quartz*, January 9, 2021; https://www.thetrumparchive.com/.

34. Katherine Riley and Stephanie Stamm, "How Twitter, Facebook Shrank President Trump's Social Reach," *Wall Street Journal*, January 15, 2021.

35. "Making a Leader," U.S. Memorial Holocaust Museum, http://www.ushmm.org /propaganda/themes/making-a-leader.

36. John W. Dean and Robert A. Altemeyer, *Authoritarian Nightmare: Trump and His Followers* (Brooklyn, NY: Melville House, 2020), 125.

37. Ralph M. Goldman, *From Warfare to Party Politics: The Critical Transition to Civilian Control* (Syracuse, NY: Syracuse University Press, 1990), 1.

38. Nick Niedzwiadek, "The 9 Most Notable Comments Trump Has Made About Accepting the Election Results," *Politico*, September 24, 2020, https://www.politico.com /news/2020/09/24/trump-casts-doubt-2020-election-integrity-421280.

39. Molly Jong-Fast, "What Happens If Trump Actually Refuses to Accept the Election Results?" *Vogue*, October 10, 2020.

40. Sam Gringlas, Scott Neuman, and Camila Domonoske, " 'Far from Over': Trump Refuses to Concede as Biden's Margin of Victory Widens," *NPR*, November 7, 2020.

41. "Trump Team Pressed Ariz. Officials," *Minneapolis StarTribune*, July 4, 2021.

42. "#StopTheSteal: Timeline of Social Media and Extremist Activities Leading to 1/6 Insurrection," Atlantic Council's DFRLab, February 10, 2021, https://www.justsecurity .org/74622/stopthesteal-timeline-of-social-media-and-extremist-activities-leading -to-1-6-insurrection/.

43. "Transcript: President Trump's Phone Call with Georgia Election Officials," *New York Times*, January 3, 2021, https://www.nytimes.com/2021/01/03/us/politics/trump -raffensperger-georgia-call-transcript.html.

44. "Post-Election Lawsuits Related to the 2020 United States Presidential Election," *Wikipedia*.

45. Brian Naylor, "Read Trump's Jan. 6 Speech, a Key Part of Impeachment Trial," NPR, February 10, 2021.

46. Catherine Barret Abbott, "The Reverend Jim Jones and Religious, Political, and Racial Radicalism in Peoples Temple," PhD diss., University of Wisconsin–Milwaukee, 2015, https://dc.uwm.edu/etd/1037.

17. THE PARTY IN PERIL

1. On June 4, Facebook set his ban at two years.

2. Aaron Zitner, Siobhan Hughes, and John McCormick, "GOP Splits Over Its Path After Trump," *Wall Street Journal*, January 11, 2021.

3. Politico Staff, "Read Liz Cheney's Full Statement in Support of Trump's Impeachment," *Politico*, January 12, 2021.

4. Catie Edmondson and Nicholas Fandos, "House Republicans Choose to Keep Liz Cheney in Leadership Post After Her Vote to Impeach Trump," *New York Times*, February 3, 2021.

5. "Statement Following Meeting with President Trump," Kevin McCarthy for Congress, January 28, 2021, https://mccarthyforcongress.com/statement-following-meeting-with-president-trump/.

6. "Donald Trump CPAC 2021 Speech Transcript," *Rev* (blog), February 28, 2021, https://www.rev.com/blog/transcripts/donald-trump-cpac-2021-speech-transcript.

7. Elaina Plott and Jonathan Martin, "Conservative Conference Sets Its Tone: Go Light on Policy and Heavy on Trump," *New York Times*, February 2, 2021.

8. Plott and Martin, "Conservative Conference Sets Its Tone."

9. Steve Peoples and Jill Colvin, "Bowing to Trump? GOP Brings Leaders, Donors to His Door," *Minneapolis StarTribune*, April 10, 2021.

10. Kristina Peterson, "GOP Spars Over 2020 Campaign at Party Retreat," *Wall Street Journal*, April 28, 2021.

11. Nicholas Fandos and Catie Edmonson, "Republican Leaders Tell the Truth but the Party Is Tired of Hearing It," *New York Times*, May 5, 2021.

12. Catie Edmundson, "G.O.P. Replaces a Trump Critic with a Trump Convert," *New York Times*, May 15, 2021.

13. Siobhan Hughes, "Mitch McConnell Says He Would Support Trump If He's GOP's 2024," *Wall Street Journal*, February 25, 2021.

14. Steve Peoples and Gary D. Robertson, "'What Does GOP Stand For? Right Now, It's All Trump," *Minneapolis StarTribune*, June 7, 2021.

15. John Boehner, *On the House: A Washington Memoir* (New York: St. Martin's, 2021), 247.

16. "Paul Ryan Reagan Library Speech Transcript May 27: Future of GOP," *Rev* (blog), May 28, 2021, https://www.rev.com/blog/transcripts/paul-ryan-reagan-library-speech-transcript-may-27-future-of-gop.

17. Ryan Carter, "In Land of Reagan, Mike Pence Defends His Jan. 6 Actions While Lauding Trump's Years in Office," *Daily News*, June 24, 2012.

18. "Never Trump Movement," *Wikipedia*.

19. "Newspaper Endorsements in the 2016 United States Presidential Election," *Wikipedia*.

20. Stuart Stevens, *It Was All a Lie: How the Republican Party Became Donald Trump* (New York: Knopf, 2020), 4, 36.

21. Lewis L. Gould's books on the Republican Party and its presidents include *The Presidency of William McKinley* (Lawrence: Regents Press of Kansas, 1980); *The Spanish-American War and President McKinley* (Lawrence: Regents Press of Kansas, 1982); *William McKinley: A Bibliography* (with Craig H. Roell) (Westport, CT: Meckler, 1988); *The Presidency of Theodore Roosevelt* (Lawrence: Regents Press of Kansas, 1991); *Grand Old Party: A History of the Republicans* (New York: Random House, 2003); and *The Republicans: A History of the Grand Old Party* (New York: Oxford University Press, 2014).

22. Gould, *The Republicans*, 2014, 5.

23. Lewis L. Gould, email, January 23, 2021.

24. Stevens, *It Was All a Lie*, 201.
25. Frank Annunziata, "The Revolt Against the Welfare State: Goldwater Conservatism and the Election of 1964," *Presidential Studies Quarterly* 10 (Spring 1980): 257.
26. Annunziata, "The Revolt Against the Welfare State," 259.
27. Stevens, *It Was All a Lie*, 174.
28. Thomas E. Mann and Norman J. Ornstein, *It's Even Worse Than It Looks*, rev. ed. (New York: Basic Books, 2016), xxiv.

18. A REPUBLICAN EPIPHANY

1. "Letter from a Member of the Convention," *Chicago Tribune*, August 13, 1868. A *Tribune* story on July 3, 1862, referred to "the grand old party of Pierce and Buchanan," who were both Democrats, so the phrase was applied to other parties, but rarely.
2. *Chicago Tribune*, March 12, 1879; emphasis added.
3. Peggy Noonan, "America Needs the GOP, and It Needs Help," *Wall Street Journal*, April 10, 2021.
4. With the Korean scholar Jin-Young Kwak, I studied 212 countries with and without party systems in 2007 for their performance on six measures of "governance" defined by the World Bank. This is from our concluding paragraph: "After controlling only for country size and wealth, we find that countries without elections and political parties consistently rate lower on all six indicators of country governance. . . . We also find that countries with competitive party systems rate higher on all six indicators except Political Stability." Kenneth Janda with Jin-Young Kwak, *Party Systems and Country Governance* (Boulder, CO: Paradigm, 2011), 178.
5. Geoffrey Kabaservice, *Rule and Ruin: The Downfall of Moderation and the Destruction of the Republican Party, from Eisenhower to the Tea Party* (New York: Oxford University Press, 2012), 388.
6. Kabaservice, *Rule and Ruin*, xix.
7. Qtd. in John Kenneth White, *What Happened to the Republican Party?* (New York: Routledge, 2014), 72.
8. Parts of this chapter draw heavily from Kenneth Janda, *A Tale of Two Parties: Living Amongst Democrats and Republicans Since 1952* (New York: Routledge, 2021), chap. 3.
9. Henry Barbour et al., *Growth and Opportunity Project* (Washington, DC: Republican National Committee, 2013); emphasis added. The report was originally posted at https://gop.com/growth-and-opportunity-project but later removed. It was preserved at https://online.wsj.com/public/resources/documents/RNCreport03182013.pdf.
10. "RNC Platforms and Reports," http://www.americancatalyst.org/reference--pubs .html.
11. Barbour et al., *Growth and Opportunity Project*, 1.
12. Barbour et al., *Growth and Opportunity Project*, 4.
13. Barbour et al., *Growth and Opportunity Project*, 7.

14. Barbour et al., *Growth and Opportunity Project*, 14; emphasis added.

15. *Washington Post*, June 16, 2013.

16. A Google search on January 10, 2020, returned this result: "Growth and Opportunity Project—Republican National . . . https://gop.com/growth-and-opportunity-project." No information is available for this page.

17. Joseph Aistrup, *The Southern Strategy Revisited: Republican Top-Down Advancement in the South* (Lexington: University Press of Kentucky, 1996), 5.

18. Aistrup, *The Southern Strategy Revisited*, 27–28.

19. Nathan Layne, "Trump Knocks Immigration, Urges Voters for Republicans in Ohio rally," Reuters, June 27, 2021.

20. The total votes cast for president come from the clerk of the House of Representatives. The partisan division of the votes was calculated from percentages reported in the 2016 and 2020 American National Election Studies.

21. Gideon Rahat, "Candidate Selection: The Choice Before the Choice," *Journal of Democracy* 18 (January 2007): 163.

22. Assaf Patir, Bnaya Dreyfuss, and Moses Shayo, "On the Workings of Tribal Politics," January 26, 2021, 2, https://scholar.harvard.edu/files/dreyfuss/files/tribal_politics_v13.pdf.

23. Patir, Dreyfuss, and Shayo, "On the Workings of Tribal Politics," 5.

24. Barry Goldwater, *The Conscience of a Conservative* (Princeton, NJ: Princeton University Press, 1960), 8.

25. In an email to me on December 29, 2021, the political scientist John Pitney wrote about President Reagan: "After his often-quoted 'government is the problem' line (prefaced by the words 'In this present crisis'), he said: 'Now, so there will be no misunderstanding, it is not my intention to do away with government. It is, rather, to make it work—work with us, not over us; to stand by our side, not ride on our back. Government can and must provide opportunity, not smother it; foster productivity, not stifle it.' Both as governor and president, he was more practical than either his partisan critics or partisan cheerleaders let on." That was true, but "government is the problem," not Reagan's qualification, became the Republican message.

26. Ronald Reagan's speeches are available at https://www.reaganfoundation.org/ronald-reagan/reagan-quotes-speeches/.

27. Kathleen S. Swendiman, "Mandatory Vaccinations: Precedent and Current Laws," *Congressional Research Service*, March 10, 2011. In *Jacobson v. Massachusetts*, 197 U.S. 11 (1905), the Supreme Court ruled, "The rights of the individual in respect of his liberty may at times, under the pressure of great dangers, be subjected to such restraint, to be enforced by reasonable regulations, as the safety of the general public may demand."

28. Kate Pickert, "Keep Your Gov't Hands off My Medicare," *Time*, October 21, 2010.

29. Trip Gabreil, "G.O.P. Ignores Working Class It Won Over," *New York Times*, February 5, 2021.

30. Gabreil, "G.O.P. Ignores Working Class It Won Over."

31. Aaron Zitner, "Republicans' Blue-Collar Agenda Is Still a Work in Progress," *Wall Street Journal*, May 8, 2021.

32. Amy Fried and Douglas B. Harris, *At War with Government: How Conservatives Weaponized Distrust from Goldwater to Trump* (New York: Columbia University Press, 2021).

33. John Boehner, *On the House: A Washington Memoir* (New York: St. Martin's, 2021), 247.

34. Arnold Offner, *Hubert Humphrey: The Conscience of the Country* (New Haven, CT: Yale University Press, 2018), 3.

35. White, *What Happened to the Republican Party?*, 102, 121.

36. Miles Taylor and Christine Todd Whitman, "We Are Republicans. There's Only One Way to Save Our Party from Pro-Trump Extremists," *New York Times*, October 11, 2021.

EPILOGUE: THE NEXT REPUBLICAN ERA

1. Kenneth Janda, *A Tale of Two Parties: Living Amongst Democrats and Republicans Since 1952* (New York: Routledge, 2021).

2. "Ipsos/Reuters Poll: The Big Lie," May 21, 2021, https://www.ipsos.com/sites/default/files/ct/news/documents/2021-05/Ipsos%20Reuters%20Topline%20Write%20up-%20The%20Big%20Lie%20-%2017%20May%20thru%2019%20May%202021.pdf

3. Clinton Rossiter, "Conservatism," in *The International Encyclopedia of the Social Sciences*, ed. David L. Sills (New York: Macmillan/Free Press, 1968), 3:290–95.

4. Rossiter, "Conservatism," 291.

5. Rossiter, "Conservatism," 292.

6. The value tradeoffs between order, freedom, and equality are discussed in Kenneth Janda et al., *The Challenge of Democracy* (Boston: Cengage, 2021), chap. 1.

7. Barry M. Goldwater, *The Conscience of a Conservative* (Princeton, NJ: Princeton University Press, 1960), 5–6.

8. Indeed, Wayne Allyn Root, the 2008 vice presidential candidate of the Libertarian Party and Barry Goldwater devotee, titled his book *The Conscience of a Libertarian* (New York: John Wiley, 2009). Chapter 1 was labeled "It's All Familiar: The Journey Begins with Barry Goldwater."

APPENDIX A: VALIDATING THE CODING

1. Richard G. Browne, "National Party Platforms and Their Significance," PhD diss., Northwestern University, 1936.

2. Edward F. Cooke, "Origin and Development of Party Platforms," *Social Studies* 51 (1960): 174–77.

3. Browne, "National Party Platforms and Their Significance," lists all party planks by election years on 48–50.

4. Browne, "National Party Platforms and Their Significance," 34–35.

5. Browne, "National Party Platforms and Their Significance," 52.

6. Browne, "National Party Platforms and Their Significance," 54.

7. Browne, "National Party Platforms and Their Significance," 256.

8. Why did Browne fail to classify and analyze the 1,666 platform planks so laboriously assembled in 1936? Perhaps because it *was* 1936, when political scientists then lacked the knowledge, tradition, and tools for empirical research. Regardless of the reason, I am grateful for his dogged collection of data on party planks. Almost a century after he collected them, his planks are readily transformed into a database for contemporary analysis. Despite not clearly defining his unit of analysis (the plank), Browne's painstaking and comprehensive research on U.S. party platforms offers detailed insights into positions taken by the two major parties over the last half of the nineteenth century and the first third of the twentieth.

BIBLIOGRAPHY

Abbott, Catherine Barrett. "The Reverend Jim Jones and Religious, Political, and Racial Radicalism in Peoples Temple." PhD diss., University of Wisconsin Milwaukee, 2015. https://dc.uwm.edu/etd/1037.

Agadjanian, Alexander. "When Do Partisans Stop Following the Leader?" *Political Communication* 38 (2021): 351–69.

Ahler, Douglas J., and Gaurav Sood. "The Parties in Our Heads: Misperceptions About Party Composition and Their Consequences." *Journal of Politics* 80 (April 2018). https://www.journals.uchicago.edu/doi/abs/10.1086/697253.

Aistrup, Joseph. *The Southern Strategy Revisited: Republican Top-Down Advancement in the South.* Lexington: University Press of Kentucky, 1996.

Aldrich, John. *Why Parties?* Chicago: University of Chicago Press, 1995.

Alesina, Alberto, Edward Glaeser, and Bruce Sacerdote. "Why Doesn't the US Have a European-Style Welfare System?" National Bureau of Economic Research, Working Paper 8524, October 2001.

Alsop, Stewart. "Can Goldwater Win in 64?" *Saturday Evening Post*, August 24, 1963, 23.

Annunziata, Frank. "The Revolt Against the Welfare State: Goldwater Conservatism and the Election of 1964." *Presidential Studies Quarterly* 10 (Spring 1980): 254–65.

Antonsen, Jon R. "The Platform Strategy: Concession to Win Elections." *Scholarly Horizons: University of Minnesota, Morris Undergraduate Journal* 5, no. 1 (2018). https://digitalcommons.morris.umn.edu/horizons/vol5/iss1//.

Associated Press. "Trump Team Pressed Ariz. Officials." *Minneapolis StarTribune*, July 4, 2021.

Atlantic Council. "#StopTheSteal: Timeline of Social Media and Extremist Activities Leading to 1/6 Insurrection." Atlantic Council's DFRLab, February 10, 2021. https://www.justsecurity.org/74622/stopthesteal-timeline-of-social-media-and-extremist-activities-leading-to-1-6-insurrection/.

Aull, Charles. "Fox News Republican Debate." *Ballotpedia*, August 6, 2015. https://ballotpedia .org/Fox_News_Republican_debate_(August_6,_2015).

Axelrod, Robert. "Where the Votes Come From: An Analysis of Electoral Coalitions, 1952–1968." *American Political Science Review* 66 (March 1972): 11–20.

Bagby, Wesley M. "The 'Smoke Filled Room' and the Nomination of Warren G. Harding." *Mississippi Valley Historical Review* 41 (March 1955): 657–74.

Bailey, Philip M., and Ledyard King. "'I Know the Topic Is Cancel Culture.' What Rep. Liz Cheney Said in Her House Floor Speech About Trump." *USA Today*, May 11, 2021.

Ball, Terence, and Richard Dagger. "Ideologies, Political." In *The Encyclopedia of Political Science*, vol. 3, ed. George Thomas Kurian. Washington, DC: CQ Press.

Bañón, Verónica Carmen. "Parties, Identity, and Brands in Political Marketing." Master's thesis, George Washington University, 2011.

Banville, John. "How Reactionaries Have Ruined Our World. Review of *The Shipwrecked Mind: On Political Reaction*, by Mark Lilla." *Guardian*, December 14, 2016. https://www .theguardian.com/books/2016/dec/14/the-shipwrecked-mind-on-political-reaction-by -mark-lilla-review.

Bara, Judith. "A Question of Trust: Implementing Party Manifestos." *Parliamentary Affairs* 58 (2005): 585–99.

Barbour, Henry et al., *Growth and Opportunity Project*. Washington, DC: Republican National Committee, 2013. https://online.wsj.com/public/resources/documents /RNCreport03182013.pdf.

BBC. "Death Penalty: How Many Countries Still Have It?" *BBC News*, December 11, 2020.

Beer, Samuel H. "In Search of a New Public Philosophy." In *The New American Political System*, ed. Samuel H. Beer et al., 5–44. Washington, DC: American Enterprise Institute for Public Policy Research 1978.

Bennett, David H. *The Party of Fear: From Nativist Movements to the New Right in American History*. Rev. ed. Chapel Hill: University of North Carolina Press, 1988, 1995.

——. "The Witches' Brew: The Origins of the Trump Base, the Trumplican Party, and the Politics of Resentment." Unpublished paper, Syracuse University, January 2021.

Bernstein, Mary. "Identity Politics." *Annual Review of Sociology* 31 (2005): 47–74.

Bishop, Bill, with Robert G. Cushing. *The Big Sort: Why the Clustering of Like-Minded Americans Is Tearing Us Apart*. Boston: Houghton Mifflin, 2008.

Black, Earl, and Merle Black. *The Rise of Southern Republicans*. Cambridge, MA: Harvard University Press, 2002.

Boehner, John. *On the House: A Washington Memoir*. New York: St. Martin's, 2021.

Borchard, Gregory. *Abraham Lincoln and Horace Greeley*. Carbondale: Southern Illinois University Press, 2011.

Brake, Robert J. "The Porch and the Stump: Campaign Strategies in the 1920 Presidential Election." *Quarterly Journal of Speech* 55 (1969).

Brenan, Megan. "Trump Still Scores Highest as Strong Leader, but Less So Now." *Gallup News*, August 16, 2017. https://news.gallup.com/poll/216260/trump-scores-highest-strong -leader-less.aspx.

Brimicombe, Allan. "Text Mining the Election Manifestos." *British Society of Criminology Newsletter* 76 (Summer 2015): 6.

Brinkley, Douglas, *The Wilderness Warrior: Theodore Roosevelt and the Crusade for America*. New York: HarperCollins, 2009.

Brown, Archie, *The Myth of the Strong Leader: Political Leadership in the Modern Age*. London: Vintage, 2018.

Browne, Richard G. "National Party Platforms and Their Significance." PhD diss., Northwestern University, 1936.

Brownstein, Ronald. "Bush Breaks With 140 Years of History in Plan for Wartime Tax Cut." *Los Angeles Times*, January 13, 2003. https://www.latimes.com/archives/la-xpm-2003-jan-13-na-outlook13-story.html.

Bryce, James. *The American Commonwealth*. Vol. 2. London: MacMillan, 1888.

Budge, Ian, and Richard I. Hofferbert. "Mandates and Policy Outputs: U.S. Party Platforms and Federal Expenditures." *American Political Science Review* 84 (March 1990): 111–31.

Bühlmann, Marc, and Hanspeter Kriesi. "Models for Democracy." In *Democracy in the Age of Globalization and Mediatization*, ed. Hanspeter Kriesi et al., 44–68. New York: Palgrave, 2013.

Bureau of the Budget. *Historical Tables, FY2021*. Washington, DC, 2020.

Burge, Ryan P. *The Nones: Where They Came From, Who They Are, and Where They Are Going*. Minneapolis, MN: Fortress, 2021.

Burke, Edmund, *Thoughts on the Cause of the Present Discontents*. 1770.

Byrne, Julie. "Roman Catholics and Immigration in Nineteenth-Century America." National Humanities Center. http://nationalhumanitiescenter.org/tserve/nineteen/nkeyinfo/nromcath.htm.

Campbell, Angus, Warren E. Miller, Philip E. Converse, and Donald E. Stokes. *The American Voter*. Chicago: University of Chicago Press, 1960.

Carter, Ryan. "In Land of Reagan, Mike Pence Defends His Jan. 6 Actions While Lauding Trump's Years in Office." *Daily News*, June 24, 2012.

Cavna, Michael. "How 'Doonesbury' Predicted Donald Trump's Presidential Run 29 Years Ago." *Washington Post*, June 23, 2016.

Chait, Jonathan. "Conservatives and the Cult of Trump." *National Interest*, February 6, 2018.

Chartrand, Robert, Kenneth Janda, and Michael Hugo, eds. *Information Support, Program Budgeting, and the Congress*. New York: Spartan, 1968.

Chicago Tribune. "Letter from a Member of the Convention." *Chicago Tribune*, August 13, 1868, 4.

Civic, Melanne A., and Michael Miklaucic. "Introduction: The State and the Use of Force." In *Monopoly of Force: The Nexus of DDR and SSR*, ed. Melanne Civic and Michael Miklaucic. Washington, DC: National Defense University Press, 2011.

Clark, Cory J., and Bo M. Winegard. "Tribalism in War and Peace: The Nature and Evolution of Ideological Epistemology and Its Significance for Modern Social Science." *Psychological Inquiry* 31 (2020): 1–22.

Cobb, Jelani. "How Parties Die." *New Yorker*, March 15, 2021.

Conger, Kimberly H. "Party Platforms and Party Coalitions: The Christian Right and State-Level Republicans." *Party Politics* 16 (2010): 651–68.

Converse, Philip E. "The Nature of Belief Systems in Mass Publics." In *Ideology and Discontent*, ed. David E. Apter. New York: Free Press, 1964.

Cooke, Edward F. "Drafting the 1952 Platforms." *Western Political Quarterly* 9 (September 1956): 699–712.

——. "Origin and Development of Party Platforms." *Social Studies* 51 (1960): 174–77.

Cotter, Cornelius P., and Bernard C. Hennessy. *Politics Without Power: The National Party Committees*. New York: Atherton, 1964.

Crevits, Rens. " 'I Will Be the Greatest Jobs President That God Ever Created.' " The God Strategy and the 2016 Primaries." MA thesis, Universetit Gent, 2016.

Crockett, David A. "Dodging the Bullet: Election Mechanics and the Problem of the Twenty-Third Amendment." *PS: Political Science and Politics* 36 (July 2003): 423–26.

D'Angelo, Nicholas. "In Reckless Pursuit: Barry Goldwater, a Team of Amateurs, and the Rise of Conservatism." Honors thesis, Union College, 2014.

Dangremond, Sam. "Who Was the First Politician to Use 'Make America Great Again' Anyway?" *Town and Country*, November 14, 2018.

Darwich, May. "Casting the Other as an Existential Threat: The Securitisation of Sectarianism in the International Relations of the Syria Crisis." *Global Discourse* 6 (2017): 712–32.

David, Paul T. "Party Platforms as National Plans." *Public Administration Review* 31 (May–June 1971): 303–15.

De Alba Ulloa, Jessica, and Rodolfo Reta Haddad. "Immigrant Politics. Analyzing U.S. Presidential Elections Through Immigration and Hispanics." *Revista Mexicana de Análisis Político y Administración Pública* 5 (January–June 2016): 119–62.

de Grazia, Alfred, ed. *Congress: The First Branch of Government*. Washington: American Enterprise Institute for Public Policy Research, 1966.

Dean, John W., and Robert A. Altemeyer. *Authoritarian Nightmare: Trump and His Followers*. Brooklyn: Melville House, 2020.

Detweiler, Philip F. "Congressional Debate on Slavery and the Declaration of Independence, 1819–1821." *American Historical Review* 63 (April 1958): 598–61.

DiBranco, Alex, and Chip Berlet. "The Ideological Roots of the Republican Party Shift to the Right in Election 2016." Paper presented at the 2016 American Sociological Association annual meeting in Seattle, Washington.

Dionne, E. J., Jr., Norman J. Ornstein, and Thomas E. Mann. *One Nation After Trump: A Guide for the Perplexed, the Disillusioned, the Desperate, and the Not-Yet Deported*. New York: St. Martin's, 2017.

Domke, David, and Kevin Coe. *The God Strategy: How Religion Became a Political Weapon in America*. New York: Oxford University Press, 2010.

Downs, Anthony. *An Economic Theory of Democracy*. New York: HarperCollins, 1957.

Druckman James N., et al. "The Role of Race, Religion, and Partisanship in Misperceptions About COVID-19." *Group Processes & Intergroup Relations* 24 (2021): 638–57.

Druckman, James N., and Matthew S. Levendusky. "What Do We Measure When We Measure Affective Polarization?" *Public Opinion Quarterly* 83 (Spring 2019): 114–22.

Drury, John, and Steve Reicher. "The Intergroup Dynamics of Collective Empowerment: Substantiating the Social Identity Model of Crowd Behaviour." *Group Processes & Intergroup Relations* 2 (1999): 381–402.

Du Mez, Kristin Kobes. *Jesus and John Wayne: How White Evangelicals Corrupted a Faith and Fractured a Nation.* New York: Liveright, 2020.

Eccleshall, Robert. *Political Ideologies: An Introduction.* 3rd ed. London: Routledge, 2003.

Edmondson, Catie, and Nicholas Fandos. "House Republicans Choose to Keep Liz Cheney in Leadership Post After Her Vote to Impeach Trump." *New York Times*, February 3, 2021.

Edmundson, Catie. "GOP Replaces a Trump Critic with a Trump Convert." *New York Times*, May 15, 2021.

Edwards, Lee. "Book Review: *To Make Men Free* by Heather Cox Richardson." *Wall Street Journal*, September 19, 2014.

Ellis, Joseph J. *Founding Brothers.* New York: Vintage, 2002.

Epstein, Leon. "Political Parties in Western Democratic Systems." In *Essays in Political Science*, ed. Edward H. Burehrig, 97–130. Bloomington: Indiana University Press, 1966.

Erikson, Robert S. "The Influence of Newspaper Endorsements in Presidential Elections: The Case of 1964." *American Journal of Political Science* 20 (May 1976): 207–33.

Fagan, E. J. "Marching Orders? U.S. Party Platforms and Legislative Agenda Setting, 1948–2014." *Political Research Quarterly* 71 (2018): 949–59.

Fandos, Nicholas, and Catie Edmonson. "Republican Leaders Tells the Truth but the Party Is Tired of Hearing It." *New York Times*, May 5, 2021.

Ferguson, Thomas, Benjamin Page, Jacob Rothschild, Arturo Chang, and Jie Chen. "The Economic and Social Roots of Populist Rebellion: Support for Donald Trump in 2016." New Institute for Economic Thinking Working Paper 83, October 2018.

Fine, Terri Susan. "Interest Groups and the Framing of the 1988 Democratic and Republican Party Platforms." *Polity* 26 (Spring 1994): 517–30.

——. "Party Platforms as Tools of Presidential Agenda Setting." *White House Studies* 3 (Spring 2003).

Fishel, Jeff. *Presidents and Promises: From Campaign Pledge to Presidential Performance.* Washington, DC: Congressional Quarterly, 1985.

Fried, Amy, and Douglas B. Harris. *At War with Government: How Conservatives Weaponized Distrust from Goldwater to Trump.* New York: Columbia University Press, 2021.

Friedman, Lisa. "Republicans Begin to Tackle an Issue They've Long Scorned: Climate Change." *New York Times*, June 24, 2021.

Funk, Cary, and John Gramlich. "10 Facts About Americans and Coronavirus Vaccines." Pew Research Center, September 20, 2021.

Gabreil, Trip. "GOP Ignores Working Class It Won Over." *New York Times*, February 5, 2021.

Galvin, Daniel J. "Presidential Partisanship Reconsidered: Eisenhower, Nixon, Ford, and the Rise of Polarized Politics." *Political Research Quarterly* 66 (2013): 46–60.

Gaufman, Elizaveta. "The Trump Carnival: Popular Appeal in the Age of Misinformation." *International Relations* 32, no. 4 (2018): 1–20.

Geddes, Barbara, Joseph Wright, and Erica Frantz. *How Dictatorships Work.* Cambridge, MA: Harvard University Press, 2019.

Gemenis, Kostas. "What to Do (and Not to Do) with the Comparative Manifestos Project Data." *Political Studies* 61 (2013): 3–23.

Gerring, John. *Party Ideologies in America, 1826–1996.* Cambridge: Cambridge University Press, 1998.

Ginsberg, Benjamin. "Elections and Public Policy." *American Political Science Review* 70 (March 1976): 41–49.

Goldman, Ralph M. *From Warfare to Party Politics: The Critical Transition to Civilian Control.* Syracuse, NY: Syracuse University Press, 1990.

Goldwater, Barry M. *The Conscience of a Conservative.* Princeton, NJ: Princeton University Press, 1960.

Gould, Lewis L. *Grand Old Party: A History of the Republicans.* New York: Random House, 2003.

——. *The Presidency of Theodore Roosevelt.* Lawrence: Regents Press of Kansas, 1991.

——. *The Presidency of William McKinley.* Lawrence: Regents Press of Kansas, 1980.

——. *The Republicans: A History of the Grand Old Party.* Oxford: Oxford University Press, 2014.

——. *The Spanish-American War and President McKinley.* Lawrence: Regents Press of Kansas, 1982.

Gould, Lewis L, with Craig H. Roell. *William McKinley: A Bibliography.* Westport, CT: Meckler, 1988.

Green, Donald, Bradley Palmquist, and Eric Schickler. *Partisan Hearts and Minds: Political Parties and the Social Identities of Voters.* New Haven, CT: Yale University Press, 2002.

Green, Michael S. *Lincoln and the Election of 1860.* Carbondale: Southern Illinois University Press, 2011.

Grieco, Elizabeth. "Americans' Main Sources for Political News Vary by Party and Age." Pew Research Center, April 1, 2020.

Gringlas, Sam, Scott Neuman, and Camila Domonoske. " 'Far from Over': Trump Refuses to Concede as Biden's Margin of Victory Widens." NPR, November 7, 2020.

Hamilton, Andy. "Conservatism." *Stanford Encyclopedia of Philosophy,* Spring 2020 ed.

Hammock, Rex. "The 150-Year History of the Term 'Small Business.' " *Small Business* (blog), December 27, 2019. https://smallbusiness.com/history-etcetera/history-of-the-term-small-business/.

Harmel, Robert. "The How's and Why's of Party Manifestos: Some Guidance for a Cross-National Research Agenda." *Party Politics* 24 (November 2018): 229–39.

Harmel, Robert, Alexander C. Tan, Kenneth Janda, and Jason Matthew Smith. "Manifestos and the "Two Faces" of Parties: Addressing Both Members and Voters with One Document." *Party Politics* 24 (May 2018): 278–88.

Harmel, Robert, Matthew Biebert, and Kenneth Janda. *American Parties in Context: Comparative and Historical Analysis.* New York: Routledge, 2016.

Hartz, Louis. *The Liberal Tradition in America.* New York: Harcourt, Brace & World, 1955.

Hassan, Steven. *The Cult of Trump: A Leading Cult Expert Explains How the President Uses Mind Control.* New York: Simon & Schuster, 2019.

Hawdon, James, Shyam Ranganathan, Scotland Leman, Shane Bookhultz, and Tanushree Mitra. "Social Media Use, Political Polarization, and Social Capital: Is Social Media Tearing the U.S. Apart?" International Conference on Human-Computer Interaction HCII 2020, July 2020, 243–60.

Hofstadter, Richard. *Anti-Intellectualism in American Life.* Berkeley: University of California Press, 1963.

Hollingsworth, Shelby. "The Realignment of the Political Parties: 1877 to 1964." MA thesis, Southern Connecticut State University, 2019.

Houghton, Walter R. *History of American Politics (Non-Partisan) Embracing a History of the Federal Government and of Political Parties in the Colonies and United States from 1607 to 1882.* Chicago: F. T. Neely, 1883.

House of Commons Library. "The History of the Parliamentary Franchise." Research Paper 13.14, March, 2013.

Howison, Jeffrey D. *The 1980 Presidential Election: Ronald Reagan and the Shaping of the American Conservative Movement.* New York: Routledge, 2014.

Huang, Edric, Jenny Dorsey, Claire Mosteller, and Emily Chen. "Understanding Anti-Intellectualism in the U.S., and How It Is Literally Killing Us." *Studio ATAO*, November 13, 2020. https://www.studioatao.org/post/understanding-anti-intellectualism-in-the-u-s.

Huang, Jon, Samuel Jacoby, Michael Strickland, and K. K. Rebecca Lai. "Election 2016: Exit Polls." *New York Times.* November 8, 2016.

Huddy, Leonie, Lilliana Mason, and Lene Aaroe. "Expressive Partisanship: Campaign Involvement, Political Emotion, and Partisan Identity." *American Political Science Review* 109 (February 2015).

Huffington Post. "'God Bless America' in Presidential Speeches Has a Little-Known, Uncomfortable Beginning." *Huffington Post*, January 28, 2014. https://www.huffpost.com/entry/god-bless-america_n_4676177.

Hughes, Siobhan. "McConnell Eyes a Role in Primaries." *Wall Street Journal*, February 16, 2021.

——. "Mitch McConnell Says He Would Support Trump If He's GOP's 2024 Nominee." *Wall Street Journal*, February 25, 2021.

Hurst, Allison L. "Languages of Class in US Party Platforms, 1880–1936." *Journal of Historical Sociology* 23 (December 2010): 542–69.

Hutchinson, Edward Prince. *Legislative History of Immigration Policy, 1789–1985.* Philadelphia: University of Pennsylvania Press, 1981.

Igielnik, Ruth, Scott Keeter, and Hannah Hartig. "Behind Biden's 2020 Victory." Pew Research Center, June 30, 2021. https://www.pewresearch.org/politics/2021/06/30/behind-bidens-2020-victory/.

Ignazi, Piero. *Party and Democracy: The Uneven Road to Party Legitimacy.* Oxford: Oxford University Press, 2017.

Irving, Dianne N. "When Do Human Beings Begin? 'Scientific' Myths and Scientific Facts." *International Journal of Sociology and Social Policy* 19 (1999): 22–36. https://www.bbc.com/news/world-45835584.

Jacobson, Gary C. "Driven to Extremes: Donald Trump's Extraordinary Impact on the 2020 Elections." *Presidential Studies Quarterly* 51, no. 3 (May 2021): 1–30.

Janda, Kenneth. "Computer Applications in Political Science." In *AFIPS Fall Joint Computing Conference*, vol. 31 of *AFIPS Conference Proceedings*, 339–45. Washington, DC: AFIPS/ACM/Thomson, 1967).

——. *Data Processing: Applications to Political Research*. Evanston, IL: Northwestern University Press, 1965.

——. *Political Parties: A Cross-National Survey*. New York: Free Press, 1980.

——. *A Tale of Two Parties: Living Amongst Democrats and Republicans Since 1952*. New York: Routledge, 2021.

Janda, Kenneth, Jeffrey Berry, Jerry Goldman, Deborah Schildkraut, and Paul Manna. *The Challenge of Democracy: American Government in Global Politics*. 15th ed. Boston: Cengage, 2021.

Janda, Kenneth, with Jin-Young Kwak. *Party Systems and Country Governance*. Boulder, CO: Paradigm, 2011.

Jones, Robert P. *White Too Long: The Legacy of White Christianity in American Christianity*. New York: Simon & Schuster, 2020.

Kabaservice, Geoffrey. *Rule and Ruin: The Downfall of Moderation and the Destruction of the Republican Party, from Eisenhower to the Tea Party*. New York: Oxford University Press, 2012.

Kapur, Sahil. "Trump's 'Cult-Like' Grip on GOP Keeps Most Party Members in Line." *Bloomberg News*, June 13, 2018.

Karni, Annie. "No One Attacked Trump More in 2016 Than Republicans. It Didn't Work." *New York Times*, August 13, 2019.

Kavanagh, Dennis. "The Politics of Manifestos." *Parliamentary Affairs* 34 (Winter 1981).

Kernell, Samuel, and Laurie L. Rice. "Cable and the Partisan Polarization of the President's Audience." *Presidential Studies Quarterly* 41 (December 2011): 693–711.

Knight, Kathleen. "Transformations of the Concept of Ideology in the Twentieth Century." *American Political Science Review* 100 (November 2006).

Kostadovina, Tatiana, and Barry Levitt. "Toward a Theory of Personalist Parties: Concept Formation and Theory Building." *Politics and Policy* 42 (2014): 490–512.

Krabbendam, Hans. "Review of Daniel K. Williams, *God's Own Party: The Making of the Christian Right*." *European Journal of American Studies*, Reviews 2011-2, document 16. https://journals.openedition.org/ejas/9394.

Kraushaar, Josh. "The Crackup of the Republican Party." *National Journal*, January 19, 2021.

Krogstad, Jens Manuel, Amina Dunn, and Jeffrey S. Passel. "Most Americans Say the Declining Share of White People in the U.S. Is Neither Good nor Bad for Society." Pew Research Center, August 23, 2021.

Krouwel, Andre. "Party Models." In *Handbook of Party Politics*, ed. Richard S. Katz and William Crotty, 249–69. London: Sage, 2006.

Kruse, Kevin M., and Julian Zelizer. "How Policy Decisions Spawned Today's Hyperpolarized Media." *Washington Post*, January 17, 2019.

Layne, Nathan. "Trump Knocks Immigration, Urges Voters for Republicans in Ohio Rally." *Reuters*, June 27, 2021.

Lee, Frances E., *Beyond Ideology: Politics, Principles, and Partisanship in the U.S. Senate*. Chicago: University of Chicago Press, 2009.

Legal Information Institute. "Second Amendment." https://www.law.cornell.edu/wex/second_amendment.

Lewis, Verlan. *Ideas of Power: The Politics of American Party Ideological Development*. Cambridge: Cambridge University Press, 2019.

———. "The Problem of Donald Trump and the Static Spectrum Fallacy." *Party Politics* 27 (2021): 605–18.

Lozada, Carlos. "Show Me Your Identification." *Outlook, Washington Post Book Review*, October 18, 2018. https://www.washingtonpost.com/news/book-party/wp/2018/10/18/feature/.

Maier, Pauline. *Ratification: The People Debate the Constitution, 1787–1788*. New York: Simon & Schuster, 2010.

Maisel, L. Sandy. "The Platform-Writing Process: Candidate-Centered Platforms in 1992." *Political Science Quarterly* 108 (Winter 1993–1994): 671–98.

Mankiw, N. Gregory. *Principles of Economics*. 7th ed. Boston: Cengage Learning, 2014.

Mann, Thomas E., and Norman J. Ornstein. *The Broken Branch: How Congress Is Failing America and How to Get It Back on Track*. Institutions of American Democracy. Oxford: Oxford University Press, 2006.

———. *It's Even Worse Than It Looks: How the American Constitutional System Collided with the New Politics of Extremism*. Rev. ed. New York: Basic Books, 2016.

Mansergh, Lucy, and Robert Thomson. "Election Pledges, Party Competition, and Policy-making." *Comparative Politics* 39 (April 2007): 311–29.

Market Research. "Favorite Programs of Republicans & Democrats." *E-POLL Market Research* (blog). February 4, 2019. https://blog.epollresearch.com/2019/02/04/favorite-programs-of-republicans-democrats/.

Martin, Jonathan. "Overthrow of a Party Leader Risks Worsening Republicans' Headaches." *New York Times*, May 13, 2021.

Martorelli, Michael A. "From Tariffs to Taxes." *Financial History*, Spring 2019. https://www.moaf.org/publications-collections/financial-history-magazine/129/_res/id=Attachments/index=0/From%20Tariffs%20to%20Taxes.pdf.

Martosko, David. "Trump Trademarked Slogan 'Make America Great Again.'" *Daily Mail*, May 12, 2015.

Marx, Karl, and Friedrich Engels. *Critique of the Gotha Programme*. New York: International Publishers, 1938.

Mason, Jeff, and Doina Chiacu. "Trump Promises Tariffs on Companies That Leave U.S. to Create Jobs Overseas." *Reuters*, August 27, 2020.

Mason, Lilliana. "'I Disrespectfully Agree': The Differential Effects of Partisan Sorting on Social and Issue Polarization." *American Journal of Political Science* 59 (January 2015): 128–45.

———. "Losing Common Ground: Social Sorting and Polarization." *Forum* 16, no. 1 (2018).

———. *Uncivil Agreement: How Politics Became Our Identity*. Chicago: University of Chicago Press, 2018.

Mason, Lilliana, and Julie Wronski. "One Tribe to Bind Them All: How Our Social Group Attachments Strengthen Partisanship." *Advances in Political Psychology* 39 suppl. 1 (2018): 257–77.

Matthew Robert Bonito. "Sons of Abraham: A History of the Republican Party, Richard Nixon's Southern Strategy, and the Formation of Twenty-First Century Conservatism." MA thesis, Southern Connecticut State University, 2018.

McCarthy, Kevin. "Statement Following Meeting with President Trump." Kevin McCarthy for Congress, January 28, 2021. https://mccarthyforcongress.com/statement-following -meeting-with-president-trump/.

McVeigh, Rory, and Kevin Estep. *The Politics of Losing: Trump, the KKK, and the Mainstreaming of Resentment*. New York: Columbia University Press, 2019.

Merriam, Charles, and Harold Gosnell. *The American Party System*. New York: Macmillan, 1929.

Mohr, Charles. "Goldwater Gets Ideas from Many." *New York Times*, March 31, 1964.

Motyl, Matt. "Party Evolutions in Moral Intuitions: A Text-Analysis of US Political Party Platforms from 1856–2008." Unpublished manuscript.

Myles, Gareth D. *Public Economics*. 1995; Cambridge: Cambridge University Press, 2001.

Naylor, Brian. "Read Trump's Jan. 6 Speech, a Key Part of Impeachment Trial." NPR, February 10, 2021.

Nelson, Polsby. "An Emerging Republican Majority? Review Essay." *Public Interest* 17 (Fall 1969): 119–22.

Neumann, Sigmund, ed. *Modern Political Parties: Approaches to Comparative Politics*. Chicago: University of Chicago Press, 1956.

Newman, Father Jay Scott. "Evangelical Catholicism." http://stmarysgvl.org/wp-content /uploads/2016/08/Evangelical-Catholicism-Explained.pdf.

Niedzwiadek, Nick. "The 9 Most Notable Comments Trump Has Made About Accepting the Election Results." *Politico*, September 24, 2020. https://www.politico.com/news/2020/09 /24/trump-casts-doubt-2020-election-integrity-421280.

Noonan, Peggy. "America Needs the GOP, and It Needs Help." *Wall Street Journal*, April 10, 2021.

Offner, Arnold. *Hubert Humphrey: The Conscience of the Country*. New Haven, CT: Yale University Press, 2018.

Oprysko, Caitlin. "Biden, Sanders Unity Task Forces Release Policy Recommendations." *Politico*, July 8, 2020. https://www.politico.com/news/2020/07/08/biden-sanders-unity -task-force-recommendations-353225.

Ostrogorsky, Moisey. *Democracy and the Organization of Political Parties*. Vol. 2. Garden City, NY: Doubleday Anchor, 1964.

Overberg, Paul, and John McCormick. "Census Data Show America's White Population Shrank for the First Time." *Wall Street Journal*, August 12, 2021.

Patir, Assaf, Bnaya Dreyfuss, and Moses Shayo. "On the Workings of Tribal Politics." January 26, 2021. https://scholar.harvard.edu/files/dreyfuss/files/tribal_politics_v13.pdf.

Payne, Lee W. "'If Elected, I [Still] Promise': American Party Platforms—1980–2008." *Journal of Political Science* 41 (2013): 33–60.

Peoples, Steve, and Gary D. Robertson. "What Does GOP Stand for? Right Now, It's All Trump." *Minneapolis StarTribune,* June 7, 2021.

Peoples, Steve, and Jill Colvin. "Bowing to Trump? GOP Brings Leaders, Donors to His Door." *Minneapolis StarTribune,* April 10, 2021.

Peterson, Kristina. "GOP Spars Over 2020 Campaign at Party Retreat." *Wall Street Journal,* April 28, 2021.

Petry, Francois, and Benoit Collette. "Measuring How Political Parties Keep Their Promises: A Positive Perspective from Political Science." October 2007. Later published in L. M. Imbeau, ed., *Do They Walk Like They Talk?* Dordrecht: Springer, 2009.

Phillips, Kevin P. *The Emerging Republican Majority.* New Rochelle, NY: Arlington, 1969.

Philpot, Tasha S. *Race, Republicans, and the Return of the Party of Lincoln.* Ann Arbor: University of Michigan Press, 2007.

Pickert, Kate. "Keep Your Gov't Hands Off My Medicare." *Time,* October 21, 2010.

Pitney, John J., Jr. *Un-American: The Fake Patriotism of Donald J. Trump.* Lanham, MD: Rowman & Littlefield, 2020.

Plott, Elaina, and Jonathan Martin. "Conservative Conference Sets Its Tone: Go Light on Policy and Heavy on Trump." *New York Times,* February 2, 2021.

Pomper, Gerald M. *Elections in America: Control and Influence in Democratic Politics.* New York: Dodd, Mead, 1968.

——. "'If Elected, I Promise': American Party Platforms." *Midwest Journal of Political Science* 11 (August 1967): 318–52.

Pomper, Gerald M., with Susan S. Lederman. *Elections in America: Control and Influence in Democratic Politics.* 2nd ed. New York: Longman, 1980.

Popkin, Samuel, et al. "What Have You Done for Me Lately? Toward an Investment Theory of Voting." *American Political Science Review* 70 (September 1976): 779–805.

Porter, Kirk H., and Donald Bruce Johnson. *National Party Platforms, 1840–1964.* Urbana: University of Illinois Press, 1966.

Powell, Nathan J. "The Myth of the Russian Existential Threat." MA thesis, Maxwell Air Force Base, AL, January 2016/April 2016). https://apps.dtic.mil/sti/pdfs/AD1031566.pdf.

Putnam, Robert D. *Bowling Alone: The Collapse and Revival of American Community.* New York: Simon & Schuster, 2000.

Putnam, Robert D., with Shaylyn Romney Garrett. *The Upswing: How American Came Together a Century Ago and How We Can Do It Again.* New York: Simon & Schuster, 2020.

Quinn, Kimberly A., Andrea K. Bellovary, and Christopher E. Cole. "The Tribe Has Spoken: Evidence for the Impact of Tribal Differences in Social Science Is Equivocal." *Psychological Inquiry* 31 (2020): 35–41.

Rahat, Gideon. "Candidate Selection: The Choice Before the Choice." *Journal of Democracy* 18 (January 2007): 157–70.

Rakich, Nathaniel, and Elena Mejía. "Where Republicans Have Made It Harder to Vote (So Far)." *FiveThirtyEight,* May 11, 2021. https://fivethirtyeight.com/features/republicans-have-made-it-harder-to-vote-in-11-states-so-far/.

Reagan, Ronald, with Richard G. Hubler. *Where's the Rest of Me?* New York: Duell, Sloan and Pearce, 1965.

REV. "Donald Trump CPAC 2021 Speech Transcript." *Rev*, February 28, 2021. https://www .rev.com/blog/transcripts/donald-trump-cpac-2021-speech-transcript.

Richardson, Heather Cox. *To Make Men Free: A History of the Republican Party.* New York: Basic Books, 2014.

Riley, Katherine, and Stephanie Stamm. "How Twitter, Facebook Shrank President Trump's Social Reach." *Wall Street Journal*, January 15, 2021.

Root, Wayne Allyn. *The Conscience of a Libertarian.* New York: John Wiley, 2009.

Ross, Justine Gail Margarethe. "An Introduction to Party Brand: Lessons from Business-Marketing as Applied to the United States' Major Political Parties, 1976–2012." PhD diss., University of California–Riverside, 2018.

Rossiter, Clinton. "Conservatism." In *The International Encyclopedia of the Social Sciences*, ed. David L. Sills, 3:290–95. New York: Macmillan/Free Press, 1968.

Rovere, Richard H. "The Campaign: Goldwater." *New Yorker*, September 25, 1964. https:// www.newyorker.com/magazine/1964/10/03/the-campaign-goldwater.

Royed, T. J., and S. A. Borelli. "Parties and Economic Policy in the USA. Pledges and Performance, 1976–1992." *Party Politics* 5 (2018): 115–27.

Ryan, Paul. "Paul Ryan Reagan Library Speech Transcript May 27: Future of GOP." *Rev*, May 28, 2021.

Safire, William. *Safire's Political Dictionary.* New York: Random House, 1978/2008.

Saramaki, Sara. "American Parties' 'Policies Towards Europe in the Post–Cold War Era: A Comparative Analysis of the Democratic and Republican Party Platforms." MA thesis, University of Helsinki, 2020.

Schattschneider, E. E. *Party Government.* New York: Rinehart, 1942.

Schlesinger, Joseph A. *Political Parties and the Winning of Office.* Ann Arbor: University of Michigan Press, 1991.

Severo, Richard. "Lyndon LaRouche, Cult Figure Who Ran for President 8 Times, Dies at 96." *New York Times*, February 13, 2019.

Sheppard, Si. *The Partisan Press: A History of Media Bias in the United States.* Jefferson, NC: McFarland, 2008.

Shils, Edward. "Charisma." in *The International Encyclopedia of the Social Sciences*, ed. David L. Sills, 2:386–90. New York: Macmillan/Free Press, 1968.

Shoemaker, Robert. "Male Honour and the Decline of Public Violence in Eighteenth-Century London." *Social History* 26 (May 2001): 190–208.

Silver, Adam. "Consensus and Conflict: A Content Analysis of American Party Platforms, 1840–1896." *Social Science History* 42 (Fall 2018): 441–67.

Smith, Craig Allen, and Kathy B. Smith. "A Rhetorical Perspective on the 1997 British Party Manifestos." *Political Communication* 17 (2000): 457–73.

Smith, David G. "Liberalism." In *The International Encyclopedia of the Social Sciences*, 9:276. New York: Macmillan/Free Press, 1968.

Snyder, James M., Jr., and Michael M. Ting. "An Informational Rationale for Political Parties." *American Journal of Political Science* 46 (January 2002): 90–110.

Spencer, Wallace Hayden. "American Major Party Platforms: A Comparative Analysis." MA thesis, University of Arizona, 1967.

Stapelbroek, Koen. "Pillarization." In *The Encyclopedia of Political Science*, vol. 4, ed. George Thomas Kurian. Washington, DC: CQ Press, 2011.

Stevens, Stuart. *It Was All A Lie: How the Republican Party Became Donald Trump*. New York:. Knopf, 2020.

Stone, Walter J., Ronald B. Rapoport, and Alan I. Abramowitz. "The Reagan Revolution and Party Polarization in the 1980s." In *The Parties Respond: Changes in the American Party System*, ed. L. Sandy Maisel. Boulder, CO: Westview, 1990.

Stout, David. "Harry Dent, an Architect of Nixon's 'Southern Strategy,' Dies at 77." *New York Times*, October 2, 2007.

Stuttaford, Andrew. "Where (Some of) Lincoln's Words Came From . . ." *National Review*, November 19, 2013.

Swan, Jonathan. "The Cult of Trump." *Axios*, February 5, 2018. https://www.axios.com/cult -trump-base-maga-republicans-gop-b96102cb-7cb9-46f2-9763-b014e68a261a.html.

Swendiman, Kathleen S. "Mandatory Vaccinations: Precedent and Current Laws." Congressional Research Service, March 10, 2011.

Tajfel, Henri, and John Turner. "An Integrative Theory of Intergroup Conflict." In *The Social Psychology of Intergroup Relations*, ed. W. G. Austin and S. Worchel. Monterey, CA: Brooks/Cole, 1979.

Taylor, John B. *Economics*. 4th ed. Boston: Houghton Mifflin, 2004.

Taylor, Miles, and Christine Todd Whitman. "We Are Republicans. There's Only One Way to Save Our Party from Pro-Trump Extremists." *New York Times*, October 11, 2021.

Thackeray, David, and Richard Toye. "An Age of Promises: British Election Manifestos and Addresses 1900–97." *Twentieth Century British History* 31, no. 1 (March 2020).

Thomson, Robert, et al. "The Fulfillment of Parties' Election Pledges: A Comparative Study on the Impact of Power Sharing." *American Journal of Political Science* 61 (July 2017): 527–42.

Tribune News Services. "O'Neill Says Cheney Told Him, 'Deficits Don't matter.' " *Chicago Tribune*, January 12, 2004.

Tyson, Alec, and Brian Kennedy. "Two-Thirds of Americans Think Government Should Do More on Climate. Bipartisan Backing for Carbon Capture Tax Credits, Extensive Tree-Planting Efforts." Pew Research Center, June 23, 2020.

Van Berkel, Jesse. "Rift Grows as Walz Weighs Mask Rule." *Minneapolis StarTribune*, July 13, 2020.

Victor, Jennifer Nicoll, and Gina Yannitell Reinhardt. "Competing for the Platform: How Organized Interests Affect Party Positioning in the United States." *Party Politics* 24 (2018): 265–77.

Vidal, Felix Camila. "The Republican Party and Its 'Conservative Ascendancy': An Analysis of Its National Platforms (1960–2012)." Paper delivered at Political Studies Association 65th Annual International Conference, Sheffield City Hall and Town Hall, March 30–April 1, 2015.

Weaver, Warren, Jr. "The Emerging Republican Majority." *New York Times*, September 21, 1969.

Weiss, Brenna, and James Pasle. "Only 3 Countries in the World Protect the Right to Bear Arms in Their Constitutions: The US, Mexico, and Guatemala." *Business Insider*, October 2017. https://www.businessinsider.com/2nd-amendment-countries-constitutional -right-bear-arms-2017-10.

Wenzelburger, Georg, and Reimut Zohlhöfer. "Bringing Agency Back Into the Study of Partisan Politics: A Note on Recent Developments in the Literature on Party Politics." *Party Politics*, March 2020.

White, John Kenneth. *What Happened to the Republican Party?* New York: Routledge, 2014.

White, Theodore. *The Making of the President.* New York: Atheneum, 1961.

Wildavsky, Aaron. "The Goldwater Phenomenon: Purists, Politicians, and the Two-Party System." *Review of Politics* 27 (July 1965): 386–413.

Williams, Daniel K. *God's Own Party: The Making of the Christian Right.* New York: Oxford University Press, 2010.

Yanofsky, David. "Where to Read Donald Trump's Tweets Now That Twitter Has Closed His Account." *Quartz*, January 9, 2021. https://www.thetrumparchive.com/.

Zitner, Aaron. "Republicans' Blue-Collar Agenda Is Still a Work in Progress." *Wall Street Journal*, May 8, 2021.

Zitner, Aaron, Slobhan Hughes, and John McCormick. "GOP Splits Over Its Path After Trump." *Wall Street Journal*, January 11, 2021.

INDEX